SPILLANE

KING OF PULP FICTION

SPILLANE
KING OF PULP FICTION

A BIOGRAPHY

MAX ALLAN COLLINS
& JAMES L. TRAYLOR

THE MYSTERIOUS PRESS
NEW YORK

SPILLANE: KING OF PULP FICTION

Mysterious Press
An Imprint of Penzler Publishers
58 Warren Street
New York, N.Y. 10007

First Mysterious Press edition

Interior design by Maria Fernandez

Library of Congress Control Number: 2022917459

ISBN: 978-1-61316-379-5
eBook ISBN: 978-1-61316-380-1

10 9 8 7 6 5 4 3 2 1

Printed in the United States of America
Distributed by W. W. Norton & Company

For our favorite Veldas

"You can kill a man with a hammer
or you can build a house with a hammer."

—Mickey Spillane

CONTENTS

The Spillane Files

A TIP OF THE PORKPIE HAT

Since the publication of our initial book on Mickey Spillane, *One Lonely Knight: Mickey Spillane's Mike Hammer* (Popular Press, 1984), we have continued to closely follow and explore the writer's life and career. While our *Mickey Spillane on Screen* (McFarland, 2012) was a logical continuation of our work, the goal has always been to produce a full-scale biography worthy of this fascinating figure who made such an impact on popular culture worldwide.

During Mickey's lifetime, such a biography was impossible—Spillane made it clear to us he intended to one day write his own story. In a sense he did, spending much of his larger-than-life life in the public eye, despite a preference for privacy and a low-key existence. But while he cooperated fully with co-author Collins on an award-winning documentary, *Mike Hammer's Mickey Spillane* (1999), Mickey wrote only a few pages of a long-promised autobiography (included in this book).

As with many, if not all, fiction writers, however, Spillane created through his storytelling a veiled autobiography, written primarily in a colorful first-person point of view, on the one hand invoking a blue-collar, common-man sensibility and on the other a pulp-fiction "tough guy" argot.

Collins collaborated with Spillane not only on the biographical documentary, but on such projects as the *Mike Danger* comic-book series and numerous anthologies, and is currently working to finish the wealth of uncompleted novels, stories, and screenplays in the late writer's files. (Mentions of Collins in the text will in most cases be represented as MAC.)

Co-author Traylor has continued to write about Spillane in various articles, reviews, and biographical entries (sometimes alone, sometimes with Collins), including for *The St. James Guide to Crime & Mystery Writers* and *The Strand*.

Together we have written about Spillane in such magazines as *Mystery Fancier*, *Armchair Detective*, *Mystery Scene*, *Journal of Popular Culture*, *Videoscope*, *Video Watchdog*, and *Psychotronic Video*.

The authors have corresponded with and/or interviewed an array of individuals notably associated with Spillane. These include Spillane's youngest daughter, Caroline Spillane Hill; Ruth Boyer, his classmate at Kansas State Teacher's College, Manhattan, Kansas; Doris Sloan, one of Spillane's young friends from Newburgh, New York; Jon Gerrity, son of writer Dave Gerrity, Spillane's longtime friend, also from Newburgh; George Wilson, Spillane's "buddy" dating to the days of the Army Air Corps in Greenwood, Mississippi; Don Watts, who became Spillane's friend after the writer moved to South Carolina in the early 1950s and who took more than one hundred trips with Mickey; Harold Cooke, the North Carolina trooper whom Spillane joined on moonshine raids; Gene Powell, "adopted" by Spillane in the late 1950s; Shirley Eaton, Spillane's costar in the film *The Girl Hunters*; actress Lee Meredith, the Miller Lite "Doll," who shared wonderful stories of her long association with Mickey as a Miller Lite All-Star; TV producer Jay Bernstein, Mickey's Hollywood friend and collaborator; Stacy Keach, star of three Mike Hammer TV series and multiple made-for-television films; Paul Vernon, producer of Mickey's fishing videos and his associate in conservation efforts; and Jane Rogers Spillane, Mickey's gracious widow.

The collected papers and records of publishers E. P. Dutton (at Syracuse University) and Signet/New American Library (at New York University) were likewise at times both fascinating and frustrating. The insight of the editors and publishers at these two venerable houses contributed greatly to our understanding of the Spillane phenomenon.

Together and separately, we interviewed Mickey Spillane on numerous occasions. Uncredited Spillane quotes here are taken from the five hours of interviews conducted by Collins with the writer in 1998 for the 1999 documentary. Ayn Rand expert Shoshana Milgram Knapp provided a recording of Rand and Spillane on Mike Wallace's TV program. Rare prose pieces were shared by dedicated Spillane historians, including Lynn Myers, co-editor with Collins of *Primal Spillane*, the collected comic-book filler stories. Myers has generously allowed us to include personal anecdotes of his visits with Spillane and his close friends, including Dave Gerrity.

Several film noir historians and devotees have offered help and advice. These include *Shadow* pulp expert Will Murray, who provided additional clues about the mysterious "Frank Morris," who—in the waning years of the pulp magazines—contributed stories that were likely written by Spillane. Pulp historian, novelist, and Spillane authority Stephen Mertz—who knows as much about the writer's progenitor Carroll John Daly as anyone—was especially insightful. Special thanks to David McDonald, who joined Traylor on his road trip to visit with Spillane's daughter Caroline, and Robert Berntsen, who served as Traylor's tour guide on his trip to visit Newburgh and the apple country of upstate New York.

Various Internet websites provided information, including sites devoted to several actors who portrayed Mike Hammer—the late Darren McGavin, the late Biff Elliot, and Stacy Keach, who has done numerous projects with co-author Collins. Some sites, such as the Internet Movie Database Pro and Turner Classic Movies, are more reliable than others; and Spillane's old high school, Erasmus Hall, and alma mater, Kansas State College, have sites with valuable information about their famous student. (A more complete rundown on Internet sources is included with our bibliography.)

We have from Spillane's personal files hundreds of photos going back to Spillane as an infant, including nearly one hundred photos from the beach and college days. The estate has given access to these photos and approved their use. Other photos come from the collections of Collins and Traylor.

Mickey Spillane inspired the co-authors in many ways: a love of mystery fiction and the "tough guy" PI; an appreciation of the style of writing known as hard-boiled that has come to be called noir (by way of French film critics referencing publisher Gallimard's *Serie Noire*); and of course our high regard for the talent and artistry of this multimedia giant. At every opportunity, Mickey encouraged our best efforts, all the while sharing his humanity, generosity, and down-to-earth nature. This book reflects not just our love for his work, but for the man, with thanks for his encouragement and friendship.

Certainly that has colored our view of his life and work. Mickey did not sugarcoat his fiction, however, and we hope to follow his hard-nosed lead in the nonfiction ahead.

CHAPTER ONE

MICKEY SPILLANE'S
MIKE HAMMER

In the second half of the twentieth century, almost overnight, Frank Morrison "Mickey" Spillane became the most popular mystery writer in the United States, rivaled internationally only by Great Britain's Agatha Christie.

Rising from the obscurity of low-end comic-book writing, Spillane rode high on bestseller lists in much the way working-class Elvis Presley came to dominate the pop music charts. In the early 1950s, the writer had become—again, almost overnight—the pariah of mystery fiction, vilified by reviewers and social critics, derided and even despised by many of his would-be peers. Yet according to the *Chicago Tribune*, by 1980 seven of the top fifteen bestselling fiction titles until then were his, with estimates of global sales around two hundred million.

Despite several self-imposed absences from publishing novels, Spillane maintained an unparalleled identification with hard-boiled fiction, surpassing even Dashiell Hammett and Raymond Chandler. And like the venerated creators of Sam Spade and Philip Marlowe, whose work preceded Spillane's, the creator of Mike Hammer was far less prolific than many of his contemporaries. His name stayed in the public eye through his private eye's television series and the writer's own self-spoofing appearances in a long-running series of beer commercials.

Ultimately, Mickey Spillane came to be regarded as an icon of crime fiction, the controversy over his censor-baiting novels subsiding even as he mellowed into a senior citizen whose underlying rage now rarely bubbled over. His final public image was that of a self-amused celebrity who dismissed his own incredibly popular fiction as "the chewing gum of modern literature."

Recognition had been long in coming, but in 1983 he received the Eye, the lifetime achievement award from the Private Eye Writers of America, and in 1995 was named a Grand Master by the Mystery Writers of America. Finally, after more than fifty years, the traditional mystery establishment acknowledged Spillane's overwhelming contribution to their genre.

Spillane's enthusiastic and loyal readers never required the endorsement of either his rival mystery writers or the critical establishment. To his "customers" (as he described them), Mickey Spillane was, until the end of his remarkable career, a true embodiment of the Greatest Generation, a World War II veteran from humble beginnings who did very well indeed. From New York publishing to Hollywood filmmaking, as a writer and actor and (as he often described himself) an entertainer, he excelled both as a hypnotic storyteller and a commanding personality.

The short take on Spillane has always been "sex and violence." Looking back at what was viewed by critics as "dirty" in his early work now seems almost laughably tame. Just as bedroom doors had closed in books and movies for decades before anything much happened, so did the doors leading up to supposed Spillane sex scenes—though occasionally those doors might slam or get kicked down.

Spillane did not indulge himself with erotic content until much later in his career (*The Erection Set*, 1972, *The Last Cop Out*, 1973), in the Harold Robbins/Jacqueline Susann era, when provocative sensuality was an expected ingredient of an "airport" bestseller. But in the 1940s and '50s, Spillane's detective having physical relationships with various women was itself a door the writer kicked down. Hammett had implied such shenanigans in *The Maltese Falcon* (1929), but stopped short of steamy descriptions leading up to them. Private eyes in mystery fiction just didn't do that sort of thing.

The great Rex Stout, asked about his detective Archie Goodwin's sex life in *P.S.* magazine, said frankly, "He has, probably, in the course of these stories, probably screwed between fifteen and twenty girls." But Nero Wolfe's papa went on to say sex is "the most boring thing you could possibly write about." (The cover of the magazine in which the interview appeared, however, depicted the final striptease of Spillane's *I, the Jury*.)

Chandler, who had little nice to say about Spillane ("Nothing but a mixture of violence and outright pornography"), did not allow Philip Marlowe to get in bed with a woman (in *The Long Goodbye*, 1953, and *Playback*, 1958) until Mike Hammer had made such activities permissible and even expected.

The other accusation against Spillane has aged far less. Film noir expert Eddie Muller says of the writer's startling action scenes, "The violence is like pornography," wherein clinical descriptions of carnage merge with the author's surrealistic urban poetry.

"I rolled on top of him," Spillane writes in *My Gun Is Quick*, "and took his head like a sodden rag and smashed and smashed and smashed and there was no satisfying, solid stomp, but a sickening squashing sound that splashed all over me."

Such bone crunching and blood splattering unsettled readers, just as Spillane intended. Another unsettling feeling, less easily discerned, rises from the friction between what seems a simplistic black-and-white view of a world in which the actions of Spillane's protagonist result in a disturbingly gray outcome.

But Hammer's ends-justify-the-means rationalization works only in the moment. While it may only seem fair that life's questions be easily answerable, in reality they are nothing of the kind. The inner turmoil Hammer faces follows his response to a complex problem with a simple answer—violent retribution—and results in intense emotional, psychological, and even spiritual ramifications.

The Spillane mix as presented in the key half-dozen Mike Hammer novels published between 1947 and 1952 was far more than sex and violence. They present a postwar Manhattan at once gritty and surreal, a place as dangerous as the jungles of the Pacific Theater, a nightmare dreamscape where gangsters and crooked politicians and Communist cells make a mockery of everything fighting men had fought for, where women are as willing as they are desirable and men as tough and hard as a hammer and nails.

The pace of Mike Hammer's first six cases is fast if not always coherent, a fever dream narrative with verbs and nouns and even adjectives tumbling from its antihero's cigarette-dangling lips like bullets from a machine gun or, in quieter moments, the moody rhythms of rain in the city at night. And when the bullets aren't flying, that rain is coming down—sometimes both at once in a dizzying dance of, yes, sex and violence but also noir atmosphere. Spillane, Ross Macdonald said ruefully, was the only real poet twentieth-century America had.

This, too, is from *My Gun Is Quick*: "There was still a threat of rain in the air. Overhead the clouds were gray and unruffled, a thick, damp blanket that cut the tops off the bigger buildings and promised to squat down on the smaller ones. From the river a chill drove in wave mist that covered everything with tiny wet globules. Umbrellas were furled, ready to be opened any instant; passengers waiting for buses or standing along the curb whistling at taxis carried raincoats or else eyed the weather apprehensively."

"Mike Hammer," Mickey Spillane often said, "is a state of mind."

But who was . . . who *is* . . . Mike Hammer? And who besides the parade of bimbos and boozers and dames and dimwits and slobs and suckers and villains and victims lives in the skyscraper cliffs and dingy pads and dank gin mills of the big bad city?

The man behind the pebble-glassed door inscribed *Michael Hammer Investigations* is a traumatized veteran of the war in the Pacific. He is in business with a lovely ex-cop, Velda Sterling (her last name not revealed till the posthumous *The Goliath Bone*, 2008), who serves as secretary and backup PI. His best friend is Captain Pat Chambers of Homicide, who provides the rational ego to Hammer's raging id. Pat and Mike were in the army together and at the police academy, although that rarely comes up. Hammer settles scores using the methods of combat and of the bad guys themselves, or as Spillane said, "He's a good guy, but he wears the black hat."

Of the thirteen Hammer novels published during his creator's lifetime, six are considered key by fans and detractors alike: *I, the Jury* (1947); *My Gun Is Quick* (1950); *Vengeance Is Mine!* (1950); *One Lonely Night* (1951); *The Big Kill* (1951); and *Kiss Me, Deadly* (1952).

Dashiell Hammett in five novels defined and refined the tough American mystery novel, particularly with *The Maltese Falcon*, his lone novel-length Sam Spade mystery. Raymond Chandler in seven Philip Marlowe novels developed the private eye as modern-day knight and pipe-smoking poet. And Mickey Spillane in his first six novels thrust his protagonist into a postwar loss of innocence that included brutal vengeance and sexual promiscuity, paving the way for decades of antiheroes from James Bond to Dirty Harry, from John Shaft to Lisbeth Salander.

To consider Mike Hammer's pivotal six novels—and other Spillane works to follow—discussion is required of their shocking, surprising (at the time at least) conclusions. So much a part of Spillane's technique, the "socko" ending demands attention, and we must set aside the conventional mystery-fiction etiquette of not revealing "who done it."

"When you're writing a story," Spillane said, "think of it like a joke. What's a great punch line? Get the great ending then write up to it."

In *I, the Jury*, Mike Hammer pledges at the crime scene to avenge the murder of Jack Williams, the foxhole buddy who lost an arm saving the private eye's life in the South Pacific. Trained as a policeman, honed to toughness by a brutal war, Hammer vows revenge—nothing will stop him from killing Jack's murderer, no matter who it might be. But what if it turns out to be psychiatrist Charlotte Manning, Hammer's newfound love? Will the detective fulfill the promise of the novel's title?

"He's never had sex with this girl," Spillane said in 1998. "She comes over to kiss him . . . now if he kisses her, she's going to reach behind him for a gun and blow his head off. But he stays true to his promise."

Hammer shoots her in her "naked belly."

The naked, dying Charlotte asks, "How c-could you?"

His curtain-line response—"It was easy"—becomes a psychological scar for the detective, a metaphor for the lost innocence of postwar America, and one of the most famous last lines in fiction.

My Gun Is Quick opens with Hammer talking directly to the reader (and most likely to Spillane's editors in New York publishing). He compares the reading of thrillers to the ancient Romans watching slaves being killed for mass sport. Spillane's skillful preamble is designed to help readers willingly suspend their disbelief over the course of the wild and wooly tale to follow:

> *When you sit at home comfortably folded up in a chair beside a fire, have you ever thought what goes on outside there? Probably not. You pick up a book and read about things and stuff, getting a vicarious kick from people and events that never happened. You're doing it now, getting ready to fill in a normal life with the details of someone else's experiences. Fun, isn't it? You read about life on the outside thinking about how maybe you'd like it to happen to you, or at least how you'd like to watch it. . . .*
>
> *But remember this: there are things happening out there. They go on every day and night making Roman holidays look like school picnics. They go on right under your very nose and you never know about them. Oh yes, you can find them all right. All you have to do is look for them. But I wouldn't if I were you because you won't like what you'll find. Then again, I'm not you and looking for those things is my job. They aren't nice things to see because they show people up for what they are. There isn't a coliseum any more, but the city is a bigger bowl, and it seats more people. The razor-sharp claws aren't those of wild animals but man's can be just as sharp and twice as vicious. You have to be quick, and you have to be able, or you become one of the devoured, and if you can kill first, no matter how and no matter who, you can live and return to the comfortable chair and the comfortable fire. But you have to be quick. And able. Or you'll be dead.*

In *My Gun Is Quick*, Hammer suffers from immense guilt, but true to his wartime code, he feels he did the right thing by executing the femme fatale who murdered his best friend. When a young prostitute Mike befriended is killed by a hit-and-run driver, the detective goes to work for one of the rich elite on Long Island. Investigating the woman's death, Hammer encounters (and beds) several surrogate Charlottes, who are killed because of their association with him.

The real killer, Mike learns, is his highly respected client, who has chosen to protect his esteemed reputation by eliminating anyone he perceives as a threat, familial relationships aside. Trapped in a burning building with the aristocratic murderer, Mike finds the will to execute the evil one just as the fireman's ladder arrives to rescue them. Hammer promises the rich killer a pauper's grave.

"I won't deprive myself of the pleasure of killing you," Hammer tells Arthur Berin-Grotin. "I'll kill you so I can live with myself again."

The Mike Hammer stories are about corruption, and how difficult it is to root out ingrained evil in a society, evil often protected by—and sometimes an outgrowth of—money and power. *My Gun Is Quick* is ultimately about Hammer's fiery execution of a greedy man, who not only betrayed a friend but his own family.

Hammer has killed another of the evil ones, those he considers it his duty to destroy. He has killed again, but not without justification, and he has sought redemption the only way he knows: through vengeance.

Vengeance Is Mine! finds Mike avenging the death of another army buddy, this one murdered with Hammer's own gun. Following a lead that his friend had been dating a model, Mike enters the rarefied world of high fashion, ultimately falling for stunning golden-haired Juno, whose resemblance to Charlotte all but sends Mike into a trance.

In his dreams, Mike is rescued by Velda, whose "raven-black" hair indicates the duality of the real love their deeper relationship embodies. But Charlotte "wouldn't stay dead," and before Mike comes to terms with his need for Velda, he falls into Juno's velvet trap—she has told him that sex with her would be something new and unusual for him. And in that sense she has not lied—Mike discovers "Juno was a man!"

Spillane's justly famous ending—withholding a key fact until the last word of the novel—made a lasting impact with readers.

At once unusual and yet the most representative of the first six Hammer novels, *One Lonely Night* pits Hammer against "Commies" in their most stereotypical 1950s sense. Often used to brand both Spillane and Hammer as rabidly anti-Communist—and indeed the writer was no fan of the Soviet Union—*One Lonely Night*'s Commies are bad guys in the sense of the Indians in John Ford's *Stagecoach* (1939) or perhaps the Blue Meanies in *Yellow Submarine* (1968). Yet *One Lonely Night* is Spillane's single strongest work, the first of the Hammer books written after he began to feel swept up in the hysterically negative critical tide.

Hammer suffers public humiliation at the hands of a judge ("He was little and he was old with eyes like two berries on a bush") who has very reluctantly acquitted the private eye of murder on grounds of self-defense. The detective walks in the rain onto the George Washington Bridge, his mood near suicidal. A young woman runs onto the bridge, pursued by an armed man, who Hammer shoots and kills. Mistaking Hammer for "one of them," she hurls herself off the bridge.

Feeling responsible, Hammer investigates, infiltrating a Communist Party cell and becoming involved with Ethel Brighton, a young society woman naively helping fund it. Lee Deamer, a super-patriot politician mounting a McCarthyesque purging of Communists in government, is being blackmailed by his twin brother, Oscar, an insane-asylum escapee thought to be a murderer.

When Oscar, pursued by Hammer and others, dies under the wheels of a subway train, the matter seems closed. Hammer recovers some stolen government documents ("the latest in the process for the annihilation of man") but Russian agents kidnap his beloved Velda, tying her from the ceiling by her wrists for a naked torture session to pry from her the location of the documents. Hammer bursts in with a machine gun.

"They heard my scream," Hammer tells us, "and the awful roar of the gun and the slugs tearing into bone and guts and it was the last they heard.

They went down as they tried to run and felt their insides tear out and spray against the walls."

With Velda rescued, Hammer meets with Lee Deamer on the George Washington Bridge. By now he knows Lee is actually Oscar, Lee's demented brother, the "head Commie." Hammer burns the documents, strangles Deamer, leaves the body on the bridge, where snow slowly covers it. The novel closes—as it opened—with a wonderful Spillane image: "Nobody ever walked across the bridge, especially not on a night like this. Well, hardly nobody."

The plot is outlandish, a dark dream, and is marked by Hammer coming to terms with his role as society's mad avenger—he decides God has put him on earth to purge it of evil. Not exactly Raymond Chandler's chess-playing, poorly paid knight. . . .

Even more telling is Spillane revealing the murderer as a Joe McCarthy surrogate. Spillane's critics often linked Hammer to the reckless, demagogic Wisconsin senator, as if the detective and his actions were the manifestation of McCarthyism.

Asked about McCarthy years later, however, Spillane said bluntly, "McCarthy was a nit-head. He didn't know what was going on. He was a slob."

The Big Kill continues Spillane's depiction of the archetypal deceptive female. Hammer takes under his wing a child whose crying father, William Decker, had left the baby in a dingy bar and walked outside into a rainstorm to face death at the hands of mobsters. Enraged by this senseless murder and the resulting orphan, Hammer once again sets out to deliver rough justice.

The detective soon discovers Decker was a small-time thief trying to go straight who, going out on one last job to raise money for his desperately ill wife, has inadvertently lifted some blackmail documents. During the search for the documents, Spillane injects Hammer into some of the most brutal scenes of violence in all the Hammer canon.

Mike meets a beautiful older woman, retired actress Marsha Lee, whose apartment Decker had burgled. Meanwhile, babysitter Hammer notes uncomfortably that the child displays a fascination with guns; his little charge reaches for Hammer's "rod," tries to touch it every time he sees it. Hammer is successful in keeping the firearm away from the infant until baby William saves Hammer's life by accidentally shooting the evil Marsha.

As *Kiss Me, Deadly* begins, Hammer is riding in his souped-up "heap" on a mountain road when a young woman, beautiful sanitarium escapee Berga Torn, jumps in front of his car and flags him down, refusing to get out of his way. Hammer helps Berga make it through a roadblock before thugs waylay them, sapping Hammer, who becomes a groggy witness as the woman is tortured to death. Then the thugs place her body and Hammer in his car and roll it off a cliff. Hammer wakes in a hospital and pledges to Pat and Velda he will find the killers.

Mike tangles with hood after hood, seeking a missing box of valuable narcotics. Velda is again kidnapped and rescued, and Mr. Big taken down. But ultimately, Hammer must deal with Berga's roommate, Lily Carver, who has been reluctant to sleep with Mike. This proves to have been because her torso is one massive burn scar, revealed when she opens her robe after an alcohol bath (*"A horrible caricature of a human!"*).

Gloating, she shoots Hammer with his own .45. On the floor, possibly dying, Hammer asks for a final cigarette, which she grants. When she leans over for a goodbye kiss—"Deadly . . . deadly . . . kiss me"—Hammer ignites her rubbing alcohol–soaked body. He crawls away from the flames: "The door was closed and maybe I had enough left to make it."

The six novels reveal the gradual progression of Hammer's self-analysis in dealing with the "easy" answer at the end of *I, the Jury*, which obviously wasn't easy at all.

In *My Gun Is Quick*, Hammer tries to atone for having killed a woman by attempting to redeem two prostitutes (Red and Lola), both of whom die, despite his best efforts.

In *Vengeance Is Mine!*, Hammer is tortured by the memory of Charlotte and swears never to kill a woman again, a problem resolved by the dark humor of Charlotte's doppelganger proving to be a transvestite.

In *One Lonely Night*, Hammer, haunted by the judge who reprimanded him for his wholesale slaughter and vigilante pursuits, struggles with the rights and wrongs of killing, coming to the somewhat hysterical conclusion that God put him on earth "to kill the scum . . . so that others could live."

In *The Big Kill*, Hammer for the first time does not execute the murderer, the killer dying accidentally at the hand of a child—God punishing the guilty through the innocent.

In *Kiss Me, Deadly*, worn down by his own excesses, Hammer says, "I'm getting old in the game—I don't care anymore." Though he does execute Mr. Big, the villain's female accomplice is killed by the private eye in actual self-defense.

In these six seminal novels—and in the subsequent Hammer mysteries, with decelerating intensity—Spillane hammers the theme of revenge, usually expressing it in terms of his protagonist's outrage, merging two distinct character types into one, the hero and the avenger. This combination is what causes many critics, both yesterday and today, to be appalled by Hammer's actions: both the avenger and hero have distinct roles assigned to them by tradition.

The hero is normally categorized as good, and the avenger as bad; but in Hammer, Spillane fuses the two. When a hero kills in self-defense, rarely does a reader or critic have a moral or ethical objection. Mike Hammer—who at times kills in what amounts to cold blood—presents a problem for most critics and some readers: frankly, how to react to a character who is supposed to be the hero going around killing people.

In a 1979 interview, Spillane said that Hammer, as a character, needed to get past killing Charlotte Manning—a cleansing was called for, a ridding of his guilt over avenging the death of his friend Jack in so terrible a fashion. Hammer needed to find, in the aftermath of the treacherous femme fatale's death, a woman he could love . . . and trust.

Velda first comes alive as a character in *Vengeance Is Mine!* Though she is a licensed investigator and carries a gun, in the first two novels she is essentially the stereotypical secretary, suffering an unrequited love for her private-eye boss.

"She's big and beautiful," Hammer tells us, "and she's got a brain that can figure the angles while mine only figures the curves."

But in the third book, Hammer presents Velda with the ultimate test: "If you had [a] gun in your hand pointed at somebody's belly, could you pull the trigger?"

The understood but unstated part of the question—an application of Hammer's unwritten but inviolable code—is whether Velda is capable, in a life-or-death situation, of killing . . . whoever the adversary might be. Velda of course passes the test, telling Mike it would take her only one shot.

In that same novel, Hammer is swept up in Juno's charms, this mortal woman who reminds him of the queen of the lesser gods and goddesses. Yet when he's with Juno, there's something about her he doesn't like, although he does not understand why. His subconscious tries to navigate the conundrum for him (as it often does in Spillane) by way of a dream.

"I slept the sleep of the dead," Hammer tells us. And he screams at Charlotte, "I'll kill you again if I have to!" But soon in the dream, golden-haired Charlotte is confronted by a woman with raven-black hair. Mike trusts the raven-haired woman and soon he hears himself "saying over and over, 'Velda, thank God! Velda, Velda, Velda. Velda.'"

Hammer, in his dreams at least, is coming to terms with loving Velda, even if for now he must continue to execute Charlotte again and again. And every time he and Velda meet it's as if he's seeing her for the first time, each description more loving and elaborate.

"She was a big luscious woman," Hammer says of her in *Kiss Me, Deadly*. "Velda. Tall, with hair like midnight. Beautiful, so it hurt to look at her. . . . She was everything you needed just when you needed it, a bundle of woman whose emotions could be hard or soft or terrifying, but whatever they were it was what you wanted."

But Charlotte refuses to "stay dead," her memory bearing increasingly on Mike and Velda's relationship. While Velda loves him and tells him so, Hammer is afraid to admit he feels the same, as if by some perverse twist of fate it would mean Velda, too, would die.

"No kiss of death for you," he tells her. "There've been two women now. I said I loved them both." He's referring to Charlotte and Lola. ". . . [B]oth died, but not you, kid."

Even with the stop-and-start nature of their relationship, Velda's growing importance in Hammer's world heals him and redeems him, makes him less a misanthrope and more a rounded human being. Of course, the later novels present a better-balanced Hammer, though he is not as compelling as the young, mentally unbalanced protagonist, who so resonated with postwar readers.

Hammer and Velda are remarkably complicated characters to encounter in a series of melodramatic private-eye yarns.

But the same could be said of their creator.

TOP LEFT: Young Frank Morrison Spillane with his parents, Catherine and John. TOP RIGHT: Morrison Spillane at twelve. CENTER: High school graduation portrait. BOTTOM LEFT: Captain of the Breezy Point lifeguards. BOTTOM RIGHT: Football at Fort Hays Kansas State College, 1940.

CHAPTER TWO

STORYTELLER
IN THE MAKING

Frank Morrison Spillane was born in Brooklyn, New York, on Saturday, March 9, 1918, the son of Catherine Anne and John Joseph Spillane, close enough to midnight to make the actual date of birth, fittingly enough, a mystery.

"I was christened in two churches," Spillane said, "and neither took."

Baptized with the middle name "Michael" in his father's Catholic church and "Morrison" in his mother's Presbyterian one, the couple's only child grew up in an outlying, rather rural section of Elizabeth, New Jersey.

"I was a month old and I moved to Elizabeth, New Jersey, and took my mother and father with me," Spillane said in 1998. "I had a good upbringing—farmland, a lot of fun . . . chickens, cats, dogs."

His father ("as Irish as Paddy's pig," his son said) called the boy "Mick," which evolved over the years into the familiar nickname of the Spillane byline. His mother had another preference.

"*Baaaabe!* Babe, she'd yell it out the window," her grown son recalled. "I was the only Irish kid in a Polish neighborhood."

The Spillanes raised their son with a balance of affection and a firm hand. Mickey's father, small and slender and outgoing, was a bartender who bounced from job to job, including shipyard worker and clerking in a hardware store. Mickey's mother, large and pleasant and placid, devoted herself to baking—cookies, shortbread, and (according to her son) "the best scones in the world." The highly educated Mrs. Spillane, whose maiden name was Irvine, spoke of relatives in Scotland, including Mickey's grandfather, a university professor in Edinburgh.

"My mother taught me to read and write a little before I went to school," Spillane recalled. "I was reading books when other kids were learning their ABCs."

In 1955, Spillane told *Redbook* magazine he was "not a model student, but a good one." A rather stuffy older teacher asked him, "How do you ever expect to make a living when you have to count on your fingers?" Young Mickey replied, "I'll hire somebody to count for me."

His interest in money, and his knack for making it, expressed itself early on. When a miniature golf course opened near his house, he built a rival course in his yard and rented out his lemonade stand to a pal. Once, when a truck hit a rut and hundreds of small baskets designed for berries bounced out, he scavenged them and planted pansies in them. After nurturing the flower-filled baskets in the cellar all winter, he dispatched his friends to sell them when Easter rolled around. His father, alarmed by all the folding money his son suddenly had, hoped his good boy hadn't gone bad. Mick hadn't robbed the poor box, had he?

"When I was a little kid," Spillane told *Armchair Detective* in 1979, "I used to hear my mother say to my father, 'Jack, if only we were free and clear.' And I used to wonder, what did that mean?"

Clearly it was important to be free and clear, and when as an adult he found out what that meant, Spillane became free and clear, all right.

"I don't owe anybody any money," he said in 1979.

The writer always looked back fondly on his childhood, speaking with such passion of his Flexible Flyer in those cold snowy East Coast winters that the sled might have been his *Citizen Kane*–style Rosebud. Throughout his life, his battered old childhood toy chest remained with him, a repository for the physical remains of lingering memories.

"We made our own toys," he told *Armchair Detective*. "We were pretty satisfied with what we had." And if a toy did arrive in a box, Spillane said, he'd rather play with the box. He saw his own kids do the same.

Elizabeth "wasn't as grown up as it is now," Mickey told *True* magazine's Mark Murphy in 1952. "It was hilly around there and we would go out in the woods in winter and ski. We used anything—old boards, barrel staves—even skis sometimes."

He and his pals would ski down the embankments to a railroad cut, the footbridge over which, Spillane said, reverting to tough mystery-writer mode, "was a swell spot for suicide."

Times were poor, he told another interviewer, adding, "You had to fight to keep what you had." His mother had sent him to grammar school in a lovely handmade Buster Brown outfit that required him to "fight his way to school and back."

But his bent for storytelling created a less overtly violent method of self-defense.

"I loved to terrorize the kids," Spillane said of the ghost stories he would spin, and sometimes stage, for his young peers. "'Cause I was a kid myself. You knew you did a good job when the mothers would come to your mom and say 'He scared my child! Today my kids came home crying to me!'"

In the hardware store where his father was working between bartending gigs, the boy caught sight of his first typewriter when he was eight or nine.

"I loved the sound it made," he told *Vanity Fair* in 2003. "I used to type on it. I knew I was going to be a writer."

Mickey appears to have been a typical American boy of the period, his interest in sports eclipsed only by a love for reading. He was attracted to adventure stories and swashbuckling romances—*Treasure Island*, *The Count of Monte Cristo*, and *The Three Musketeers*. Throughout his life, he would cite Alexander Dumas as his favorite author and Anthony Hope's *The Prisoner of Zenda* as his most-loved novel, rereading it every year.

"When I was a little kid," he said, "we had moved into a school where there was a library that ran underneath the windows—and I remember the teacher saying, 'Children, someday you'll be able to read this book,' and she held up a copy of *Moby-Dick*. And I said to the teacher, 'I like this book!' She says to me, 'You certainly didn't read this book!' And I said, 'Call me Ishmael.' She could never get over that!"

With the exception of *A Christmas Carol*, he did not care for Charles Dickens. "In school we were supposed to read *David Copperfield*. I told the principal, 'That's just to get the dolts to read.' I read more in a week than most of them will read in their lives."

In high school he was drawn to pulp fiction of all genres—Western, horror, science fiction, and especially adventure, particularly Carroll John Daly's wild and wooly detective yarns. He began writing the same kind of thing himself.

The budding storyteller's yen for adventure, nurtured by his reading habits, was triggered by a beloved uncle, Billy Turk, a New York police inspector, who may well have inspired the creation of Captain Pat Chambers of Homicide and perhaps Mike Hammer himself.

"I went to take out some books one day from the big library downtown," Spillane recalled, "and the librarian said, 'You can't take this out, it's from the adult section!' Finally, another librarian came up and she said, 'Oh no, he can take them out. He reads them and brings them back.'"

The boy who was called Babe by his mother and Mick by his father was known at school, among his teachers at least, as Morrison. And in June 1924, in Queens, New York, Morrison Spillane made the honor roll at Public School 88. Two years later, he entered Theodore Roosevelt School in Elizabeth.

And at Woodrow Wilson School on Friday evening, June 14, 1929, Morrison appeared as "King of the Weeds" in *The Stolen Flower Queen*—an early instance of an urge to perform. Many years later, Spillane—who held on to a picture of the acting troupe at their spring operetta—would make *King of the Weeds* the title of his penultimate Mike Hammer novel (completed by MAC in 2014).

Around the same time, Spillane began pursuing an interest that, like writing, would be with him throughout his life. Asked by an interviewer what he'd have been if not a writer, Spillane unhesitatingly said, "Commercial pilot."

"All I ever wanted to do," he said, "was fly."

At thirteen, the boy began to hang around the Newark airport, where he would help clean up the airplanes, scrounge up spare parts, pump up tires—everything and anything a kid might be able to do.

"And one day," he recalled, "this pilot said, 'Hey kid, I want you to clean up that engine out there.'"

But this time young Mickey stubbornly said, "I'm not going to do it."

The pilot asked why not, and the boy said, "I want a ride."

That ride was the first of many, and before long the pilot would hand Mickey the control wheel and say, "All yours, kid."

"And I'm flyin'," Spillane said, as gleeful a lifetime later as a thirteen-year-old kid. Learning to handle small aircraft at so young an age would one day prove to determine Mickey Spillane's wartime future in sometimes frustrating ways.

In June of 1932, when young Mickey graduated from Theodore Roosevelt Junior High in Elizabeth, he had already begun writing for publication and money.

"This was at the time of the Depression," Spillane said, "when they started Prohibition." Kids, the writer said, "get to know things," hanging around neighborhoods, crawling under garages, learning where "all the bootleggers hid their stuff." He said he'd started at this early date to write about gangsters and bootlegging for the *Elizabeth Daily Journal*.

Years later he would casually inform *Vanity Fair*'s Cliff Rothman that he'd been a crime reporter as a teenager for the Elizabeth paper. At times he would mention being a crime beat reporter to interviewers, neglecting to add he'd been a high school kid at the time.

"I'd make carbon copies of stories I was writing," Spillane said, "and turn one copy in as a school writing assignment."

Around the time Mickey was ready to start high school, the Spillane family moved to Church Avenue in East Flatbush. At Brooklyn's St. Erasmus High School, Mickey excelled in English (despite his dislike of Dickens) but also sports—swimming and football, where he played both halfback and quarterback.

Spillane occasionally cited 1935 as the year he turned pro, after gradua-tion. But the Erasmus yearbook of January 1936, *The ACADEMY*, includes a picture of handsome young "Spillane, Morrison," having entered the school in September 1935. His ambition was to go to Rutgers and become a doctor, the yearbook predicting an auspicious future: "Here's one who could amount to much."

Spillane's first professional job, the writer told *Vanity Fair*, was for an entertainment magazine, reporting on burlesque at the Apollo Theater—a foreshadowing of the scantily clad beauties who would adorn countless Mike Hammer paperback covers.

How much more work he may have done for the *Daily Journal* is unknown, but around then Spillane began seriously submitting to magazines—the pulps and "slicks" as well as newspaper syndicates and radio. His markets included contests, Sunday supplement articles, and pulp magazines, with a particularly unusual writing stint coming at Coney Island, where in 1936 early television broadcasting was in its infancy.

He said to interviewers that he sold a story to *Collier's*, a top market for fiction, and other slicks as well, all under pen names forgotten by posterity . . . and by Spillane himself.

"I don't know the titles of the magazines I wrote for," he told comics writer Roy Thomas in an *Alter Ego* interview in 2001. "I had a lot of the old magazines and whatnot on my shelves, and then [Hurricane] Hugo pretty much destroyed it all [in 1989]."

What would seem the most natural market for Mickey Spillane—the pulp magazines—may have proved elusive. Some old friends say his luck was strictly hit-and-miss there, which would have been frustrating, as Spillane's favorite crime writer was *Black Mask* star Carroll John Daly, the largely forgotten writer credited with creating the private eye of fiction. Daly's Race Williams is often called the template for Mike Hammer.

Describing him as "the sensational young author of the Mike Hammer series," a writing magazine in 1951 suggested Spillane had come up through the pulps and believed "an apprenticeship in the pulps is one of the fastest ways of learning the writing craft." The writer told the magazine that he knew "a lot of pulp writers making more money than a good proportion of current novelists."

"There are only a certain number of basic plots," Spillane went on. "All stories are an elaboration on these plots and a good background in writing pulp fiction gives you the benefit of stockpiling these elaborations in your mind plus the ability to twist them into elaborations not yet used."

In the late 1930s, the young man spent his winters writing and doing odd jobs, and his summers as a lifeguard at Long Island's Point Breeze beach. With fellow lifeguards Homer Lane, Ray Wilson, and Jack McLynn, under captain Lou Cheiffo, Spillane patrolled the sands at the end of Flatbush Avenue. Soon he was heading up the unit, practicing—and teaching—the American Red Cross techniques of lifesaving and water safety.

One rescue made by Spillane himself holds an ironic resonance. No one in the mid-twentieth century was more associated with beaches than Long Island bodybuilder Charles Atlas, whose health and fitness course was widely advertised (often in comic books) as having transformed the former Angelo Siciliano from "a 97-pound weakling" getting sand kicked in his face to a prime physical specimen. Spillane pulled the much larger man from the waters with characteristic skill and ease.

"We had the safety record for Atlantic Coast bathing," Spillane remembered, and said he'd also rescued several players from the Dodgers baseball team. "For seven years we didn't have a drowning."

Spillane polished his storytelling skills on the beach, sitting around lazy summer-night campfires with other boys and girls, spinning ghost stories, delighted to again be "scaring hell out of [his friends]."

Caught up in a summer romance, the popular lifeguard made the *Point Breeze News* gossip column: "Wilma S and Mickey S make a nice couple—don'tcha think?" And not for the last time, either: "A little birdie told me that Mickey S. really loves that delicious creature that walks down to see him from Rockaway Point each day."

Throughout the years, Spillane held on to snapshots of himself and his best girl at the beach. And he always spoke warmly of Wilma Sterling, whose last name and physical description he gave to Velda, the pistol-packing partner/secretary who was the love of Mike Hammer's life.

As the fall of 1938 approached, the Breezy Point lifeguard began thinking ahead to college.

"I had started to go to Rutgers with my buddy, Ray Wilson," he recalled. "But they wanted us to do nothing but swim and play ball. I said, 'Gee, there's no education value here. I don't want to go into this on an athletic scholarship.'"

Nonetheless, when Spillane enrolled at Kansas State College in Fort Hays, it was in part to join his buddy Ray Wilson, who was on the football team; soon the Breezy Point pals were Phi Delta Chi fraternity brothers. For the next two years, football and intramural swimming took precedence over Mickey's prelaw studies.

"I was a good football player," Spillane said. "But that was back in the old days. We had leather helmets, we didn't have face masks."

His main nonathletic pursuit remained fiction writing.

"I started writing stuff for *Liberty Magazine* and *Saturday Evening Post*," he recalled, insisting he'd been making more money with freelance writing than the dean of the college in salaried education. As in his junior high and high school days, Mickey turned in carbon copies of what he was selling to magazines in New York to his instructors at Kansas State.

Spillane always claimed to have started with the higher-end publications and worked his way down to the pulps, working under various pseudonyms—possibly including Frank Morris, although this particular pen name has never been confirmed—and apparently contributing short fiction everywhere from *Collier's* to *Hollywood Detective*.

Tracking down Spillane's late '30s and early '40s fiction in both the pulps and the slicks has been a frustrating and largely futile task for researchers.

Kansas State classmate Ruth Boyer remembers Spillane talking about receiving checks for stories he'd written, but her friend Mickey never shared the names of any of the magazines who'd bought them. Apparently Mickey's success in the magazine field—whether slick or pulp or both—was lucrative enough for him to drop his ambition to become a lawyer and concentrate instead on writing.

Of course, Spillane as his own mythmaker may have exaggerated—or even invented—having worked in both markets. The writer often spoke of "making a living" writing for New York magazines while at college, but the details always remained hazy. Spillane did specifically mention passing himself off as an unwed mother numerous times for *True Story* magazine.

According to Spillane's crony Ray Gill, the writer's most outrageous "lies" were often slightly inflated truths—that he did indeed begin his writing career in junior high working for the Elizabeth, New Jersey, newspaper and soon thereafter began writing for the pulp magazines under various names. In the 1930s, selling to the pulps and romance magazines could provide the equivalent of two or three months of wages for the average working man.

Whether Spillane really did, as he often said, make more money as a writer than the dean of Kansas State as an educator is perhaps questionable. Storytellers do, after all, tell stories.

According to his friend and editor Bob Curran, Mickey "played varsity football and studied just enough to stay in school." But after two years at Fort Hays, Spillane decamped to Brooklyn, taking a seasonal Christmas job in 1940 selling closeout haberdashery in the Gimbel's department store basement. He became beer drinking buddies with another temporary clerk, Joe Gill, who also drank in Spillane's claims to be selling fiction to one market after another.

Big, tough, and affable, himself an aspiring writer, Gill offered to take Mickey over to meet his brother Ray at something called Funnies, Inc.

TOP LEFT: First appearance of the character that would become Mike Hammer (*Green Hornet*, December 1942 issue, published several months earlier). BOTTOM LEFT: "Captain Mickey Spillane of the Point Breeze Life Guards" appears in the August 1942 issue of *Blue Bolt* thanks to writer Ray Gill and artist Harold De Lay. TOP RIGHT: Wilma S., Mickey's Breezy Point girlfriend who was the model for Velda Sterling, Mike Hammer's partner. BOTTOM RIGHT: Mick in fedora, comic-book days.

CHAPTER THREE

SEE YOU IN THE FUNNIES

I was in the first group of writers," Spillane told *Alter Ego* magazine, "when we first started comic books."

In the early 1930s, comic books in America reprinted comic strips from the "funnies," Sunday color sections and daily pages of black-and-white strips, the latter usually colorized for republication. Gradually, original material worked its way in, with costumed "long underwear" heroes (as they were known in the business) flying through the stories and off the newsstands. By 1940, DC (Detective Comics, Inc.) was selling hundreds of thousands of copies of their *Superman* and *Batman* titles with Fawcett's *Captain Marvel* not far behind. And that was only the first exciting episode.

Packagers of comic books began to spring up, providing content for publishers. Among the most successful was Lloyd Jacquet's Funnies, Inc., at West Forty-Fifth Street in Manhattan, a shop producing scripts and artwork for various comics characters, among them Human Torch, Sub-Mariner, and Blue Bolt.

As an editor working for Jacquet, Ray Gill—"a good artist and good writer," Spillane said—was happy to meet his brother Joe's buddy Mickey, whose precocious previous writing experience made him a natural recruit.

"Ray said, 'Come on, give comics a try,'" Mickey told comics luminary Roy Thomas in 2001. "So I went up with Ray and I started—*bam!*—right into Funnies, Incorporated."

Comic books provided a new breeding ground for artists and writers at a time when (Spillane said) "you were either a great commercial artist or you were nothing," where writers who couldn't get into novels (before the paperback boom) "could find an outlet for their work."

Working on the seventeenth floor, the artists were at drawing boards in their area with the writers at typewriters in theirs ("Bangin' stuff out," Spillane said). Breezy Point cronies giggled about the lifeguard's new job, but Mickey had the last laugh, because "that's where the money was."

Initially, Spillane shared an office with Ray Gill. The space adjacent was "crammed with junk like Fibber McGee's closet." The new writer got Jacquet's permission to clean out the room—the boss clearly thinking the task an impossibility—but Mickey and Joe Gill pulled it off. It was an all-day proposition, but when they were done, "a new Woodstock typewriter was in there, a desk, a great chair. . . ." Now everybody wanted that space, but Spillane laid claim.

"We used to work at all hours," he said. "All these new experiences were pretty exciting and enjoyable. I was never a comic book reader till I got into the business itself."

Artist Dan Barry (*Tarzan*, *Flash Gordon*) recalled Spillane as "a handsome cocky Irishman who seemed to be out most of the time. Search parties were always out looking for him at the great bars around Forty-Fifth Street."

But Spillane—who said he worked at home more than in the office—wasn't loafing. According to Bob Curran, the young writer soon had revamped the system for scripting comics, developing a method of outlining a story, making each sentence a picture and every paragraph a page.

Jacquet was, by Spillane's estimation, "a very strange man," who emphasized his resemblance to General Douglas MacArthur by smoking a corncob pipe. The writer considered this somewhat pompous character "second-rate," because Jacquet did not seize the moment and go into publishing himself.

"Some of us liked to work without noise," Spillane wrote in a letter to Jerry DeFuccio, *Mad* magazine's longtime associate editor, "so we got in the office at 6:30 (beating out rush-hour traffic) and quit at noon. We had weekends to ourselves and gave Lloyd the screaming jumps. He'd see us apparently goofing off and say, 'Where are the pages?' Naturally, we'd say as off-handedly as we could, 'Already delivered.'"

Spillane and the other writers delighted in Jacquet thinking they had fouled up his schedule. The boss paid "lousy," the writer said. Comics scripters learned, on the sly, to work directly for Timely's Martin Goodman and other publishers, including Novelty Press, the comic-book imprint of Curtis, publisher of the *Saturday Evening Post*. Novelty's titles *4-Most*, *Blue Bolt*, and *Target* used countless Spillane scripts.

"I was working as an independent entrepreneur," he said. A courier servicing several publishers would come directly in need of stories. "And I'd already have something written! We knew these things would come up."

Despite running such end runs, and occasional frictions with Jacquet, Spillane rose to an editorial position, a post he held from December 1941 to September 1942. According to his army records, Spillane "was an editor, wrote scripts and was in charge of make-up prior to [issues] being sent to publisher." The latter word covers a lot of ground, what with Funnies, Inc., doing no publishing itself, working instead for the mushrooming number of comic-book lines often associated with existing magazine publishers.

In 1939, Goodman contracted Funnies, Inc., to assemble a comic book with original science-fiction material—*Marvel Comics*, a name that would become familiar worldwide, though not for several decades. After one issue, the title was changed to *Marvel Mystery Comics.*

Carl Burgos's Human Torch appeared in a first issue filled with costumed heroes in the mode of the already wildly popular Superman and Batman. That first *Marvel* issue also included cartoonist Bill Everett's creation, Prince Namor, the Sub-Mariner. Over the years, Spillane, who occasionally scripted the feature, took delight in pointing out that Namor is Roman spelled backward.

Although he occasionally collaborated on scripts with Ray Gill, Spillane seems to have hung out more with artists than his fellow scribes and editors.

"We all ate at the same chintzy places," he said, "and went to strange art shows together and threw paper helicopters out the seventeenth floor of Funnies, Inc., that made the city slickers wonder what the hell all those space critters were up there. We even made the *Daily News* and *Mirror*."

He told of walking along Broadway with cartoonist Mike Roy—who would draw the first *Mike Danger* stories and illustrate the syndicated comic-strip versions of *The Saint* and *Nero Wolfe* in the 1950s—and spotting an art gallery window's posting of an open competition for "best painting." After wandering in and having a look around, Spillane told Roy, "You can do better than these guys."

Roy smiled, mulled that, and headed home. By the next morning he had submitted a painting—not yet dry—and took top honors, Spillane claimed, as well as a $1,000 grand prize.

A theatrical producer's office was next to door to the Funnies, Inc., studios. When the producer bemoaned to his neighbors that a truckload of expensive sets had been destroyed in a vehicular accident, Mike Roy and other comic-book artists got together and whipped up replacements for the producer, ensuring the show would go on.

"These guys were great!" Spillane told Thomas. "They were the leaders in the field, and you've got to remember that when they were doing these things, printing and reproduction . . . were not as good as they are today." Some cartoonists worked with brushes, others with pens, or a combination thereof—"A lot of different techniques!"

"I was always amazed at the abilities of an artist," Spillane said. "It's incredible what they can do, and as they improve, they get so much better."

The writer acknowledged that the later work of top talents like Bill Everett and Carl Burgos was superior to their initial "primitive stuff," which was nonetheless "fun to look at." Sixty years later, he got a big kick out of collectors showing him the early versions of the Sub-Mariner and the Human Torch, who were still famous, and Sergeant Spook and Sub-Zero, now long forgotten.

"Later [the artists] evolved," Spillane pointed out, being capable of some "pretty fancy artwork." Ed Robbins, the future artist of the *From the Files of . . . Mike Hammer* comic strip, "was a pen man" who later became a respected portrait and landscape painter.

A number of women worked as artists in the comics field, including Genevieve Mills, whose pseudonym was Tarpé Mills. A glamorous woman who had worked as a model, she and Spillane—both born in 1918—may have known each other at Erasmus High in Brooklyn. Her comic strip, *Miss Fury*, about a costumed female action hero, began (as *The Black Fury*) in 1941, predating *Wonder Woman* by six months.

Mills contributed to various comic-book titles at Timely and Novelty, where Spillane was a frequent contributor. In her Greenwich Village apartment, she posed as Miss Fury (and other women in her stories) before a full-length mirror.

"She'd be in the nude," Spillane told Thomas, chuckling. "She'd use herself for a model! The guys used to love to deliver the pencils to her. 'Wait a minute, I'll put something on.' 'Don't bother, lady!'"

Spillane specialized in the "filler" short stories needed to satisfy postal regulations requiring a minimum of two pages of prose per comics issue. Among the many pieces Spillane produced was a lifeguard story featuring Captain Mickey Spillane.

"You got twenty-five dollars a shot for two pages of these things," Spillane recalled. "And [they] would take up to a half hour to write, you know. But at that time, twenty-five bucks was a lot of money. You could write four a day and you're getting one hundred dollars a day when a hard-workin' man out there is making thirty-five dollars . . . a week!"

And the filler stories were the only comic-book features where a writer regularly got a byline, at which time Frank Morrison Spillane replaced his first and middle name with his nickname. Mickey Spillane, the writer recalled with a smile many years later, got a nice big byline in dozens of comic books where other writers remained largely anonymous.

The young writer also scripted numerous comics stories about superheroes, some of whom would become American icons (as, of course, would Mike

Hammer). Writing credits beyond the two-page fillers were rare, but Mickey often managed to get the artists to slip his name somewhere into the artwork.

Looking back, Spillane listed some of the characters he scripted: Sub-Mariner, the Human Torch, Captain America—"Oh—a whole kit and kaboodle of 'em." For the most part he didn't recall which artist had drawn what feature, although he recalled Sid Greene (later a DC standby) drawing Target and the Targeteers.

Spillane did not, as has on occasion been asserted, write Batman ("I never wrote for DC") or Plastic Man for Everett M. "Busy" Arnold and Will Eisner at Quality. Batman co-creator Bob Kane and Spirit creator Eisner were acquaintances of his, but nothing more.

In the August 1942 issue of *Blue Bolt*, writer Ray Gill showcased "Captain Mickey Spillane of the Point Breeze Life Guards" in an Edison Bell story, with Mickey recognizable on camera in the art by Harold De Lay. The lifeguard hero contributed to the issue himself—a Sergeant Spook story and a text filler.

Spillane wrote scripts for *4-Most, Target*, and *Marvel Mystery Comics*, and such features as the Angel, Target and the Targeteers, the Cadet, and Jap Buster Johnson (a feature unlikely to be revived). For Novelty Comics, he scripted Dick Cole and Blue Bolt.

One market allowed him to revisit some of his childhood favorites. "When *Classic Comics* first came out . . . you would take a book like *Count of Monte Cristo*. I wrote that one and [Jack] Kirby drew it." Some sources credit him with adapting *The Three Muskeeters*, the climax of which prefigures the ending of *I, the Jury*.

When expert comics historian Thomas began throwing names of Golden Age cartoonists and writers at him, Spillane remembered encountering most but had little specific to share.

"We kind of worked at distances," he said.

Spillane would write a story and before long the penciled artwork, and possibly the inked version, would come back to him. He would check everything, looking for mistakes in the artwork or the lettering and make notes requesting changes.

"And that was it!" he told Thomas. "You never knew the guy on the other side. You'd know all *about* them, you talked to them over the phone and whatnot, or they'd call you for corrections and so forth. But you'd never have any personal relationship."

But now and then the worlds of artist and writer collided. A "fire and water" theme involving Timely's Human Torch and Sub-Mariner seemed a natural, though such a crossover between features had never been done in the comic books. A two-issue slugfest between the hot-and-cold-running heroes was planned, spanning *Marvel Mystery Comics* #8 and #9.

Ray Gill told Jerry DeFuccio that a team including Spillane, Bill Everett, Carl Burgos, Ed Robbins, Robin King, writer-editor-art-director John Compton, and Gill himself assembled in one small apartment to put together the two-issue Torch/Mariner "battle series." Sub-Mariner creator Everett's mother did the lettering, and one writer—possibly Spillane—sat typing in an unfilled bathtub.

Spillane reported one writer rushing in with coffee while "Ray Gill came popping in" with ideas outlined on a chart.

"It was fun, it was hectic, and it worked," the writer recalled. "But it was always like that at Funnies, Inc."

An assumption has been made by some comics historians—guesswork based on Spillane's later Mike Hammer reputation—that the writer scripted the more violent stories involving Sub-Mariner, Captain America, and the Human Torch. As Thomas puts it, "Huge armies of Germans and Japanese would be slaughtered by Sub-Mariner and the other Timely [Marvel] heroes."

Spillane said none of that was his work, and why would it be? During most of his tenure at Funnies, Inc. (and freelancing comics on the side), America had not yet entered World War II. And once Spillane had gone into the service, he would only sporadically—"when I needed any money"—send scripts in.

At Funnies, Inc., Spillane met future Marvel Comics superstar and publisher Stan Lee. They were good friends. He told Thomas, "Stan always said he could write at three typewriters at once. He's a two-fingered typist, like me."

Lee rose to prominence in the field quickly. "He had a flair for being in that comic book industry," Spillane said. "I kind of got out of it because there were better things to be done."

Many years later, Spillane said of his time as a comic-book writer and editor, "They were the happiest days of my life." He wistfully added, "I could walk anywhere and nobody knew who I was."

The beginnings of Mike Hammer can be traced to Spillane's Funnies, Inc., days. Among the artists he worked with there was Harry Sahle, another veteran of "long underwear" comics, a versatile cartoonist who, with Bob Montana, is credited with establishing the distinctive look of the *Archie* comics characters. Ray Gill was one of the main writers of that feature.

Here things become somewhat fuzzy.

Spillane's story was this: he created the prototype of Mike Hammer before the war as a proposed comic-book character, "Mike Danger," which he and Sahle had ready to go when Mickey had to ship out. And the only surviving example of Sahle's Mike Danger art, a mock-up cover depicting a snarling Hammer-like private eye, might well date to that pre-war period.

After all, as Ray Gill said in 1953, Spillane had been kicking around the idea of Mike Hammer for ten or twelve years: "He already had the thing written [in his mind]. All he had to do was put it on paper."

But Gill dates the production of the Mike Danger comic-book stories as much later—part of a postwar effort by former Funnies, Inc., employees to either publish their own comics or sell them to established publishers. (More about this later.)

Further muddying the waters is the comics story "Mike Lancer and the Syndicate of Death," published as a back-up feature in *Green Hornet* #10, December 1942. This is undoubtedly the first published appearance of the "grim-faced, gunslinging private detective" who would become Mike Hammer. The script certainly sounds like Spillane's work, as when Mike dispatches a hood, saying, "And that saves the state's electric bill!"

Spillane would later claim Sahle had jumped the gun, submitting the story without his knowledge, changing "Danger" to "Lancer." In correspondence with DeFuccio, after being provided with a copy of *Green Hornet* #10, Spillane only says, "What a pleasure it is, seeing Sahle's art again."

At the time of the "Mike Lancer" story's publication, Spillane was indeed serving in the military. But he was also known even then to occasionally sell stories to his usual markets, and for that matter was still working as an editor at Funnies, Inc., as late as September 1942, although he'd entered the army in May.

It is a certainty, however, that on December 8, 1941—the day after the Japanese attack on Pearl Harbor—Mickey Spillane and many of his friends in the comics industry arrived late for work at the Funnies, Inc., office.

They'd been lining up to enlist.

TOP LEFT AND RIGHT: Second Lieutenant Frank M. Spillane, flight instructor, 1943. BOTTOM LEFT: Mickey and Mary Ann on the town. BOTTOM RIGHT: A letter to freelancer Spillane from a Timely Comics editor.

CHAPTER FOUR

STATESIDE WARS

On December 8, 1941, Mickey Spillane lined up with his Funnies, Inc., pals on Whitehall Street in lower Manhattan only to get caught up in the crush of eager volunteers swarming enlistment centers in numbers that could not be processed all at once. Army records show Spillane's date of processing as May 9, 1942; furloughed, he would not enter active service until October 19, which explains his continued editorial position at Funnies, Inc., through September.

It also indicates the "Mike Lancer" story in the December issue of the *Green Hornet* comic book—on newsstands on October 6, 1942—was likely a sale Spillane made himself, or at least one Harry Sahle made with his writer's knowledge. (As with most periodicals, the month on the cover of a comic book indicated the final date of designated sale.)

An apparent Spillane insider wrote an anonymous, somewhat mean-spirited men's magazine article in 1953, saying the young pulp writer had his sights set on the Air Corps with "visions of swishing through the skies in his fighter and blasting Jerries and Japs to bits," further speculating that Mickey would probably stay awake at nights during basic training, "dreaming how he would be America's Ace of Aces."

As an Aviation Cadet, Spillane trained at Advance Flying School in Mariana, Florida, from May 9, 1942, to July 27, 1943. His Air Corps commission became official on July 28, his military occupational specialty (MOS) and code listed as "Fighter Pilot, Single Engine, 1055."

But Second Lieutenant Frank Morrison Spillane would fight his war stateside, winning his wings and gold bar as an Instructor of Cadets in Basic Training at the Greenwood Basic Flying School in Greenwood,

Mississippi. Spillane, eager to see action, was sorely disappointed when his adolescent flying training at Newark airport and his affable communication skills conspired to convince his superiors that the young pilot was ideally suited for teaching.

Or, as that anonymous insider had put it in the 1953 article, "The guy with the long white beard and star-spangled vest pointed a bony finger at Mick and said, '. . . You're going to stay here in the States and teach other guys how to fly and knock Jerries and Japs from the skies.'"

From July 1943 until January 1945, Spillane was a flight instructor at the Greenwood Army Airfield, where the unit motto was "Prepare for Combat." Mickey's students remembered him (Marion Hargrove reported in his 1955 *Redbook* article) as "a disturbingly dynamic young lieutenant, a capable and conscientious pilot, and a popular teacher."

The Greenwood Army Air Force Company Yearbook includes a page of photographs of the instructors. On the bottom row are Frank M. Spillane, Second Lieutenant, Flight Instructor, and George R. Wilson, Second Lieutenant, Flight Instructor, a drinking buddy who become a lifelong friend.

"I thought he was a bullshitter," Wilson told *Vanity Fair*, "a Brooklyn type fast-talker. But I found out he was a pretty amiable guy."

The writer-turned-pilot forged many lasting friendships in the army. In Greenwood, he met Charlie Wells and Earle Basinsky, who would become published mystery writers with the help of their pal's postwar fame. Friend Nat "Sporty" Drutman recalled warmly Mickey taking in stray cats to give them mess-hall milk. In 1965, Spillane would dedicate his novel *Bloody Sunrise* to Nat Drutman "and the days of the Kaydets and the AAF when the blue yonder was really wild and even wilder when you got shot out of it."

Spillane often called himself a country boy, citing the rural nature of the section of Elizabeth, New Jersey, where he was raised. But he'd been a lifeguard in Queens and a comic-book scripter in Manhattan, and was enough of a city boy for Greenwood, Mississippi, to have seemed a whole new world to him.

At the eastern edge of the Mississippi Delta, about one hundred miles from capital city Jackson and one hundred thirty miles south of Memphis,

Tennessee, the once-prosperous little town of about fifteen thousand was nearing the end of its reign as a center of cotton production. Nonetheless, a sign at the bridge over the Yazoo River continued to brag of Greenwood's status as the "World's Largest Inland Long-Staple Market," and Front Street, with its cotton factories and related businesses, was still known as Cotton Row.

Such a small, quiet town must have been a shock to the system for boisterous big-city arrivals like Spillane and so many others at the airfield. Grand Boulevard with its three hundred oak trees had been deemed one of America's ten most beautiful streets by the US Chambers of Commerce and the Garden Clubs of America. The oaks had been planted in 1916 by a local garden club headed up by a member of the Daughters of the American Revolution. And the turmoil of the Civil Rights movement was a decade away.

Of course, as with every city and town in America, daily living in Greenwood had been changed by the war, the home front seeing the usual war-bond and scrap-metal drives but also the housing of foreign prisoners of war. The influx of military must have hit the sleepy community like a bombshell; but the base was also a boon. At its height, the Greenwood Army Airfield would be home to more than 3,500 service men and women and employ hundreds of local civilian workers, at a time when cotton cultivation and processing was becoming mechanized, displacing thousands.

City boy Spillane connected with local girl Mary Ann Pearce at the Greenwood USO; though she was a secretary at the base, this was apparently where they first met. He fell hard, writer Adams reported, for "the sweet-looking, soft-spoken, wholesome Baptist girl." Quiet, even serene, Mary Ann was a "soft-eyed brunette" (as Spillane crony Dave Gerrity described her) who may have reminded Mickey of Wilma Sterling back at Breezy Point. Petite and pretty with a winning smile, Mary Ann wore dark-rimmed glasses that gave her the look of the kind of schoolteacher boys get a crush on.

Spillane and Mary Ann were married in her church. On his third baptism, Spillane went the "full-immersion" route, leaving both Catholicism and the Presbyterian church behind. She was nineteen, he was twenty-seven. They lived off the base on George Street in Greenwood in what was likely a rental property.

Mickey had a certain bluster the Greenwood girl either found amusing or put up with, or more likely both. When his boastful oratory got out of hand, Mary Ann would accuse him of "popping off" and he would take it. But when he said no woman was going to tell him what to do, she'd just smile and say to an observer, "From time to time you see him pulling his rank."

That anonymous insider reflected, in his somewhat snide fashion, "And so it was that again Mick was thrown into a mundane way of life. The wings on his blouse had made him feel big, but he would have felt like a giant with a couple of rows of ribbons . . . and a score of swastikas on the side of his plane."

Not long before the marriage, Spillane had finally trained for combat missions, taking the P-40 Fighter Gunnery Transition Course conducted at Napier Field, Dothan, Alabama. By August 29, 1945, his official paperwork noted the following particulars: "FIGHTER PILOT, SINGLE ENGINE. Was pilot of a P-51. Has approximately 1600 hours flying time. Took transition training in P-40s and P-51s. Was single-engine pilot instructor for 18 months."

At last, before the end of the war, he received a combat fighter assignment in P-51s; but there is no record of him seeing combat. On October 8, 1945, he was promoted to First Lieutenant in the Air Corps, and enlisted in the Air Corps Reserve for five years.

His stateside war was over.

The couple lived at 808 Beverly Road, Brooklyn, New York, almost certainly his parents' address, as Spillane would continue to use it for business purposes after he and Mary Ann no longer lived there. (808 is Mike Hammer's office number in the Hackard Building.) Spillane set out immediately to get back into the comic-book business, but things had changed.

"They had a bunch of creeps come in there," he told Roy Thomas, "and they took over all of our stuff . . . so we decided we've got to get them out."

Because the comics writers and artists who'd gone into the military had been freelancers, comics shops including Funnies, Inc.—now called Lloyd Jacquet Studios—did not have to give them their jobs back.

"So we went in," Spillane continued, "and [said] 'We'll do it for half the price.' We wiped these guys out of their spots, and they bitched and yelled, but tough! We got back in the business, and then our prices went up."

But the writer had soured on working for Jacquet and other packagers. He got together with his old pals Ray and Joe Gill—now skilled writers and editors in the comics trade—and went into business, renting a storefront on Vanderveer Place in Brooklyn. They brought along several artists from the Funnies, Inc., days, including Mike Roy and Harry Sahle, and set up their own comic-book factory.

The Vanderveer Place district, at the time, was largely residential, the neighborhood abuzz, wondering about the group of men sequestered in an office "crammed with filing cabinets, typewriters and drawing boards." Snoops discovered garbage cans rife with used beer cans and crunched cardboard coffee cups.

When a couple of cops came around wanting to know what was going on, Spillane said, "We are writing comic books." He was always polite to the police.

"Oh, a wise guy?"

The question was repeated.

So was the answer.

The comic-book guys didn't ask for a warrant when the cops searched the place, one officer keeping an eye on the suspicious characters, the other tossing the joint.

At the end of that effort, the second cop said to the first, "You know what these guys are doing?"

The other cop said he didn't.

His partner shrugged and said, "They're writing comic books."

According to that anonymous insider, what they were writing wasn't especially innovative: "They created new characters, which were actually the same characters they had written about before with different names. They wrote stories and had them executed into art."

Bobbing along alone in this sea of unoriginality was something unusual for the comic-book medium—Spillane's Mike Danger, brutal, tough, a good guy with bad-guy methods.

"Meet Mike Danger"—drawn by Mike Roy and (according to some sources) possibly Sam Burlockoff—features a small cast of recurring characters that would one day be familiar to millions of mystery readers—a secretary named Velda and Mike's cop buddy Pat Chambers, still a uniformed officer here. Other familiar aspects of the private eye's world include an office in the Hackard Building and a .45 under Mike's left arm. Velda even says, "I'll watch the angles—you watch the curves!"

"Murder at the Burlesque" is drawn by unknown and lesser lights but utilizes first-person narration in a now familiar way, with Mike on a kill-crazy, violent tear. Both stories would eventually be published (without Spillane's permission or even knowledge) by short-lived Key Publications in issues #3 and #4 of an obscure crime comic book, *Crime Detector*, in 1954.

The intent of the comics factory had been to go into publishing. They even had some financial backing. But, according to Roy, "One of the business partners disappeared with about $25,000 in cash."

That left the Brooklyn storefront comics factory with only one option: try to sell their finished comic-book material to established publishers. And no one was interested, perhaps (as the caustic insider said) "because [those publishers] already had the same characters with different names."

And somehow Spillane's early draft of a character who would become as well-known in the second half of the twentieth century as Tarzan or Batman got lost in a jumble of hackneyed offerings.

In his *Climax* magazine story, "The Amazing Success of Mickey Spillane," Henry Adams speaks of the storefront operation as a random collection of battered typewriters and beat-up desks. When Spillane would generously haul in six-packs of cold beers to pass around to the boys, he'd sound off about one tabloid outrage or another.

"Murder Incorporated's latest victim," Spillane said, tossing the *Daily News* on his desktop. "A plain Joe Citizen. A poor little shoemaker with a wife and three kids, who wasn't bright enough to keep his trap shut about something he happened to see. This is a hell of a city. It stinks!"

If Mickey was a detective on the case, he sure as hell wouldn't fool around.

"I'd tail the torpedo that pulled this till I had him cornered," Spillane told his pals, lighting up a Lucky. "Then I'd let him have a slug in the belly and kick his teeth in while he was lying there, bleeding to death."

"Cripes!" one of his buddies said. "What's eating you?"

Spillane had come back from his Greenwood, Mississippi, war with a new chip on his shoulder. He had that special form of survivor's guilt that afflicted GIs who spent the duration stateside. Though he eased some over the years, never seeing action was a sore point with Spillane, and friends knew not to bring it up. That included even the likes of Don Watts, his close friend in South Carolina, who decades later helped rebuild the house that Hurricane Hugo destroyed. Watts had served on the oil tanker *Cepochet*.

And right there in the storefront office with Mickey sat his buddy Joe, who had joined the Coast Guard and served in Saipan and the Philippines.

In Mississippi, Spillane had looked forward to returning to "the big city." Once there, however, he discovered he didn't like it much.

"Everybody was trying to take us," he told Hargrove, then listed various petty grievances which had inspired him to "get out—get away from these cliff dwellers—and move somewhere where people aren't like this."

Jon Gerrity believes this postwar anti–New York City attitude was at least partially the result of a beating Spillane took in a street fight.

Sub-Mariner man Bill Everett told Roy Thomas in an interview that Spillane came home angry from the war—that Mickey got "mad" and wrote a novel. Spillane took exception to that.

"I needed the money!" he told Thomas.

And in 1946 he had the kind of postwar dream that required a pile of it to come true.

A compulsive exerciser, Spillane sat among his fellow toilers in the comics field absently using a hand-spring grip. He'd been playing some semipro football and been nicknamed the Man in the Iron Mask because he wore a face guard on his helmet to protect an already much-broken nose.

Suddenly he said, "I've found the spot where I figure to spend the rest of my life."

"Yeah," somebody cracked, "a view of the Hudson from a barred window in Sing Sing."

"Nuts! It's an old hayfield on the river, eight miles from Newburgh, where the air is sweet and clean."

His friends listened wide-eyed as he informed them he'd bought the property from a family he knew upstate; he'd gotten a VA loan. The acreage was near an army base and West Point, sixty miles from New York City, and his army buddy George Wilson was already clearing it with a brush hook. He and George would build a house for Mickey and Mary Ann (and George and his wife). It was a plan designed for privacy and for beating the postwar housing shortage.

According to Henry Adams, Spillane's comic-book cronies reminded him he knew not a damn thing about building a house.

"Haven't you ever heard of the Portland Cement Company?" he asked them, indignant. He'd been sent a pamphlet with all the instructions. But Spillane still needed one thousand dollars for materials.

"You'll never make that kind of money freelancing comic books," pointed out a fellow freelancer, in a position to know.

Inarguably, Mickey Spillane's writing career was stuck in a serious low-paying limbo in the summer of 1946. With his dream of building a house in mind, he began feverishly writing stories for *The Angel* and other teenage comic books.

In a July 8, 1946, letter, Al Sulman—story editor of Timely Comics—told Spillane: "Received your three teen-age stories this morning. . . . I am accepting them, in spite of the fact that they are too damn long."

Sulman's complaint about the length of Spillane's scripts is a rare instance of the writer getting criticism for being too verbose.

The editor continued, "I'll have to do plenty of editing on them, in order to cut them down to my required length, that is, 1400 words for teen-age stories. And when I say 1400 words, I do *not* mean 1457, 1458, or 1469 . . . I mean *1400*!"

On the letterhead, Martin Goodman is listed as publisher of Timely Comics, their headquarters in the "empire state building new york city" [*sic*]. The bottom of the stationery features "America's leading comic characters: Captain America, Bucky, Human Torch and Sub-Mariner."

Less than two weeks later, Sulman gave Spillane the bad news about the synopses of his three stories: the editor's superior "does not care for any of these stories . . . he says they are the old stereotyped, pulp magazine plots."

One story foreshadows Mike Hammer's nightmare landscape: "The Devil His Due." A "rich financier" has sold his soul to the devil for success, payment due on his fiftieth birthday. He hires the Angel to protect him on this fatal day, but Old Nick captures them both, takes them to Hades, chains them, and makes them "do impossible tasks at whip point."

Sulman's comments could not be more out of step with Spillane's postwar success to come: "Portrayal of *Devil* and *Hell* is objectionable. Sadistic whippings and beatings *not* good idea." The editor told Spillane that higher-up Frank Torpey wanted "something timely and topical, with a moral." Yes, the Timely bigwig wanted something timely. . . .

Torpey would later speak of Spillane in glowing terms: "Any time we wanted a story by three o'clock—or a whole book in forty-eight hours—we'd call on Mickey."

Living in a tent now on his hayfield property, waiting to be financially able to begin construction of his cement-block house, Spillane sat at a battered typewriter with a cat on his lap and wrote more of the twenty-five dollar each filler stories he was still able to place.

"There was George, my wife, and me in the same tent," he told Thomas, "and our main course was sugar beets. We'd make like it was turkey or string beans or whatnot. . . . We'd eat groundhogs. We'd have to wait for the dog—the dog would try to bite you when you tried to take his groundhog away. . . ."

It was the only kind of meat they had for three months. Mary Ann—"Baby," Mickey called her—cooked it over an open fire, but refused to partake.

At night, at an unsteady table, by the light of a Colcman lamp, Spillane would type on "an L.C. Smith with a backspace that didn't work and a couple of keys that were shot that I paid $15 for."

A thousand bucks was a lot of twenty-five dollar text fillers. A novel would pay $250, he'd heard. Maybe he could do something with that rejected Mike Danger character.

Mystery stories paid better than comic books, didn't they?

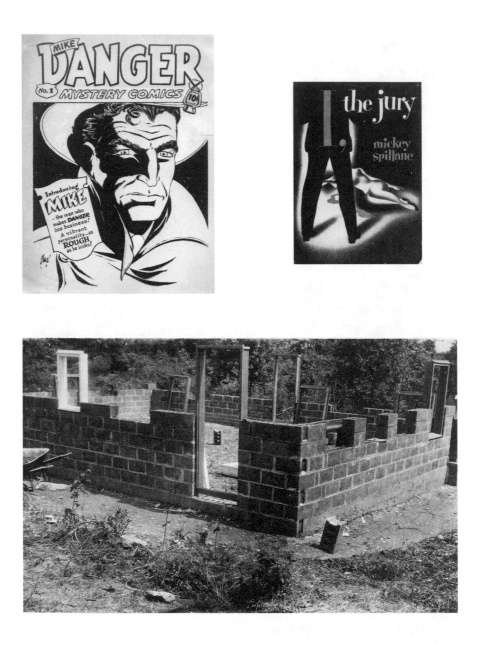

TOP LEFT: Harry Sahle's mock-up of a Mike Danger comic-book cover for Spillane to shop around with sample stories. TOP RIGHT: First edition hardcover of *I, the Jury* (1947). BOTTOM: Thanks to a $1,000 advance and a VA loan, Spillane starts building his house.

CHAPTER FIVE

I, THE NOVELIST

During World War II, paperback books were distributed free to servicemen, who could easily tuck the booklets into a pocket or a backpack. These were reprints of hardcover bestsellers and genre titles, particularly mystery, but also classics. The format was oblong and smaller—from 5 ½" to 6 ½" long and from 3 ⅞" to 4 ½" high—than the reprints produced by Pocket Books in the USA and Penguin in Great Britain, those mass-market, pocket-sized paperback books that had revolutionized the publishing industry in the 1930s. An astonishing 122,951,031 books were given away free to the men and women of the armed forces.

"Some of the publishers think that their business is going to be ruined," broadcaster H. V. Kaltenborn told his listeners in 1944. "But I make this prediction. America's publishers have cooperated in an experiment that will for the first time make us a nation of book readers."

It occurred to Mickey Spillane that returning soldiers and sailors—and for that matter pilots—would become accustomed to reading the cheaply produced, portable paperback books at the established twenty-five-cent price point.

The same had already proven true with ten-cent comic books, sold in military base PXs and ideal for even barely literate GIs. They were easily transportable reading material, and offered the same popular genres as the movies of postwar America. Romance, war, horror, crime, and science fiction were flourishing with a new adult audience.

Spillane felt that original paperbacks—a logical extension of pulps and compatible with the reprints distributed free to servicemen—would be the next big thing: for writers, a less stuffy market than the traditional hardcover publishers; for readers, a much more affordable cover price.

"This [would be] the new concept coming up," Spillane said in 1998. "Something brand new and different."

He would have preferred to write *I, the Jury* directly for the paperback market, but instead did so with the conventional New York publishers in mind. "I wrote it for the hardback market," he said, "because that was the only way in."

How long it took Mickey Spillane to write *I, the Jury* is a mystery unlikely to be solved. Caught up in his own puckish sense of self-promotion, Spillane would proclaim over the many years that the crucial event of his writing career had been accomplished in nine days . . . or was it nineteen? Other times it became two weeks or three. His *Cavalier* editor Robert Curran, whose 1963 *Saga* profile of Mickey is among the best, put it at thirty days.

"Following the comic book format," Curran noted, "he first worked out the socko ending—the bullet in the belly for the nude blonde. Then he went back to the beginning and developed a plot that carried the action to the bullet-in-the-belly scene."

Spillane typed his novel single-spaced, Curran said, "because double-spacing meant he had to change the paper in the machine too often." The writer also thought it "looked more like a book."

Mike Lancer and Mike Danger were typically snappy comic-book names. But Spillane needed something less over-the-top and more real, yet with appropriate impact. George Wilson tells of "a joint" on Great Lake Street in Newburgh called Hammer's Bar, a hangout for Spillane, Wilson, and other buddies, including fellow writer and World War II veteran Dave

Gerrity. Over the course of the summer of 1946, Spillane adopted the Hammer name for his private-eye character.

The writer apparently divided his work on the book between his temporary home—a World War I army surplus tent—and the Brooklyn storefront comic-book factory. How Mickey made the commute is unknown, as he and Mary Ann did not own a car. Or have water, a telephone, or electricity.

"My buddy Joe Gill," Spillane recalled in 1981, "used to read the pages as they came off the typewriter."

His fellow comics scripters had hooted with derisive laughter when Spillane announced he was writing a book. Gill would read pages as they rolled off the typewriter and share them with the others in the former grocery store: "Listen to this junk, willya? This is crappy writing."

But when Gill offered to help out and correct the errors, Spillane said, "You're not going to change a word of it."

In fact, Mary Ann, back on their hayfield property, was retyping the book in traditional double-spaced fashion, doing some editing as she went.

Spillane's comic-book cronies agreed with Gill. Mickey didn't know any more about writing a novel than he did building a house! They read the pages flying out of the typewriter and found them (in Hargrove's words) "atrocious and unsalable." Spillane told them he fully intended to get a $1,000 advance and build his house and shut them up.

"What the hell do you think you're doing?" another of his cohorts asked, as the copy kept rolling from the machine. "Who's going to buy that?"

Spillane finished the draft of *I, the Jury* in early 1946. "Everybody agreed it would never sell," Spillane remembered with a grin. "You know what they say about last laughs?"

For a time, though, the verdict of his fellow comic-book pros seemed apt. Seven publishers turned down *I, the Jury*.

"They said it was too dirty," Spillane recalled, "and all that kind of stuff . . . they had never seen anything like *I, the Jury!*"

The storefront verdict wasn't unanimous. Some of his peers warmed to the rowdy yarn as Mike Hammer's adventures played out, and they had to admit the thing held your interest and was tough to lay down.

"But," as journalist Adams reported, "there was nothing to compare it to. It seemed to be in a class all by itself." This Mike Hammer thing just might take off, if the writer could find a publisher willing to take a chance on something different.

"The war," Adams observed, "had violently altered the nation's reading habits. An appetite for tougher fare had been whetted and multitudes [of ex-soldiers and sailors] who had never bought a book were now avid readers." That whetted appetite included an urge for more sexually explicit entertainment as well.

Among the storefront believers was Joe's brother, who as a Funnies, Inc., writer/editor had once upon a time seen Spillane's potential. He now offered Mickey a helping hand.

Ray took the manuscript to Jack McKenna, an executive with Duenewald Printing Corporation, who did business with Fawcett Publications. Maybe, as a favor, Jack would get the book to Roscoe Fawcett, whose outfit had made a fortune out of comic books, and who did not harbor the usual prejudices against toilers in that field.

But first McKenna had to read it himself, and—favor to a friend or no favor—the busy exec just couldn't seem to find time. As Curran relates the story, McKenna tossed the manuscript to his wife.

"You like detective stories," he told her at bedtime. "Read this one."

In the morning, McKenna's wife shook him awake. She'd just finished *I, the Jury*, having read through the night. "Read it!" she ordered him. "This is different."

McKenna couldn't put it down either.

On June 18, 1946, Spillane entered into an agreement with John Francis McKenna, now Mickey's exclusive agent representing him "in the sale of the book 'I THE JURY' and such other books as I may write" (note the absence of Spillane's characteristic comma). The hand-typed letterhead reads "MICKEY SPILLANE, 808 Beverly Road, Brooklyn, New York" (again, the probable address of his parents), and is signed with his now-familiar stylistic "M" with the upward slash, granting McKenna (of 3 Woodlawn Road, Maplewood, New Jersey) a ten-percent commission.

Now, at Spillane's urging, McKenna took *I, the Jury* to Roscoe Fawcett.

"Fawcett thought it was great," Spillane told *Vanity Fair.* "So Fawcett went to New American Library with a proposition: 'If you will print this book, I will distribute it.'"

NAL was interested but said they couldn't do it—they were a reprint house with no hardcover line. After all, they said—reminding Fawcett of the obvious—no reputable publisher put out paperback originals. But if the distributor could find a hardcover house to publish the novel, NAL would be happy to negotiate reprint rights.

E. P. Dutton was also a major client of Duenewald Printing, and the newly minted literary agent with one client found "a skeptical editor" at Dutton to take a look at the mystery that had kept Mrs. McKenna up all right.

Throughout his lifetime, Spillane took a self-satisfied glee out of reporting that almost everyone at Dutton thought *I, the Jury* was terrible. He liked to say he was the only author Dutton was ashamed to publish (a rare use of the term "author" from Spillane).

Editor in chief Nicholas Wreden agreed the book wasn't "in the best of taste," but he thought it would sell.

Spillane insisted on a $1,000 advance—the figure needed to complete his house—and, with McKenna's help, got it. That was high for a first novel from a mystery writer, but a reprint deal for $750 was quietly sealed between NAL co-founder/editor Victor Weybright and Dutton vice president John Edmondson.

Grateful as he might be for this opportunity, Spillane was not about to be rolled over. He refused to be edited beyond the most basic typos and issues of clarity.

Ray Gill explained why a first-time author with a desperate need for money would be so stubbornly controlling: "He didn't want them to refine the guts out of the story." The creator of Mike Hammer, for all his celebrated I-only-write-for-money claims, from the start cared intensely about the integrity of his work—of his art, though he would never call it that.

Despite his impeccable literary credentials, it is not really surprising that Victor Weybright would appreciate what Spillane was up to. The NAL publisher was a country boy, too, and had written stories for *Adventure*, a pulp magazine Mike Hammer's creator read as a youth.

Publishers subjected new authors, then as now, to questionnaires, and Spillane's six-page self-biography sheet for Dutton (dated December 16, 1946) reveals a good deal about Spillane's habits and attitudes at the time.

"I'm the mediumist guy I know," Mickey writes. "5'8", short brown hair, hazel eyes, size 40 suit, getting a tan (got blisters) filling in my driveway, one small denture where I lost an argument." That last detail, a typical Spillane throwaway, seems to confirm Jon Gerrity's explanation for Spillane's desire to leave New York after a nasty street-corner confrontation.

"During my Air Force career," Spillane continues on the form, "I probably hit all the states. My experiences were all memorable, most unusual, and unhappily unprintable. I can't recall anything distinctive since everything was a jumbled mass of hedonistic activity at the time."

Of course, this tongue-in-cheek response raises more questions than it answers. Years later, in 1951, a letter to his editor Marc Jaffe provides a rare glimpse into that side of the writer's lifestyle.

After a wild night at Topp's, run by Mickey's buddy Louie the Lug, Spillane reports, "Sunday, which was supposed to be quiet, wasn't. Everybody re-gathered [at Spillane's place] for a recapitulation, hauled in more beer, two delicious babes and we started over. One deep dish was a stripper and gave us an uninhibited version of arts sans censorship. One guy's gal friend, not to be outdone, tried the same act, got tangled in her panties and hit the dirt where she completed the deal snake fashion. In case you're wondering, all the wives . . . spent the afternoon taking in a movie. . . ."

Writer Marion Hargrove, himself a World War II veteran (and best-selling author of *See Here, Private Hargrove*, 1942), characterized "the house-building period" as "probably the happiest of Spillane's life, and his proudest single achievement."

Spillane told Dutton publicity director Elliott Graham that the process had begun. "With the optimism of a novice," he wrote, "armed with folders of sketches and a few tools, [I have] started to dig."

In 1981, Spillane explained his decision to move out into the sticks: ". . . [We] were going to raise kids. We weren't going to have them in the city. *All* cities are sinkholes. I knew it even then."

Ensconced in his tent on his acreage, amid scenic wooded country on the west side of the Hudson River near Storm King Mountain, Spillane and his wife, "Baby," recruited assistance for the do-it-yourself effort from weekend guests and the comic-book cronies who'd mocked Mickey. Charlie Wells from Mississippi, who according to Wilson "latched onto Mickey," pitched in. Jack McKenna and his wife, who'd been so instrumental in the sale of *I, the Jury*, were also part of the informal construction crew. Spillane called the building site "Little Bohemia."

But Spillane and Wilson did the bulk of the work over what the writer terms "an exceptional summer," hoisting the cinder blocks, mortaring them, the result a serviceable structure, a bunker without, homey within.

"We saw snow before we got out of that tent," Spillane recalled in 1998. "We had gravel on the floor for a long time. It was great if you want to throw your coffee, your dishwater . . . just throw it on the floor. It was too cold to go outside."

The coldness and lack of insulation would be diminished by knotty-pine paneling and the gravel floors upgraded to cement. But not for a while.

"There was no running water," Wilson remembered. "Everything had to be carried in. And the bathroom facilities were primitive."

They took baths in wash tubs. Brought in water in big milk cans until a neighbor named Joe Tubbs drilled a well. The crew called themselves the "52-20 Club" because they were eligible for $52 a week for twenty weeks from the federal government for their wartime service.

Eventually three buildings stood on the property—the main house with its single-lane dirt road out front, the artist's studio where George Wilson worked (called Pickwick Studios, ironically so, out of the host's dislike of Dickens), and the writer's building where Mickey worked. A small stream separated the house from the studios, on Rockcut Road, where nearby neighbors were Jehovah's Witnesses.

Years later, the writer boasted that his friends were jealous of his new home and were after him to build one for them. That's at least partially Spillane tongue-in-cheek braggadocio. But in 1946 he may have been serious—building his friends' houses would have been work he could use.

In October 1946, the Spillanes moved in, the place outfitted with army cots and porch furniture provided by Mickey's parents. The storefront comic-book factory shut down but Spillane continued to write comic-book scripts. He applied to the city editor of a Newburgh newspaper and was told he didn't look or talk like a reporter, and got shown the door. Finally, he signed on as a copywriter in the advertisement department of Schoonmaker's, a local department store—part of a jobs program, the government paying companies to hire veterans.

Mickey helped his pal Wilson get a job with him in the advertising department at Schoonmaker's store, but Wilson grew bored with writing ads for perfume and soon left Little Bohemia behind to head out to Bangor, Maine, for a job with a logging company.

Spillane stayed on as an ad copywriter (Dashiell Hammett had once done the same), commuting by bicycle or hitchhiking, for fifty bucks a week. When the bike broke, he splurged and bought a 1934 Pontiac convertible. He loved the vehicle and, making one of his less accurate predictions, pledged it would be the only car he'd ever want or need.

Day job or not, having sold a book inspired Spillane and he began work on his second Mike Hammer novel. The setting was a small town on Long Island, with Hammer dealing with corrupt local cops and the gangsters who funded them—very different from the setting and situation of *I, the Jury*, but nonetheless with references to "the Williams case." It sputtered out, perhaps because Spillane had allowed the Mike and Velda relationship to get away from him, developing too soon into the lasting love that would come much later.

Or the writer may have abandoned the novel after showing the partial manuscript to Nicholas Wreden at Dutton or Weybright at NAL, perhaps even just mentioning he was working on it. Either or both would likely have advised him that writing a sequel to a book as yet unpublished, and untried in the marketplace, was premature if not foolhardy.

Using the fragment's small-town setting and some of the characters, Spillane would in 1948 write a completed second Mike Hammer novel, *For Whom the Gods Would Destroy*, which would face its own publishing obstacles. (The false start would be completed by MAC and titled *Lady, Go Die!* for 2012 publication. Another Hammer manuscript, of around thirty single-spaced pages, dates to this period, possibly preceding *I, the Jury*; it was presented as the detective's first case in *Killing Town*, 2018, again completed by MAC.)

On January 1, 1947, *I, the Jury*, a hardcover edition priced at $2.50, saw publication. The modest printing of five thousand copies got off to a slow start.

A few reviewers noticed the novel, however, including James Sandoe of the *New York Herald Tribune*, who deemed its author "an inept vulgarian." The Criminals at Large column in the *New York Times* was negative if balanced: "The story will measure up to the expectation of those mystery fans who must have the impact 'right between the eyes!'"

The *Saturday Review* summed up in "The Criminal Record": "Lurid action, lurid characters, lurid writing, lurid plot, lurid finish. Verdict: lurid." The author's name was misspelled "Spilland."

Some of the critical reaction was positive. The *Miami Herald* said, "In a long and misspent life immersed in blood, I don't believe I've ever met a tougher hombre than Mike Hammer, private eye." The *Cleveland News* raved: "I've read dozens of tough-guy mysteries but this one tops them all."

The *Oakland Post Enquirer* warned, "This isn't good fare for the squeamish, but the writer has certainly produced a dramatic climax . . . guaranteed to chill your blood."

In the early fall of 1947, in an undated letter to E. P. Dutton publicity director Elliott Graham on John Schoonmaker & Sons, a frustrated Spillane detailed a local promotion for *I, the Jury* thanks to his employer, whose department store had a book section. The young writer was interested in anything concerning self-promotion—book signings, advertisements, general publicity.

"Some of my friends in New York have been trying to buy the book," he told Graham, but area bookstores either were out of stock or waiting for orders to be filled. "Is it really selling that well . . . or hasn't it reached some of the stores yet? I'd really like to know how it's doing if you've had any reports."

Spillane also asked Graham about getting copies of the book to the editor of the Greenwood *Morning Star* to help generate interest in his wife's hometown in Mississippi.

He wrote, "As yet, Mr. Dewey, of Dewey's Drug Store, hasn't seen the Dutton agent and has been getting a lot of requests for the book. . . . [T]here's enough local pride to carry it for a good sale."

The newly minted novelist had just recently completed an article for "house-hungry vets" for King Features. He noted that the Spillane house was nearing completion and that "right now we're in the middle of installing electricity . . . oh happy day! Writing by candle light and Coleman burners keeps words to a minimum."

Toward the end of 1947, the *San Francisco Chronicle* picked *I, the Jury* as one of the year's seven best mysteries.

But few readers noticed, and life at Little Bohemia went on, with chickens running underfoot now, providing better fare than groundhog, the ad-man husband getting to work by car, not bike or thumb, and the rat-a-tat-tat of two-finger typing raging in the night.

"After I wrote *I, the Jury*," Spillane told Thomas, "I stayed in comic books here and there, until the paperback came out."

In December 1948.

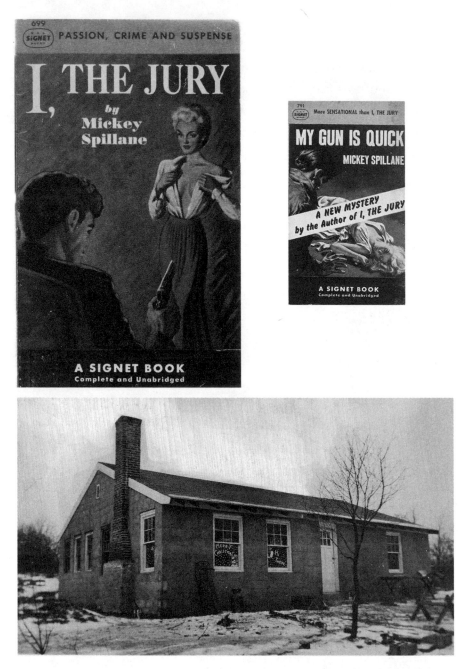

TOP LEFT: First paperback edition of *I, the Jury*, with Tony Varady cover.
TOP RIGHT: First paperback edition of *My Gun Is Quick*, with Lu Kimmel cover.
BOTTOM: The house Mike Hammer built, ca. 1949.

CHAPTER SIX

THE EVER-PRESENT MIKE

"**M**ike Hammer was," Spillane's friend and editor Bob Curran said, "what almost every ex-GI wanted to be in 1946—or maybe even what most men wanted to be."

Many returning veterans had been living "me first lives," Curran pointed out, three to four years where self-preservation was all . . . where they'd learned to fight not only other men but machines, and how to repress "their most basic appetites."

Who better than Mike Hammer to provide a postwar male wish-fulfillment fantasy? A guy who didn't have to look for sex—it came looking for him. A guy who "cut through red tape like a bayonet through Spam," who didn't stand in line or recognize rules or follow procedural handbooks. And a guy who cut bullies down to size with their own terrible tactics.

Spillane had presented this new kind of hero by way of a canny literary gimmick—he never gave a description of Hammer, whose first-person narration crawled into the heads of readers, made himself at home after raiding the icebox for a beer, and then stayed for the duration . . . of the novel. It allowed an identification between antihero and reader that was at once personal and visceral.

But every guy who fought overseas knew what Mike Hammer looked like, all right—he saw him in the mirror every morning.

"If you describe a guy as being six-foot-two, stalwart, big-muscled and dark haired," Spillane said in 1998, "how can a guy that's short and fat think that he's the hero in the story? He can't do that. But if [Hammer's] not described, that guy can be the hero in his own mind."

The five-thousand-copy hardcover print run of *I, the Jury* had sales of around 3,500, barely respectable; and the print run of NAL's label Signet was their minimum, 150,000.

But as Spillane recalled it, Roscoe Fawcett had told Signet he wanted an unprecedented half-million copies for the first paperback printing of *I, the Jury*, a request that was ignored. The underestimated initial print run barely lasted a week. On Coney Island, the books were selling like red hots. One dealer reported selling 25,000 copies in a single day.

". . . and the distributors were screaming," Spillane said, "'Where's the books? We need those books!'"

When Fawcett discovered his direct orders were ignored, heads rolled.

The morning the first royalty check arrived, providing a dizzying payday, Spillane thought it had to be a mistake.

"Right away I became rich," he told Thomas. "Now, rich at that time was $200!" Thousands of dollars on a single check *had* to be a mistake. . . .

But, of course, it wasn't. The evocative, art-deco-flavored artwork on the first paperback edition of *I, the Jury* had resonated with readers looking for something new. It depicted a seated Hammer with his back largely to the camera, his .45 trained on a seductive blonde unbuttoning her blouse—sex and violence, striptease and judgment, it was all there.

"Those who attributed Spillane's overnight success to realism couldn't have been more wrong," the anonymous insider writing for *Sir* magazine said. "Hemingway is realism. Maugham is realism. Mickey is straight surrealism bordering on fantasy."

In the spring of 1948, the writer had sequestered himself in his knotty-pine-paneled "garret" (as he put it) in the fir-hugged little building where he worked. He returned to the setting and basic idea of the abandoned Hammer novel that would eventually be completed and published as *Lady, Go Die!* Having read an article in the April 12, 1948, issue of *Life* magazine ("Warden Adopts a Young Murderer"), Mickey had come up with an idea leading to a "socko" conclusion designed to hit with the impact of *I, the Jury*'s striptease execution.

For Whom the Gods Would Destroy (destined not to be published till 1966, as *The Twisted Thing*) was Spillane's second completed Mike Hammer novel, his intended follow-up to *I, the Jury*.

Billy Parks, an ex-con friend of Hammer's, now works for scientist Rudolph York as a chauffeur. York's son, Ruston, is abducted, and corrupt sadistic cop Dilwick is convinced Parks is guilty, using third-degree tactics to get a confession. Hammer rescues Parks and is subsequently hired by Rudolph York to locate the son. York is obsessed with creating the perfectly conditioned learning machine. He's been using as his guinea pig fourteen-year-old Ruston, who has been programmed from infancy to know everything.

Hammer returns Ruston to his father, who becomes enraged at the mention of the name Mallory, which the boy has picked up from one of the kidnappers. Later that night, Hammer finds Rudolph York dead, his head split open by a meat cleaver. The detective discovers the essential clue to Rudolph York's murderer: only one person on his list of suspects knew the name Mallory. Ruston York!

Yes, Ruston is the killer—a child driven mad by his scientist father's programmed learning techniques. Hammer confronts him, but manufactured genius Ruston has already figured out that Hammer suspects him and has removed the clip from Hammer's .45. Ruston pulls his own .32 and denounces his dead father: he does not consider himself human but rather a "twisted thing" warped by science and better off dead. With that, he puts the gun barrel in his mouth and pulls the trigger.

For Whom the Gods Would Destroy strongly suggests that the vengeful Hammer of the first novel was not envisioned by his creator as the Hammer of *all* the novels—rather, *I, the Jury* appears intended to tell just that one tale of murdered-friend vengeance. In *The Twisted Thing* (as it would be published), Hammer seems comparatively grounded, not haunted by the events of *I, the Jury* as he would be in *One Lonely Night* (1951) and the other early novels. There is steamy sex (by 1948 standards), and characteristically violent action, hard-knuckled rough stuff consistent with the debut Hammer novel.

But the dominant theme is a father-and-son relationship between Mike Hammer and fourteen-year-old "child genius" Ruston York. The cold rage and hot blood that fuels the more famous Hammer novels is largely absent, and—perhaps significantly, since the abandoned version of this story had taken the relationship perhaps too far—so is Velda, the love of Hammer's life. Pat Chambers rates only a cameo appearance.

All of this indicates Spillane was intending to make Hammer a more standard tough PI, with the major twist being the placement of his Race Williams–like figure in an Agatha Christie–style classical mystery.

Also strikingly absent is Spillane's nightmare New York—the action takes place in a small resort town, where Hammer is initially involved with rescuing young Ruston from kidnappers. The tough, corrupt local cop—the memorably named Dilwick—provides the initial conflict, but the young genius's wealthy father is soon murdered, and away Hammer goes.

Hoods and a casino right out of *The Big Sleep*, and several willing voluptuous dames, provide the tough dick with further fun and games, but his detective work is also right out of Christie, including a search for missing documents more typical of Hercule Poirot than Mike Hammer.

The ending, revealing the identity of the murderer, comes in typical, abrupt, shocking Spillane style, making a lot of sense as the second such ending of the Hammer canon—and would have been a controversial, disturbing surprise if published in 1949 or '50. It still packed a punch in its delayed 1966 appearance and retains power today.

The small-town setting, the classic pulp cast—troubled millionaire, willing wenches, crooked cops, casino thugs—and the surrogate father-and-son relationship at the novel's core make *The Twisted Thing* unique among Spillane's Hammer novels, a telling glimpse into where the character might have gone had the reading public post–*I, the Jury* not taken a bloodlust fancy to Spillane and his Hammer at their most vengeful extreme.

The emotionally twisted thing who was Mike Hammer in *One Lonely Night* and the other early novels is what truly sets Spillane apart as a key hard-boiled writer. Had *For Whom the Gods Would Destroy* been published as the second Mike Hammer novel, in 1949 perhaps, it might well have taken Hammer and his creator down a more traditional, and less artistically and commercially successful, path.

Spillane's frank sexuality and his realistically brutal scenes of violence were innovative; but the retribution aspect of *I, the Jury*—the private eye as avenging hero, the combat vet who kills his lover out of loyalty to a fellow soldier's memory—is what truly set author and character apart. So had the unusual near-psychotic ravings of the antihero on the rampage. This was all new.

Similarly resonating in *I, the Jury* was the way the postwar world seemed to have let Hammer down. The private eye may have respect for the police in general and a certain policeman in particular, but he has contempt for a judicial system that allows the guilty to either escape unpunished or with so little punishment that there is no deterrent to crime. Hammer essentially views himself as a cop, an unpaid public servant, although by *One Lonely Night* he has come to consider himself an avenging instrument of God.

In Mike Hammer novels to come, Spillane will use the theme of revenge again and again, usually expressing it in terms of his detective's outrage, merging two distinct character types, the hero and the avenger. Dave Gerrity's son Jon pointed this out as a common theme from Catholic literature.

Publisher Victor Weybright could see Mickey Spillane's great potential and became concerned for the writer's future after the explosive success of *I, the Jury*, an anxiety largely based on the *For Whom the Gods Would Destroy* manuscript.

On August 23, 1949, he wrote the writer's agent, Jack McKenna—still associated with Duenewald Printing Corporation—and referred to the thirty-one-year-old Spillane as a "young genius" (perhaps an unconscious reference to Ruston York). *For Whom the Gods Would Destroy* struck Weybright as "too weird and an implausible tour de force." He recommended that "it should be put into the deep freeze until two or three more Spillane books, with the quality of *I, the Jury*, genuinely endear him to his vast audience."

Weybright felt the book would negatively impact Spillane's market and harm his ability to earn. Better, he said, for Spillane to make a "fresh start" on the novel after he's done two or three more traditional Hammer mysteries. To Weybright, "the plot is way 'off,'" and "the manuscript should be held in storage" until the Dutton and Signet forces could move "move forward with [a] fresh opus."

The publisher felt Signet, with its small list and high sales per title, was perfect for Spillane, whose "genuine potential lies in the 25 [cent] mass market." Working with Fawcett as NAL's national distributor, Weybright considered it "an incalculable advantage to have Roscoe Fawcett personally as well as professionally interested in putting Mickey Spillane in the Big League, of mass market authors of quality."

McKenna had already arranged two in-person meetings between Weybright and Spillane to discuss the next steps in the writer's market development. One such meeting took place on Friday, August 19, 1949, but no record of that conversation exists.

Weybright copied the McKenna letter to Dutton's mystery editor, Nick Wreden, who also had a keen "interest in developing Spillane's market." Wreden had decided to back Weybright in the decision not to publish *For Whom the Gods Would Destroy* at this time.

Weybright noted, "[T]he literary world abounds in ruined careers in which a poor second book erases all the promise and luster of an initial success."

In a separate letter to Wreden, Weybright characterized part-time agent McKenna as someone "who isn't very knowledgeable about publishing protocol and printing in particular."

Both these industry professionals were concerned that if they outright rejected *For Whom the Gods Would Destroy*, McKenna might give the book to "some second string, quick-buck deal that would mar the high hopes you and I have for Spillane as a literary property."

Indeed, subsequent correspondence stressed the need to avoid the word "reject," which would allow Spillane—hot off the heels of *I, the Jury*'s astounding success—to sell the manuscript to another publishing house.

Dutton and NAL *wanted* the property—just not to publish it at the present time. Had McKenna been a more experienced literary agent, he no doubt would have insisted they pay for the privilege of placing so valuable a property on the shelf.

The correspondence does not indicate whether Weybright and/or Wreden realized at this point that the missing element from *For Whom the Gods Would Destroy* was the vengeance motif. Likely their major objections were to do with the science-fiction nature of the father experimenting to increase a genius child's intelligence, and especially the idea of a murderous child.

(The homicidal Rhoda Penmark of novelist William March's *The Bad Seed* would not appear till 1955. Mickey Spillane appeared as the lawyer of the murderous mother in the indie film *Mommy*, 1995, portrayed by the original Broadway and film Rhoda, Patty McCormack.)

But the public's interest in a vengeful Mike Hammer was not lost on Spillane himself. And when he went back to work in his woods-bordered office on a new Hammer, *My Gun Is Quick*, he and his antihero returned to revenge. The writer also indicates in the novel that the events of *I, the Jury* were weighing heavily on Mike Hammer, beginning what would be something unusual at the time in mystery fiction: a detective with an ongoing history.

In the fall of 1949, Weybright informed Colonel John P. Edmondson at Dutton that NAL had received the manuscript of *My Gun Is Quick*, forwarded by Wreden, and was excited and ready to schedule it on Signet's 1950 list. In October, Weybright wrote to thank Edmondson for phoning to let him know of a magazine inquiry about the availability of Spillane's new novel for abridgement.

"I am glad that you agree that all our interests, including those of the author," Weybright wrote, "are best served by not releasing condensation rights to Spillane."

He closed by asking for "galleys as soon as possible" of the new Spillane. That both publishing houses are aware that they have an important new—if unlikely—star author on their hands is apparent in the correspondence.

In September 1949, Elliott Graham recorded in the files some salient facts about a recent conversation with Spillane, who "lives in a creative wilderness [and] deliberately maintains the woods and wild bushes in a luxuriant state around the house." Spillane issued him an invitation: "If you can find [the place], you're invited in."

By now Spillane was the father of a twelve-week-old girl, Kathy. The writer says he "answers every [fan] letter" and that "75% of his mail [is] from women." Unlike the critics, the letters do "not [have] a single unfavorable comment."

Spillane "devotes all his time to writing" and is "now working on a third book." He described his work schedule as "night and rainy days . . . keep going till tired out—with a bottle of beer and a pack of cigarettes."

In another undated letter to Graham, Spillane was once again writing blurbs for his book cover, even though he is uncomfortable with that role: "I still feel like a jerk when I try to write something about myself."

Spillane's second bio form for Dutton intriguingly presents Mike Hammer as a real person.

"Around here," Spillane writes, "Mike is sort of an ever-present but out-at-the-moment guy with everyone playing guessing games trying to figure what he'll be up to next. However, he has ideas of his own that I don't even know about. They all seem to come out when I sit down to type."

What follows is quite revealing of Spillane's creative process.

CONVERSATION WITH MIKE HAMMER AND HIS AUTHOR
MICKEY SPILLANE

It's been an hour now since Mike dropped in. He has a cut over one eye and his knuckles are raw, and he just sits there in a chair fooling with the slide of his .45. He caught me watching him over the type-writer and grinned.

"You got a nice easy life, kid," he said.

"Sure," I agreed sarcastically, "real easy . . . being cooped up here trying to make a buck. Open the door and you'll find a wife, a new baby, three dogs, four tame chickens and cats whose kittens have

kittens that have kittens. One poor goldfish too. They all want to be fed. Usually at the same time. A real easy life."

"Ah, quit crabbing. You got a house and enough jungle around you to keep out an army. You never have to wear a tie or tight shoes, either. Writing's a good racket, Mickey, all you need is an idea and a typewriter and you're in business. Look what I do for a buck." He shoved the slide back in the .45 and stuck the gun under his coat.

I felt like clubbing him with it. "Right now ideas are what I need bad, chum," I told him. "You scrape the cream of excitement off life and leave me here beating my brains out on a mill. I wish you'd push an idea my way for a change."

Mike didn't answer. He scowled and checked his watch every few minutes. He had that look in his eyes again. Something was up but he wouldn't sound off. I knew damn well he wasn't here to make small talk with me . . . not just yet.

Two minutes ago he pulled his lips back over his teeth, lost in his thoughts. He barely nodded to me when he brushed by. When I heard his car start outside I let out a laugh and put the cover back on the typewriter. I didn't need an idea now.

When he came back I'd have my whole damn story.

The Big Kill receives a record 2.5-million-copy first paperback edition, with all the previous Hammers receiving another million each.

CHAPTER SEVEN
VENGEANCE IS HIS

Mike Hammer thrillers basically have three openings: (1) a friend of Mike's has been murdered or badly assaulted; (2) Mike is the personal eyewitness of a brutal encounter or murder; or (3) Mike receives transformative information motivating him to rise out from a pit of personal depression.

Occasionally, Hammer alludes to bread-and-butter cases, but the enthusiastic and profitable reception to *I, the Jury* and its vengeance-driven detective encouraged Spillane to focus on Hammer's excursions into rage and revenge, at least in those first six novels.

In all three standard openings, Hammer swears to find the killer or killers and deliver punishment of a biblical nature ("an eye for an eye") without involvement of a court of law. Hammer becomes the instrument of God and delivers his own version of hellfire and brimstone—sometimes hands-on, other times via a clever ploy, with at least one occasion of possible divine intervention.

The protagonist's mode of delivering justice and the way he handles—and at times manhandles—the people he meets on each investigative crusade becomes the basis for Mike Hammer's code. Spillane considered the core of Hammer's character to be a willingness to go after the bad guys utilizing their own illegal and violent methods.

His authorial voice—through his first-person surrogate Mike Hammer—was influenced by personal experience and societal shift. The loss of innocence brought by World War II and the resulting changes to American life led to a new normal in the United States: increased awareness of graft and corruption in local government and law enforcement at all levels, and a more observable incidence of the influence of unlimited lawless wealth at the expense of the little guy.

The writer incorporated those societal pressures into a new consciousness, tapping into the universal mindset by expressing the unresolved rage of the reading public—male and female alike—who embraced his stories by the millions. Spillane combined his eclectic reading (including pulp fiction) and life experiences (particularly wartime) with a direct knowledge of the elemental appeal of the comic book into a new style of fiction that excited and pleased a wide swath of the reading public.

In his minibiography for Dutton, Spillane describes many of his experiences as "hedonistic" and unprintable. As so often with Spillane's public persona, he speaks the literal truth in an amused manner that takes the edge off. The Mike Hammer stories of Spillane's Golden Age (1947–52) are, despite their dark humor, deadly serious, reflecting the rage of both character and writer. Signet's usual cover copy underlines this: "A Mike Hammer Thriller!"

Spillane correctly predicted and shaped the exploding paperback-novel market. His books included the following elements, enhanced by his years of writing comic-book adventures and short filler stories. His Golden Age novels all contain certain plot elements:

- the "socko" beginning
- the slam-bang closing chapter
- the mentally twisted adversary
- the rich but corrupt businessman or a representative of society's elite set
- sexual situations outside the accepted norm of middle America (homosexuality, cross-dressing, bondage and domination, and other acts, up to and including incest)

But a Spillane book is much more than suggested by such a listing of what have become tropes. Spillane's fiction defines an American Revenge Tragedy. His world follows the tradition of Revenge Tragedy—The Tragedy of Blood—exemplified in the Elizabethan/Jacobean plays of the later 1500s and early 1600s, including Thomas Kyd's *The Spanish Tragedy* (ca. 1585–87), William Shakespeare's *Hamlet* (1599–1601), and Thomas Middleton's *The Revenger's Tragedy* (1606–7). Modern American society closely replicates the sexual attitudes and mores of that period.

Spillane's revenge thrillers include the following characters:

- The Avenger (Mike Hammer)
- The Good Woman (Velda)
- The Elite (corrupted by money or sexual perversion)
- The Police, small group of good guys
- The Corrupt Police, a much larger group
- The Mob (the Syndicate bosses, plus all the related goons and hitmen)
- The Innocent Victims
- The Insider Press Contact
- The Hooker (usually with a heart of gold)
- The DA (the district attorney, politically motivated and ignorant)
- The Desirable Debutante
- The Insider Police Contact (Pat Chambers)

Spillane turned this cast and the normal plot points of a standard detective novel into the dramatic action of a modern American revenge play.

Each Spillane novel, written at whatever point of the writer's creative life, reflects the emotional intensity of his avenging angel. The repetition of what appears to be a mundane plot becomes irrelevant to the satisfaction derived from reading a Spillane novel, all of which end with a psyche-cleansing catharsis for protagonist and reader.

By the conclusion of *I, the Jury*, the reader has learned much about Mike Hammer. The detective has a strong sense of duty and friendship, has compassion for the suffering of humankind, and is a man who finds society's means of delivering justice ineffective. He is also a violent man, a self-labeled misanthrope susceptible to great rage and quite capable of exacting a suitable revenge for the murder of a friend.

Hammer is usually described as a tough guy, without regard for any law but his own. Some critics even understandably use the title *I, the Jury* itself as evidence that he considers himself above the law. Certainly Hammer can, and does, deliver bloody justice to those he deems degenerate and evil.

In the early 1950s and beyond, Spillane's millions of readers never let these acts of vengeance deter them from snatching up and devouring each new Mike Hammer thriller and eagerly awaiting the next. This apparent lack of taste, or perhaps discernment, by a vast readership troubled Spillane's early critics, who were quick to denigrate the books and even to some extent Spillane himself.

Throughout his life, beginning in childhood, Spillane voraciously consumed classic adventure stories written by Alexander Dumas, Anthony Hope, Thomas Bulfinch, and even William Shakespeare. He was a born storyteller who would incorporate this reading into his own creative calling.

The Mike Hammer novels follow two distinct patterns, reflecting widely different influences. Most readily apparent, of course, is the hard-boiled private detective story of the pulp magazines of the 1930s and 1940s. Spillane knew and admired the work of Dashiell Hammett and Raymond Chandler. Of Hammett's novels, Mike Hammer's creator cited *Red Harvest* as his favorite, not *The Maltese Falcon*, which *I, the Jury* more directly draws upon. Of Chandler's novels, Spillane's favorite was *Farewell, My Lovely*, a title providing the direct address/punctuation style Hammer's creator often utilized in titling his novels.

But the pulp mystery writer who set the pattern for Spillane was Carroll John Daly, creator of Race Williams, the seminal hard-boiled detective whose long run began in the influential *Black Mask*. Spillane held on to copies of Race Williams stories for years; he even wrote to Daly after his success with Mike Hammer, acknowledging the pulp writer's influence on his style and subject matter.

"Dead Hands Reaching," a typical Race Williams "action mystery," appears in the November 1935 issue of *Dime Detective*. A kidnapped diamond heiress, Mary Morse, is tied up and lowered into a room from the ceiling. Race shoots the hood holding her—Gunner Slade—three times, leaving him "stiffer than a mackerel even before he followed his tommy gun to the floor." Race is aided by his sometimes ally, "the girl with the criminal mind," Florence Drummond, AKA The Flame, who reminds him: "There is no sex in crime, Race."

This Race Williams/Flame story is one of many Daly precursors for Mike Hammer/Velda narratives. Race could never quite convince himself he loved The Flame, however, while Hammer's entire literary life revolves around his love for Velda and, for a time anyway, his intention to preserve her chastity.

Early on, Velda says, "Mike, I want you." His reply is only understandable for its shabby knight's chivalry: "No, darling, it's too beautiful to spoil. Not now. Our time will come, but it must be right."

Race could love but did not know how to express it. What he did best was rescue victims and shoot bad guys—usually with startling right-between-the-eyes accuracy. Race was vain but calculating: "When better corpses are made, Race Williams will make them!" He did not suffer remorse for killing bad men. Mike Hammer is much more emotionally torn.

The Daly stories are crude by modern standards—perhaps by the standards of their own day—and their relation to Spillane best understood knowing Race Williams was a childhood favorite of his. The clumsy prose did not bother a kid in the 1930s, nor did their inspiration stunt the growth of the man of the 1950s who had a natural bent for noir poetry.

The second pattern of influence on the Mike Hammer novels is less obvious. A significant portion of the public reading the first six Hammer novels in the 1950s would have some acquaintance with the Race Williams stories. But few would discern how Spillane utilized a number of the attributes of revenge tragedy from the time of William Shakespeare, whose

Hamlet appears almost exactly in the middle of the cycle of tales of bloody revenge beginning with Thomas Kyd's *The Spanish Tragedy* and reaching a pinnacle with Thomas Middleton's *The Revenger's Tragedy*.

Just like the Mike Hammer novels of midcentury America, these plays were immensely popular in Elizabethan/Jacobean England. They appealed to the public because they told human stories—murdered fathers, murdered sons, murdered friends, lovers raped and killed or humiliated into suicide—that they could understand. They sympathized with the living who were left behind to deal with carnage and death. They were on the side of the avenger, even if a strict interpretation of the law and the moral and religious codes demanded the avenger die as well.

In many ways, the "bestselling" example of the early Elizabethan stage was Thomas Kyd's *The Spanish Tragedy, or Hieronimo is Mad Again*. This play was immensely crowd-pleasing and revived and presented many times—in effect, the popular favorite of the revenge tragedy period. It even has the avenger quote the Bible: "Vengeance is Mine!" . . . though the quote is in Latin: "*Vindicta mihi!*"

William Shakespeare's *Hamlet* followed all the precepts of revenge tragedy that appeared in Kyd's play. While Shakespeare is obviously a much better craftsman than Kyd, the material is much the same. While Spillane never mentioned Kyd's work in interviews, he did bring Shakespeare up in interviews and alluded to Hamlet's killing of Polonius as he hides behind Queen Gertrude's tapestry in her private quarters.

Hamlet's introspective nature and many asides to himself prefigure the Mike Hammer mindset. Interestingly enough, Shakespeare's immense popularity with playgoers in the pits—the cheap seats, as opposed to the more expensive box seats for the swells—corresponds with Spillane's mass-audience appeal. Millions bought the Mike Hammer mysteries in twenty-five-cent editions.

Shakespeare's contemporaries were just as offended by his success as such critically respected novelists as Raymond Chandler and Ernest Hemingway were of Spillane's. Chandler put Hammer's creator down as a writer of comic books, and Hemingway was openly contemptuous, perhaps jealous of Spillane's huge sales figures. Literary critics were just as shortsighted, unable or unwilling to comprehend why the American reading public might choose in greater numbers the more direct, unpretentious Spillane over the more seemingly artistic novelists they endorsed.

Spillane merged the hero and the avenger into one character. Even today, this leads to violent critical reactions to Hammer's violent fictional actions, usually the detective killing the murderer or some equally bad person in his search for the murderer. When a hero kills in self-defense, rarely does a reader or a critic express a moral or legal problem. But Mike Hammer often kills in what amounts to cold blood; this became an issue for many critics.

Hammer's point of view is clear: cruel killers require cruel measures. He believes he is better able to punish the killers—the evil ones—than the often-compromised police. In a society that regards a killer only as temporarily sick rather than a miscreant who has taken a life that cannot be returned, Mike Hammer represents an idea familiar to the common man: We need defense from the crazies who will not be condemned to their just reward by the legal system.

Generally, Spillane's novels are not textbook examples of the classic detective novel. Almost every suspect in *I, the Jury* is eventually murdered or killed, an at once untidy and tidy way to clear up a murder mystery. Hammer does have to determine the killer.

This parallels some of the action of revenge tragedy, which often employs a play-within-the-play to give the avenger clues about the killer and who else might be involved. Spillane transforms this motif into his dreamscape—sometimes he gets clues; other times he is chastised by someone like the judge with the two-berries-on-a-bush eyes in *One Lonely Night*.

Spillane is a master of mood, tone, and plot, immersing the reader in novels that virtually define the term "page turner." Inconsistencies tend to be either ignored or missed entirely; but that is immaterial to Spillane and inconsequential to the reader.

When Mike Hammer complains of the problems involved with rules and regulations in protecting society, he is merely reflecting a common public sentiment. The reader can share his rage at the exploitation of prostitution, of the living death of drug addiction, and the absolute inability of modern society to protect a specific individual. Mike Hammer is, in his own opinion, God's instrument for inflicting punishment on the wicked.

Yet Hammer is no political mouthpiece. Spillane uses sentiments much of the public shares with his antihero to characterize that hero. A reader does not have to agree with Hammer to get caught up in the charismatic power of a personality his creator knows very well is a troubled one.

Every Mike Hammer novel is written in the first person. At key moments, Spillane uses italics in an idiosyncratic manner to focus the reader's attention, as if alerting that reader that something is wrong or important or impending. *I, the Jury* ends this way, with Mike's description of Charlotte Manning's striptease being interspersed with all the action leading up to the promised death of the killer. On stage in a drama, the characters can similarly speak to the audience via an aside or a soliloquy.

In the revenge tragedy, the hero/avenger is reluctant to share information with other characters. Similarly, Mike Hammer does not share information with Pat Chambers or sometimes even Velda, much less any lesser creatures. But he gives the reader access.

Mike Hammer is a night creature: he's out and about in bars or bordellos, at home dreaming his not so peaceful dreams, or awake and drinking what seems to be an ungodly amount of alcohol; or he may be walking and thinking in the rain, as in Hammer's universe it is often raining. Important decisions and actions always seem to come when it's raining. The rain has a cleansing power; it may even wash away evil. . . .

A mainstay of vintage Spillane, of course, is the hooker with a heart of gold. *Time* magazine printed a quote under his picture in their review/article of December 3, 1951: "Some of my best friends are hookers." Spillane and certain cronies would cruise the bars, both in Newburgh and the Red Hook district of Brooklyn, having a good time and looking for stories.

Later, Spillane would downplay these connections, but he always displayed a nonsexual affection for, and empathy with, prostitutes, as expressed in his nonfiction account, "Sex Is My Business" (*Cavalier*, October 1956).

Several early Mike Hammer thrillers contain scenes with Mike talking to hookers, who are at times sentimentalized; here, the "working girl" tries to be as tough as nails, but the reader is not sure that's the case.

Almost proudly, the sex worker in the *Cavalier* article admits she is a nymphomaniac, using "sex as a substitute for love." She thinks it's "funny as hell to watch . . . them squirm" after they've coupled. But Spillane has figured her out: "The real why has a vengeance motive. You're getting back at them."

Tragedy has an element of protecting an elite's good name. Arthur Berin-Grotin in *My Gun Is Quick* is but one example—Hammer refuses to put the wealthy fiend, burning to death, out of his misery by shooting him. This ties many Spillane motifs in with revenge tragedy, the difference being the sixteenth/seventeenth centuries also demanded the death of the avenger.

Spillane's world has no place for dead heroes, although Hammer is at times left alive at the novel's end but still in peril, even badly wounded. The Elizabethan avenger is only valuable if he performs, if he is capable. Mid–twentieth-century Mike has been redeemed by being an ongoing avenger.

Spillane's use of personal pronouns in his titles represents a recurring motif: "I," "Me," and "Mine" appear in over half the titles. It was a trick The Beatles would use, too, in most of their early songs.

An amused Spillane once remarked he had to change his way of titling his books because he ran out of personal pronouns. He was only half kidding. A major part of his creative genius was an uncanny ability to make readers closely identify with avenger Mike Hammer.

TOP LEFT: Mickey and his children, Ward and Kathy (and dogs), 1950. TOP RIGHT: Mickey and his pal George Wilson hike the Appalachian Trail. BOTTOM: Mary Ann sweeps up in the unpretentious Spillane home.

CHAPTER EIGHT

LITTLE BOHEMIA

In 1949, Mickey Spillane began a two-year run of productivity, during which he would write five of seven novels destined to be among the top fifteen bestsellers of all time—four more Mike Hammer mysteries and one non-Hammer, *The Long Wait*.

Spillane—whom a Canadian journalist described in 1951 as a likeable young "athletic green-eyed man with a crew haircut"—would accomplish this in a frantic climate of family matters, boozy socializing, and business activity that would challenge any writer to complete a single novel.

He and his wife, Mary Ann, had welcomed their daughter Kathy into their wooded enclave on July 2, 1949, and son Ward on September 25, 1950. The three buildings of the unwalled Spillane compound were at once utilitarian and rustic, cinder block without, knotty pine within. Two cats, Calico and Patsy—and endless assorted kittens—prowled at will; five mixed-breed dogs—Gismo, Girl, Boy, Silly, and Stupid—roamed in a pack only to vanish for days.

In the living room of the main house, Spillane often could be found tussling with his two kids on a floor that now had carpet, if nothing fancy, so strewn with playthings that the contents of a toy store's shelves might have been spilled by an earthquake. At the end of the assault, the two toddlers would find themselves sentenced for a stay behind the bars of a playpen, with their father going off, saying to their mother, "Hey, Baby, I'll be in the studio."

The studio among the pines now had two desks and a drawing table for any comic-book artists who might drop by. The bar was well stocked, though mostly with refrigerated beer, and bunk beds had been built in for guests as well as for write-by-night Mickey's naps, or for him to just flop after an exhausting session at the L.C. Smith typewriter (now repaired) without making a trip all the way to the nearby house. Skis and snowshoes rode the walls, making a minilodge out of it, the original painting for the paperback edition of *I, the Jury* framed and on display. A growing, partly wall-mounted collection of small arms and rifles—fans were always sending them—was kept unloaded, many relieved of their firing pins. Among the more prized examples were a 44–70 rifle, a 7.65 Walther automatic, and a nickel-plated Smith & Wesson .38. His 1914 Navy Colt .38—which the cheerful writer posed with for grim back-of-paperback photos—was an exception: he used that for target practice.

Despite all the fire power, he made a point of saying, "I would never shoot an *animal.*" He even spoke in italics.

As Marion Hargrove reported in *Redbook*, Spillane—although a fisherman—was no fan of the hunters who "seasonally prowled the neighborhood, shooting at every sight and sound and [then] driving back toward the city with barnyard calves draped over their fenders and out-of-season birds stuffed in their hubcaps."

"They shot my dog," a fuming Spillane told Hargrove, "and Baby had to spend a day bottle-feeding the puppies. They put two bullets through the house trying to hit the tame chicken in the yard. Once they even grazed my little boy in the back of the head . . . if I could have caught them, I would have killed them."

Who could doubt that? But then there was the tale of Mickey Spillane and the spider.

"When he and George Wilson were building the house," a longtime friend said, "Mick found a spider that had built its web on the side of a lumber pile, and he made a sort of pet out of it. Wouldn't let anybody disturb the web. Even fed the spider. Then one day he saw the spider feeding itself—with a live fly—and from that day on he would have nothing to do with that spider."

Spillane indeed was a guy who could talk about killing those lousy hunters who bloodied his boy, but who could also feel empathy for both spider and fly.

Jack Stang, the big, rugged Newburgh cop whom Spillane considered a perfect embodiment of Mike Hammer, observed about his new pal, "There's violence there, but it's half a day's work to get it out. If you back him into a corner and hit him first, then he'll go berserk. But I've never seen him go looking for trouble."

Spillane described himself thusly: "Essentially, I'm a coward—who doesn't know enough to run."

A Canadian journalist described him as, "A calloused-hand type," who got more pleasure out of helping clean out a neighbor's chicken coop than writing books. His winter uniform included rubber boots, jeans, and a flannel shirt suitable for a lumberjack.

"Life can get mighty damn dull writing," he told Dutton publicity director Elliott Graham, "and since I'm still young enough not to worry about overtaxing my heart I figure on getting in a little adventure I can tell my kids about from behind a paunch an[d] a nice cold beer."

Mickey told Graham of plans he and his buddy George Wilson had to see how far they could walk along the Appalachian Trail. And how the following summer they planned to go "from here to Florida via the Inland waterways." He also hoped, when he had a couple of months free, to grab Wilson and Wells "and take off without any road maps" and look up war buddies and have "one reunion after another."

But Mickey feared that "everybody who had helled around with us [has] turned staid and stodgy. . . . What marriage and a steady job won't do to some people!"

The writer was preparing to do some more building—two rooms to "accommodate a growing family"—and planned to do "the muscle work myself between books and save money."

He closed his letter to Graham by writing, "Right now I have to concentrate on keeping my favorite character from winding up in the V.D. ward. Sometimes he gets away from me when I'm not looking and a whole chapter goes in the verboten file."

Just as Mike Hammer seems to rarely get paid, Mickey Spillane at the end of the 1940s and start of the '50s claimed not to know how much money he had. Jack McKenna gave him a thousand dollars a month to live on, paid his taxes for him, and plowed the rest away into something called the Northland Construction Company, which the writer founded.

He allowed himself some creature comforts—his car was no longer the '34 Caddy he thought would serve him forever, but a souped-up red custom convertible, suitable for a subscriber to *Hot Rod* magazine, which he was.

Spillane's sudden success also allowed him to move his parents into a bungalow between Little Bohemia and Newburgh. Having his parents nearby, he admitted, gave him a sense of security. Mickey would drive them daily for groceries and other errands—they had no car—and he and his father would rib each other good-naturedly.

Hargrove described Spillane's gray-haired, dapper little papa as looking like "a well-seasoned old master sergeant, fond of suggesting his son go out and find a job." His son's response would be to startle his father by making the automatic window go suddenly up.

Spillane may have been a guy with books to write, but he was also someone who had the money to (as Mark Murphy said in *True*) "indulge in hospitality, dungarees and plaid shirts." His hobbies, which he seriously pursued, were a macho list including skiing, fencing, fast cars, his growing gun collection, and plenty of beer-fueled conversation with the writer pals who were now always around.

Mickey, at least in those days, seemed to have a naive, trusting side. "Anybody with a half-way decent story can take Spillane," Hargrove was told. "He'll lend people his trucks, give them his money, shovel their manure, [and] read their manuscripts. . . ."

To George Wilson, who bailed out of Little Bohemia early on, many of these guys were strictly hangers-on, often taking advantage. But Spillane liked company, and he liked holding court.

These buddies were always pledging to one day knock the stuffing out of the reviewers who'd given their pal bad notices, an idea their host did not endorse. He provided beer and sent out to the Texas Red Hot restaurant in Newburgh for franks smothered in mustard, barbecue sauce, and chopped raw onions, a delicacy capable of shooting holes in stomachs as ferociously as Mike Hammer.

Mississippi boys Charlie Wells and Earle Baskinsky both managed to get two books each put out by Spillane's publishers, with elaborate cover blurbs provided by their famous friend—Wells, *Let the Night Cry* (1953) and *The Last Kill* (1955); Baskinsky, *The Big Steal* (1955) and *Death Is a Cold, Keen Edge* (1956). Spillane techniques abound, including italics and abrupt endings.

Joe Gill was still making a living writing comics and would soon lend an often unreliable hand with the short-lived comic strip *From the Files of . . . Mike Hammer* (1953–54). In the 1960s, Gill wrote (and essentially co-created) Sarge Steel, a Hammer-like private eye for Charlton Comics, a character later graduating to DC.

Newburgh resident and merchant marine Dave Gerrity—the most successful of the satellite-Spillane writers, and Mickey's lasting friend—would have eight novels published, including two Gold Medal crime novels (*Kiss Off the Dead*, 1960, and *Cry Me a Killer*, 1961) and a Signet original (*Dragon Hunt*, 1967), which includes an elaborate Spillane endorsement and a guest appearance by Mike Hammer himself.

For years, Gerrity wrote his manuscripts onboard ships and sent them to Spillane for editing. He also penned race-car novels and Mafia thrillers, and ghosted several autobiographies, including those of stripper Georgia Sothern (*Georgia: My Life in Burlesque*, 1972) and real-life PI Fred Otash (*Investigation Hollywood!*, 1976), the latter with a Spillane introduction.

Gerrity, in an interview with crime-fiction expert Lynn Myers, was honest enough to say, "You sit at Spillane's table for a couple of hours and drink beer with him and you could steal enough of his throwaway ideas to write twenty topics. . . . It looked like an easy way to make a buck."

Policeman Jack Stang—whose family owned Stang's Bar & Grill at 85 Front Street in Newburgh—had no literary aspirations, but caught the acting bug when Spillane began to envision him as the perfect screen Mike Hammer.

Now and then, Spillane would display a streak worthy of a mischievous kid when dealing with Dutton's Marc Jaffe and other editors.

"I said a perfect book is written with the climax on the last word of the last page," Spillane recalled. ". . . if you took the last word away, you wouldn't know what the book was about."

Jaffe disagreed and Spillane bet the editor "a thousand bucks" that if he submitted the new Hammer, *Vengeance Is Mine!*, without the last word, the novel would make no sense.

"I turned it in without the last word on the last page," Spillane recalled, grinning. "He said 'What was the word, what was the word!' I said, 'Give me the thousand bucks.' He gave me the thousand bucks—I gave him the word."

The last sentence of *Vengeance Is Mine!*, of course, is: *"Juno was a man!"*

"WOW!" began Victor Weybright's enthusiastic letter to Peggy Waller at Dutton about *Vengeance Is Mine!* Though desiring a few editorial changes, Weybright seemed well aware of Spillane's power as a writer.

"I don't think we can ever judge Spillane's appeal by logical mystery standards," the publisher went on. "His magic, in our market, seems to consist of a sort of existentialist vibration, to which the readers out yonder seem to be able to tune in."

Still, in a postscript he requested a meeting with "your Dutton people, Spillane and his agent, so we can offer our advice for keeping his works on the beam established by *I, the Jury.*"

Amid a whirl of family activity, bull sessions, and midnight writing, Spillane found himself engulfed in both adulation and condemnation.

A speaker representing the WAFS in Stillwater, Oklahoma, wrote: "More! More! More! Mickey Spillane is the best novelist of all time!" An Air Force sergeant in Korea snagged a ride to Tokyo to get a copy of *Vengeance Is Mine!* In Germany, the high command refused to reveal how many copies of Spillane novels had been sold in PXs to avoid reflecting badly on the army's reading tastes.

At Radcliffe College, young women organized a Mickey Spillane fan club. Seven college professors went unashamedly public with their Mike Hammer enthusiasm, and five colleges required creative writing students to read Spillane books. And Pulitzer Prize–winning Washington correspondent Arthur Krock of the *New York Times* declared himself a Spillane fan.

The *Times* mystery critic, however, felt otherwise.

The much-respected Anthony Boucher deemed Spillane's work "a vicious . . . glorification of force, cruelty and extra-legal methods that . . . might be made required reading in a Gestapo training school," (*I, the Jury*); ". . . ammunition for the various bodies crying for the suppression or control of crime writing . . . in its attempt to see how far uncensored publishing can go," (*My Gun Is Quick*); and ". . . rife with sexuality and sadism," (*The Big Kill*).

Boucher was just one among many appalled reviewers of mystery fiction; social critics, including Dr. Fredric Wertham of anti-comic-book infamy (appropriately enough), were equally alarmed. Russian-born syndicated columnist Max Lerner considered Spillane/Hammer "a menace to American civilization." Self-appointed social saviors and pundits alike accused Spillane of, as Curran said in *Saga*, "subverting society, making the switchblade fashionable, ruining the detective story in all forms and, worst of all, writing for money."

From Curran's sardonic point of view, however, the naysayers "gave Spillane his credentials."

"They get worked up," Spillane told Hargrove, "because the villain is a woman. So what? Half the people in this world are women. How many sexes have you got to choose from?" When Spillane answered his own question—two—Hargrove reminded him that, with *Vengeance Is Mine!*, the writer had already expanded those options to three.

Hammer killing the killer got another "So what?" out of his creator. He saw Hammer as no different from Zorro using a sword or Robin Hood his bow and arrow. Perry Mason knew the law, thanks to Erle Stanley Gardner, who was a lawyer himself. But what did Mike Hammer know but his .45?

A friend of Mickey's for years said, "All of his life Mick wanted money, fame, power, security. He wanted to reach a mountaintop, out of range of people who throw rocks at you. He never knew that up there you're exposed to the heavy artillery."

But when Spillane's publishers managed to lure him from Little Bohemia to bookshops and department stores for autograph signings, he would draw enormous, adoring crowds. Soldiers and civilians alike sent him fan letters. Women sent pictures of themselves—in bed.

Quickly he became part of the American vernacular. The Academy Award–winning film *Marty* (1955) included a comical dialogue exchange between two blue-collar guys about what a great writer Mickey Spillane was. A movie critic gave a piece of advice to a rising young actor: "Brando better be careful. He relies on sheer force—he is the Mickey Spillane of acting."

In Canada, a literary critic blasted a novel by another author for "sadistic concoctions *spillaning* forth from every page." Walt Kelly used his *Pogo* comic-strip characters in two Mike Hammer parodies: Meat Hamburg in "The Bloody Drip" and "Gore Blimey: the Bloody Drip Writhes Again" by "Muckey Spleen." And in 1953 Fred Astaire would be Rod Riley in "The Girl Hunt" ballet in the film *The Band Wagon*, another specific Spillane parody.

The latter didn't sting at all: Spillane's favorite films were old Fred Astaire/Ginger Rogers pictures.

Throughout his writing life, Spillane often claimed not to revise. "I don't rewrite anything," he said in 1998. "If it's not good enough the first time, it's not going to get any better by rewriting."

But at this early stage in his relationship with Dutton and NAL, Spillane apparently did consent to at least some editing and revising. He spent over three months fulfilling Weybright's requests for specific rewrites.

On May 3, 1950, associate editor Marc Jaffe wrote, "I am sending along to you under separate cover the manuscript of your revision of *Vengeance Is Mine!* I think it's a great job, and if I must say so, an improvement over the original version."

With his next Hammer, *One Lonely Night*—a machine-gun blast from Mickey and Mike aimed at their critics—he again bet Jaffe, this time that he could deliberately include a significant error the editor couldn't spot. Spillane knowingly placed the tollbooth on the wrong side of the George Washington Bridge. Thousands of fans spotted it and wrote in about it, but the editor hadn't caught it, and Spillane again won his bet.

The writer didn't specifically say this was an act of revenge toward the editor, but it may well have been a response to an attempt to correct something intentional in Spillane's prose.

"'Nobody ever walks across a bridge on a night like this. Well, hardly nobody,'" Spillane said, quoting the opening of *One Lonely Night*. "The editor takes the second 'nobody' and makes it hardly 'anybody.' I said, 'Oh, you nut.' . . . It gets you aggravated when they start changing things that are stylistic, important."

For all of Mickey's self-deprecation about being a writer, strictly an entertainer, not an author, "the chewing gum of American literature," and so on, he clearly cared about his craft from the beginning, as all real artists do.

With three bestsellers under his belt, Mickey's delivery of his new Mike Hammer manuscript spoke volumes about his unchanged, unpretentious, blue-collar lifestyle.

At Little Bohemia, he stuffed the yellow pages of the book—it had not been retyped—in a paper bag. He shoved it under the front seat of his car, where it would slide out from time to time over the next week of driving his folks to get groceries and going on other errands. He had a meeting in Manhattan lined up with Victor Weybright—who Spillane considered "as good as any [editor that] ever came out."

In Weybright's office, he handed over the paper bag with the manuscript.

"He calls the bank across the street," Spillane remembered, "gets two security guards to come up with guns. They took this thing down with their hands on the guns, to cross the street to put it in the bank safety deposit box. . . . I don't dare tell him I had it under the seat of my car for a week, kickin' it around!"

Later that summer, an inter-office NAL memo from Jaffe to the management team returned to the touchy subject of *For Whom the Gods Would Destroy*, which had—with Mike Hammer–mania continuing to build in the publishing world—suddenly become a hot, and (in a way) dangerous, property.

The book was certainly worth salvaging, Jaffe said, and required only making Ruston York somewhat older, filling a few plot holes, and adding a sex scene or two. This, Jaffe said, would make the novel a fine follow-up to *I, the Jury* and *My Gun Is Quick*.

With those changes, Jaffe felt it would be a better book than *One Lonely Night*, whose violence-justifying soliloquies (in his view) slowed things down. In *For Whom the Gods Would Destroy*, Hammer fought and killed, yes, but out of necessity, not some sadistic urge.

This apparent displeasure with *One Lonely Night* had obviously not kept the Dutton/Signet combine from publishing it, nor had the public been put off by either the novel's philosophy or brutality. And the "anti-Commie" content could not have been more topical. Tellingly, Jaffe seemed to want even more sexual content.

But in late September, Spillane requested the return of *For Whom the Gods Would Destroy*. In a face-to-face meeting with Nick Wreden and agent Jack McKenna, Spillane had refused to revise it according to editorial suggestions.

Weybright again instructed his team not to formally reject the novel, but rather keep it in cold storage. He warned that he feared McKenna—despite having been given the agent's word otherwise—might take the novel to a certain upstart borderline publisher.

Gold Medal Books was the line of original novels launched by Roscoe Fawcett to mine the gold fields the novels of Mickey Spillane had unearthed.

TOP: Mickey inspects one of his guns in his studio. LEFT: Mickey and Mary Ann at Little Bohemia. BOTTOM: Lay preacher Spillane conducts a Jehovah's Witness Bible class.

CHAPTER NINE

PRIVATE EYE WITNESS

In 1950, Mickey Spillane's daughter Kathy, going on three—who liked to answer questions with the non sequitur response, "Sexy!"—reached for a deadly plaything on a table. Knowing the Mauser pistol was unloaded—in fact lacked a firing pin—Kathy's daddy watched, fascinated, as the infant tried three times to get the weapon down from its perch, and then finally pulled the trigger.

There's no record of whether her mom, Mary Ann Spillane, witnessed this highly questionable parental decision. But a sort of permanent record was made when the writer freely admitted utilizing the idea for the climax of his fifth Mike Hammer novel, *The Big Kill*, wherein a baby, borrowing the detective's fabled .45, accidentally but fatally shoots the evil beauty about to dispatch the private eye. Less than a year later, the paperback edition of that novel would receive a record-breaking first printing of 2.5 million copies.

No doubt the pleasant, matronly woman who rang the doorbell of the Little Bohemia studio—while Mary Ann was away at a Newburgh supermarket with toddler/gun-toter Kathy in tow—would have been horror-struck had she witnessed that recent event.

But Mrs. Florence Gobel merely smiled and gestured with her handful of booklets. "Hello," she said to the writer, whom she didn't know and who didn't know her. "I won't take up much of your time."

Coincidentally (at least according to writer Henry Adams), Kathy's father had been at the typewriter working on the "smash ending" of *The Big Kill*, executing the conclusion his daughter had unintentionally provided.

In his *Climax* article, Adams claims Spillane, "just to be polite," listened for a while to the woman, whom he gathered was a member of the local Jehovah's Witnesses.

She told him that the Witnesses were missionaries not "off in the jungle somewhere," but right here in the good ol' USA, where there were "a lot of unhappy people, maybe like you, who actually want help but don't know it yet."

Finally, Mickey quietly told her this wasn't a good time and she asked if she could leave the booklets with him.

"Try to get around to reading them," she suggested, complying. "If you do, I'm sure you'll want to talk to me."

After walking her out, the writer was about to toss the tracts into the wastebasket, but could hear the woman trudging away on the driveway just outside and, feeling it unfair to dump the religious junk before she was even gone, stowed them away in his old childhood toy chest, which he used "as a catch-all." There they would stay for a year or so.

That year had been Spillane's biggest yet. *One Lonely Night* had gone through the roof and—when *The Big Kill* came out with its record-breaking print run—Signet reissued the previous four Hammer novels in new million-copy printings.

Meanwhile, Spillane had applied for active duty in the Air Force shortly after the Korean War broke out. The writer had kept his Army Air Force training up to date. By November 13, 1947, Spillane had made First Lieutenant, A/C (Air Corps), part of the Officers Reserve Corps.

In August of 1950, NAL publisher Victor Weybright informed his staff with alarm that active reservist Spillane had been called up and would go back into the army within ten days. The publisher, understandably concerned about the flow of Spillane material stopping, suggested Signet "see what can be done about arranging to re-write some of Mickey's rejections." The latter certainly refers to *For Whom the Gods Would Destroy*, but Weybright's inter-office memo is an intriguing indication that other manuscripts might have been in the NAL "deep freeze."

Apparently, however, the federal government decided not to activate Spillane's unit, which no doubt frustrated, disappointed, and irritated the writer, still anxious to prove himself in combat.

By 1951, Spillane felt he was in a rut, and in fear of being seen as a one-trick pony. While he knew that Dutton/Signet badly wanted a new Mike Hammer novel, he instead gave them a non-series entry: *The Long Wait* (1951), the only non-Hammer book of Spillane's crucial early period.

As Adams put it, "What was needed at this stage of the game was another robust, entirely different character who would strike out in a new direction."

But Spillane, otherwise pleased with the novel, felt he'd missed the mark with his new character, Johnny McBride, whose speech and behavior differed little from Hammer. Over the years, most critics and reviewers have, like Spillane, dismissed McBride as Hammer under another name, although this is not really the case.

Mike Hammer is a man who, whatever else he might be, knows exactly who he is and what he is about. But Johnny McBride is a man without an identity; in fact, "Johnny McBride" is a name he has assumed in order to clear the name of his dead best friend.

Friendship remains a key Spillane theme in *The Long Wait*; but it's only a convenient starting point for the action, the mood one of betrayal, mistrust, and confusion. Another major Spillane motif remains intact: the effect of the war on a combat veteran, who is struggling to readjust to peacetime. A number of crime and mystery films of the late '40s and early '50s used amnesia as a metaphor for the returning serviceman's hard adjustment to the postwar world—notably *Spellbound* (1945), *Somewhere in the Night* (1946), and *The Crooked Way* (1949). *The Long Wait* is certainly the bestselling novel to explore this resonant theme.

In *The Long Wait*, Johnny McBride is a man without an identity. Amnesiac George Wilson (a character named, of course, after Spillane's artist friend) is posing as the murdered McBride, trying to learn about his best friend's past and at the same time discover the facts about himself. At every turning point, he discovers he has some new talent—shooting weapons, cracking safes, fighting skills—of which he was unaware; he comes to think that back in the life he's forgotten, he must have been a criminal and perhaps even a murderer.

The object of his search through a landscape of small-town corruption and rampant gangsterism is the beauty who betrayed McBride, Vera West, "a lovely, wonderful girl with hair like new honey." She's as much of a mystery as McBride, missing for about the same time period.

He tells Vera he's suffered a "long wait" before making her pay for the shame and humiliation his friend Johnny McBride felt when she betrayed him. But she's gathered some evidence: the amnesiac hero isn't really George Wilson—he *is* Johnny McBride, the man he has been pretending to be throughout the book—so the wrong done to himself is what he's been avenging. He's not a murderer or an embezzler, but a war hero who was framed.

The Long Wait—however tough and Hammer-like its protagonist might be—has an uncharacteristically happy ending for a Spillane novel, ultimately revealing itself to be a love story. In a tentative way, at least, Spillane is striking out in a new direction. His own misgivings and insecurities about his first non-Hammer novel were a moot point at the time, because *The Long Wait* was already on his eagerly awaiting publisher's fall schedule.

After shipping the manuscript off to Dutton (Adams tells us), Spillane felt both tired and on edge. Perhaps it was his after-hours writing practices that caused it; at any rate, he found himself caught up in a cycle of insomnia. There weren't enough beers in the world before and/or after dinner to put him to sleep. If he did manage to slumber, he would sometimes wake up at two A.M. On utterly sleepless nights, he would see daylight come.

One long night, fighting a toothache, he found himself fiddling with his gun collection; he started looking for a rare gun catalogue he'd mislaid, and checked his childhood catch-all toy box. There he ran across Mrs. Gobel's booklets.

He spent the next day reading.

It turned out the Jehovah's Witnesses believed the world would end, and soon, or at least change radically. As Marion Hargrove put it in *True*, the Witnesses offered Spillane "a maximum of universal comfort and happiness in the world to follow. . . . [but with] the promise of a Utopia . . . where everybody can be trusted and liked, because everybody is good; where nobody hurts anybody else; where no one sickens or deteriorates with age or dies."

While no one who failed to find entrance to this new life would be condemned to fire and brimstone, the Witnesses did not anticipate the Earthly Kingdom of God would come about without a struggle against evil—Jesus would be returning with a sword. Brave warriors in the Battle of Armageddon were needed, and this time Spillane wouldn't have to sit it out.

Spillane was intrigued—he had studied evolution at Kansas State and felt the Witnesses made "Darwin's theory fall flat on its face." When a second group of Newburgh Witnesses came around, he let them in at once—a local refrigeration engineer and his wife, and another housewife, just average folks. They had driven past Spillane's cinder-block enclave many times, they told him, but this time they had noticed his driveway. They did not know who he was—just that they were bringing him good news.

After four months of Bible study, Mickey Spillane joined the Newburgh Company of the Witnesses. Soon, so did Mary Ann. In the fall of 1951, fully immersed in a swimming pool in Norwalk, Connecticut, he was baptized for the fourth time. This one, apparently, took—he became a lay preacher of God's Kingdom.

The Witnesses have always believed the world is about to end—"any day now," as Mark Murphy observed in *True*, going on to say, "They irritate the hell out of members of more established faiths [in believing] they have discovered 'The Truth' and it is their duty to acquaint the rest of the world with it."

In his red Ford convertible, driving Murphy around, Spillane— in the midst of fairly typical Mike Hammer sex-and-violence discourse— interrupted himself for some momentary preaching: "The eye hath not seen, nor hath the ear heard, nor can the mind conceive what My Father hath in store for you."

As Marion Hargrove noted in *Redbook*, the Witnesses did their missionary work going door-to-door "in hope of saving others from eternal oblivion." He also noted that this practice (unlike Mickey Spillane's own exposure to the faith via a knock at his door) was "often received with something less than enthusiasm." According to the author of *See Here, Private Hargrove*, the Witnesses were viewed by many "as alarmists . . . an anti-social cult."

That collective opinion seemed to derive from what Hargrove terms "a certain civic detachment"—although law-abiding taxpayers, Witnesses did not vote or salute the flag or sing the national anthem. Nor did they observe holidays like Christmas or even their own birthdays. Jury duty was out, too, and so was going to war.

As the news of the unlikely religious conversion got out, a new round of Mickey Spillane publicity—this time not generated by him or his publishers—took off. *True*'s cover was emblazoned: "MICKEY SPILLANE—SEX, SADISM & SCRIPTURES." The upper right cover of *Life* magazine shouted,

MICKEY SPILLANE:

13 MILLION BOOKS OF

SEX AND SLAUGHTER,

and—with no sense of irony or shame—Time, Inc., filled the rest of that cover with a lovely bosomy glamour girl who might have wandered right off a paperback. The in-depth, well-researched but faintly mocking *Life* article included a picture of a pious Mickey "leading a Bible class. . . . He often spends evenings on home missionary visits to his neighbors."

This would be common in the many magazine and newspaper articles about Spillane throughout the 1950s—the contrast between the controversial muscle-shirt-sporting writer of outrageously violent, sexy mysteries and the unassuming man in shirt and tie proselytizing on Newburgh street corners with a stack of *Watchtowers* in one hand and the Good Book in the other.

Toward the beginning of this onslaught, Spillane issued a statement sent to "Al Rhodes of the Newburgh News, and to the United Press," requesting that it be "used, printed, announced, etc. completely or not at all."

Spillane wrote:

> *This world of ours has become a madhouse with a million kill-crazy problems trying to be solved by even bigger kills and bigger problems. We've been knocking down the spider webs without killing the spider. But it's all a planned madhouse and I've found out who's planning it, why and what the conclusion is. All it requires to learn is a little study and a little understanding, but it takes you to the Bible and because it does, people are ready to laugh or condemn or put the finger of fanaticism on you. There are millions today associated with Jehovah's witnesses who are learning this truth and will live because of it and not for just a little while either.*
>
> *Because of what I was, what I did and the way I wrote the public, critics and columnists have slapped the stigma of the same old worldly-ism on Jehovah's witnesses, but know this . . . I haven't written a book after my old fashion since I became a publisher for Jehovah's Kingdom. And know this too . . . more books are on the way, but they won't contain the things that bolster the excuses for the moral breakdown of this present generation. I've changed my work and course of action to be in harmony with Jehovah's Kingdom and be a favorable example as one who publishes the good news of this Kingdom.*

> *This world has been screaming for leadership, it has been get-*
> *ting leadership . . . but look at where it has been led. Great, isn't*
> *it? Along with millions of others I've found the answer to the*
> *problem the world is going mad trying to solve and the answer is*
> *a greater surprise than anything you or I will ever find in fiction.*
> *The Kingdom of God so many have prayed for is not only going*
> *to be established . . . it's here! The physical proof is absolutely*
> *conclusive and open for anyone to see. Ask yourself this . . . CAN*
> *YOU LIVE FOREVER IN HAPPINESS ON EARTH? And*
> *find out what I have found out and see why I've changed. God*
> *says it can be done. Soon, too. And it's easy.*
>
> *Mickey Spillane*

Content aside, Spillane's open letter to the public includes interesting echoes from the Mike Hammer novels: "kill-crazy" of course; "bigger kills" an obvious callback to *The Big Kill*; an overall tone reminiscent of *My Gun Is Quick*'s preamble ("Great, isn't it?"); and *I, the Jury*'s famous last line with the final words here: "And it's easy."

The writer's buddies in his studio watched all this with anxious eyes—was everything about to change? The gravy train about to screech to a stop? Spillane seemed pretty much the same, as they sat around drinking beer and eating red hots and talking hot rods, sports, and shop. But they suspected that their successful pal, as Henry Adams noted in *Climax*, was "caught in a tight squeeze between the principles of Jehovah's Witnesses . . . and the only kind of writing that comes natural to him."

The Witnesses were even against killing in war—had Mickey been called up, his fellow Witnesses would have expected him to declare himself a conscientious objector. And the very idea of Mike Hammer as a man who sat in judgment of others was as repugnant to them as pornography . . . which, by the way, Spillane was frequently accused of producing, however ridiculous that charge might seem today, looking at the euphemistic descriptions and bedroom-door fade-outs of the early Hammer novels.

As time passed, Spillane would play somewhat fast and loose with the rules his church expected him to obey. For years he was a smoker and a drinker, and his fiction remained tough and sexy. But hidden in plain sight was his most egregious offense.

Until he was retirement age, Spillane would keep up his reserve commitment in the Air Force, rising to Colonel, regularly conducting training flights from Shaw AFB, South Carolina. A conscientious objector? Hardly.

At the time of the *Life* magazine article, the sales for the paperback editions of the first five Mike Hammer novels exceeded eleven million copies. Spillane's probable royalty was 2½ cents per copy sold, which jibes with the article's estimate of Spillane making about $50,000 per title—enormous money at the time.

The cheerfully patronizing *Life* article described the writer "as a bantam-sized, slightly educated, self-professed roughneck who now lives in New-burgh, N.Y., but who grew up in Brooklyn and still talks like it."

Continuing in this condescending fashion, the writer describes twenty-six-year-old Mary Ann Spillane as "a subdued little bespectacled brunette," though her photos reveal a prototype of Velda, dark-haired and very pretty, if diminutive.

The *Life* photo of the exterior of the house confirms a rustic cinder-block structure with a chimney and a scrubby yard where Spillane rides on a small wagon with son Ward while Mary Ann holds baby Kathy. A pair of dogs roam, while writer pals Joe Gill and Charlie Wells lean against a bug-eyed truck. The lifestyle of America's bestselling novelist gives off not a whiff of affluence.

Also featured is a shot of Spillane typing at a manual typewriter, one of several he owned at the time. He would tell gullible reporters he had a mistress, and then announce her name—"Miss Smith Corona." His work area appears spartan. Tellingly, a bulletin board bearing unfavorable reviews hovers over the writer for (as he says) inspiration.

In early 1952, Spillane "punctured two beer cans" for himself and visiting Canadian journalist, James Dugan. He told his visitor about going door-to-door four nights a week "bringing the truth." On Friday nights he took Bible studies.

"Since I became a Witness," Spillane said to the *Maclean's* reporter, "the attacks on my books are worse. The Witnesses all over the country have to defend me. They tie me up with this Hammer character. They pick on me personally. Hell, I'm a guy you can get along with."

An aging brown sheet from Spillane's files record the writer's thoughts that same year:

> *People ask me questions. They want to know what I'm like. What I tell them and what they see doesn't make sense sometimes. They say . . . 'where do you get your ideas?' I scrounge for them. They don't come easy. They come few and far between but they come good and when it's all out on the typewriter, fiction is only a veil for a lot that really happened.*
>
> *Do I like to write? No. I hate it. I like to think of reworking a situation that almost happened into one that actually did, then put it away in my mind for keeps. I have to eat so I write it instead.*
>
> *Are there 'messages' in my yarns? Don't be silly. I'm an entertainer, not an educator in my particular field.*
>
> *Why are your writings so popular? Because people like to be entertained and my stuff has reflected the trend of today's emotions and mental attitudes.*
>
> *Who is Mike Hammer? He isn't me. He's a composite character of people I know but people I wouldn't like to be.*
>
> *Me? I'm thirty-four, have two kids, normal, medium and wish people would stay off my neck.*

In his studio at Little Bohemia, Spillane told his Canadian guest: "I'm going to change my style entirely, but keep the books just as exciting. I'm going to take the sex out and substitute such interesting characterizations that you won't be able to quit reading. It's a real challenge to me. My style has definitely changed. I'm revising my books God's way to bring them up to par."

He admitted with a smile he feared he was cutting his throat with this whole new style.

"The first book I wrote," he said, "since I got the truth is in the typewriter there . . . *Kiss Me comma Deadly.*"

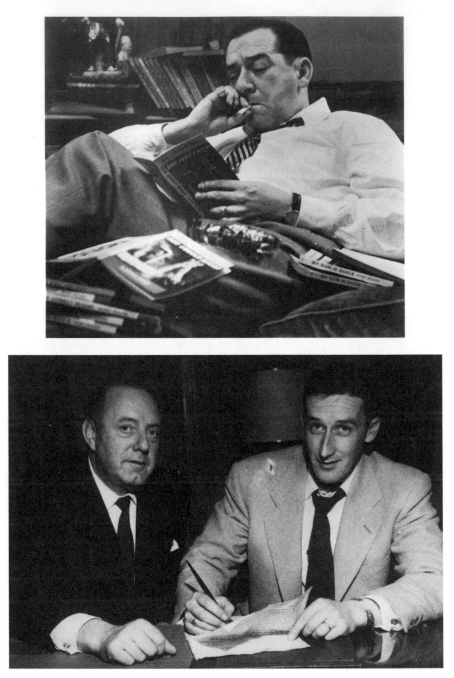

TOP: Star of radio's *That Hammer Guy*, Larry Haines—later a TV soap opera mainstay and Tony nominee—was the first actor to portray Mike Hammer. BOTTOM: Victor Saville and Spillane re-stage the signing of the writer's contract for publicity's sake.

CHAPTER TEN

TV, MOVIES, AND RADIO

Readers and critics alike over the years have been taken back and either fascinated or repulsed by the volcanic rage in the first six Mike Hammer novels. Even *The Long Wait*'s less openly psychotic Johnny McBride seems infected with postwar fury. But Spillane felt he was merely describing the state of mind of returning and struggling World War II veterans.

"When the war was over," Spillane said in 1998, "people were used to violence. You know, I was in the military—I knew what they were thinking, I knew what they were eatin' and dreamin'. That's why I didn't make Mike a pilot like I was. I made him come out of the trenches where most of the people were. And [the ex-GIs] knew what a person's mind could do to them when they came back. . . ."

As for the heat he took over sex and violence, the writer said, "[The critics] would say this man writes the most trivial garbage in the world, it's terrible, it's infused with sex and violence. . . . But sex and violence are punctuation marks in a story. The whole thing isn't written about sex and violence. There's a story involved."

His revenge on his critics: "I have gotten the worst reviews in the world. Nobody has ever gotten them as bad as me. . . . So we made this big ad out of the bad reviews, quoting from them. Then underneath we'd have a line like, this book sold six million copies. The top of the ad said, Mickey Spillane says about his new book, 'I hope this one gets lousy reviews.'"

In 1953, the first printing of the paperback edition of the new Mike Hammer rolled off the presses, with a deadly error.

"It's *Kiss Me Comma Deadly*," Spillane said emphatically in 1998. "It wasn't *Kiss Me Deadly* like it's a deadly kiss. . . . She was a deadly person and he says, 'Kiss me, deadly.'" Mickey told NAL he would not accept that cover. "You've got to put that comma back in there again."

The print run was destroyed.

Those first seven novels made Mickey Spillane a rich man, and a controversial one. He always had a love-hate affair with being a celebrity, though hobnobbing with the likes of Marlene Dietrich, Rocky Marciano, Jack Webb, Martha Raye, and Jayne Mansfield in the early 1950s seems to be something he got a kick out of—it took the edge off the critical attacks.

Spillane told Marion Hargrove, "Henry Ford made a mistake, too. He turned out Model Ts instead of Cadillacs." With a shrug he added, "Liberace had the perfect answer: 'I cried all the way to the bank.'"

Spillane became one of America's first celebrity writers, rivaling Ernest Hemingway, if lacking the critical respect afforded that other man's man. A restaurant in the Florida Keys displayed a framed photo of regular customer Hemingway; when Spillane dropped by, he was asked for a picture and it too went up on the wall. On his next visit, Hemingway demanded, "Take him down or take me down!" Down came Hemingway.

Later, after Papa bad-mouthed Spillane in *Bluebook* magazine, a TV interviewer asked Mike Hammer's papa what he thought of Hemingway, and the response—"Hemingway who?"—got peals of laughter and applause.

Television in the early 1950s was centered in New York, making it convenient for the writer to appear on such midfifties Manhattan-based shows as Steve Allen's *Tonight Show*, *The Milton Berle Buick Hour*, *The Tennessee Ernie Ford Show*, and *Hy Gardner Calling* (hosted by the show-business columnist who would become Mickey's good friend as well as a character in later Mike Hammer novels and the film version of *The Girl Hunters*).

On March 19, 1954, distinguished broadcast journalist Edward R. Murrow came to Little Bohemia to interview "the most successful mystery writer of the postwar period," and give America a look at the writer's studio and meet the wife and kids on *Person to Person*. Spillane showed off his recording equipment, talked vaguely about movie projects, and discussed the translations of his work, saying that in the UK (in a joke that gets a chuckle out of Murrow) "they even translated me into English."

"Oh, once I was doin' [the Milton Berle] Christmas TV show," Spillane gleefully recalled years later, "and the famous old actor who was going to recite 'The Night Before Christmas' was sittin' on a bar stool in front of a big crowd. In back of him there was a big movie screen where they were going to show slides of each section of [the holiday poem] to the audience."

The "very famous actor," Spillane recalled, was "drunk as a skunk."

The writer rushed to the control room and told the director, who came down and confirmed Spillane's diagnosis. When the director wondered rhetorically what could be done—they were on the commercial break of a live broadcast, after all—Mickey said, "Tell you what, I'll do it for you if you want me to."

The director asked, "Would you?"

"You got nobody else to do this."

"*Could* you do it?"

"Sure, I'll do it for you."

Spillane recalled, "So I went out and in the meantime, this director's lookin' for a script for me and the show starts. And I have a bar stool out there and in the sponsor's booth [in the back], they had glass across there. I could see the screen reflecting up there, so I could time it perfectly. So we started off and I said, 'The night before Christmas and all through . . .'"

When the director rushed down and, from the wings, threw the script at Spillane's feet, the writer kicked it back.

"And he threw it again," Spillane remembered, "and I kicked it back. In the meantime, I'm goin' on with it."

The studio audience could see Spillane repeatedly kicking the script back to the director, but the at-home audience was completely unaware.

"So I finished," Spillane recalled, "and I said, 'To all a good night.' . . . And I looked at the director, he's dripping sweat. He didn't know I knew 'The Night Before Christmas!'"

Nor did most in the viewing audience know that the hard-boiled mystery writer who had warmly recited the festive poem from memory no longer observed the holiday.

That Hollywood would come calling for the rights to the bestselling Hammer books seemed inevitable. But Spillane's success—and the strong sex-and-violence medicine of the novels—put up roadblocks. What played on the spinner racks of drug stores and tobacco shops—and was read under a teenager's covers by flashlight after lights-out—would hardly seem appropriate in your neighborhood theater.

Adapting Mickey Spillane was a challenge a seasoned filmmaker might understandably wish to avoid. How could *I, the Jury*'s signature striptease finale be staged in a manner that would pass the censors? Private eyes were a Tinsel Town staple, but also as old hat as Bogart's fedora; and the bone-crunching, blood-splashing vigilante violence of Mike Hammer that separated him from the rest of the trench-coat crowd could hardly make it past the production code.

What filmmaker would have the nerve to look past the obstacles and take advantage of the enormous success of Mike Hammer and his creator?

Unlike Mickey Spillane, Victor Saville—an art dealer's son educated at King Edward VI Grammar School in Birmingham—had seen combat. Wounded in World War I, he was invalidated out in 1916 and began his rise in the British film industry starting at the bottom, managing a small theater in Coventry by night while by day working in a film distribution office. A year later Saville was in London with the Pathé organization's features and newsreels department.

Saville and Michael Balcon had co-founded Victory Pictures in 1919 and by the late 1920s they were producing feature films for Gaumont, although Saville's first directing credit, *The Arcadians* (1927), was for his own production company. Back with Gaumont in 1931, he interspersed crime and espionage thrillers with romantic comedies and Hollywood-tinged musicals, the latter frequently featuring Jessie Matthews, star of Saville's enormously successful *Evergreen* (1934). His path to Hollywood was not unlike that of his colleague Alfred Hitchcock.

In 1936, Victor Saville Productions made several features for the celebrated Alexander Korda, including the well-regarded (and Saville-directed)
South Riding (1938). Also in 1938, he took over as head of MGM's British
arm, replacing his old partner Balcon. Having purchased A. J. Cronin's
novel *The Citadel*, he sold the rights to MGM as long as he could produce
as well; then came what would be his most successful, enduring production,
Goodbye, Mr. Chips (1939).

The producer/director spent the war years in the United States, where
he produced *The Mortal Storm* (1940) and, with Jessie Matthews again,
Forever and a Day (1943). Postwar, he remained in Hollywood, primarily
as a producer, directing only occasionally, notably the big-budget Lana
Turner–starring *Green Dolphin Street* (1947). His B-picture *Calling Bulldog
Drummond* (1951)—with fading star Walter Pidgeon taking on the role of
the British precursor to Mike Hammer—was perhaps a harbinger of what
was to come.

As "a founding father of British filmmaking," Saville seemed a highly
unlikely chaperone to escort Mike Hammer to the big screen and an eagerly
awaiting public. Saville saw in Spillane's bestsellers, despite their "raw sex
and violence," the potential for real moneymakers. And he thought he could
make a devil's bargain that would wind up funding an Oscar-worthy film
from a far more respectable bestseller, Thomas Costain's Biblical epic, *The
Silver Chalice*. It would be his American masterpiece, another classic like
Goodbye, Mr. Chips.

"I arranged a meeting with Spillane," Saville told his biographer, Roy
Moseley. "But not in an office, that was not the Spillane way. He insisted
we meet under the clock at the Pennsylvania Railway Station."

After this meeting, at once so public and yet clandestine, the American
mystery writer and the British expatriate producer "repaired to a dark bar
on Third Avenue to make a deal." They came to an agreement—a fifty/fifty
split of the profits, a partnership that fell by the wayside when Columbia
Pictures made a cash offer of $140,000 for four novels: *I, the Jury*, *My Gun
Is Quick*, *The Long Wait*, and *Kiss Me, Deadly*. Saville set aside his previous
offer and matched Columbia's.

In addition to the four films Columbia had sought, Saville apparently secured first-refusal rights to films of any other Spillane novels.

On Friday, December 19, 1952, Victor Saville announced at a press conference at the Hampshire House Hotel his "five-year exclusive contract" with Spillane and that "he [planned] to [make] two pictures a year." Hollywood gossip queen Louella Parsons wrote it up big on December 21, and showbiz Bible *Variety* covered the story on Christmas Eve. And it only underscored the distrust the Jehovah's Witness now had for the holiday.

"If Spillane had stuck to my original proposal," Saville insisted, "he would have made half a million dollars as his share of the first two pictures. He never really forgave me."

On this subject, at least, the writer and producer could agree.

But the first transfer of Mike Hammer into another medium came late in 1952, beating Hollywood and Saville to the punch. Though little remembered, a Hammer radio show—*That Hammer Guy*, later renamed *Mickey Spillane Mystery*—ran ninety-one episodes, only a dozen examples of which are known to survive.

Spillane made a deal with CBS in early 1952 that bounced to NBC—where Hammer's creator was auditioned to narrate the series—and finally to Mutual, where it debuted on December 30, without Spillane narrating.

"Not very good," was the verdict of Weybright, referring both to the show itself and Mickey's audition, when the writer played test recordings for the publisher on a Little Bohemia visit. "I would say," he went on, "[they will] neither help nor hurt the sale of his books."

But the Digital Deli Too—an excellent website devoted to "preserving the Golden Age of radio for a digital future"—notes, "It was Radio that first brought Mike Hammer to a regular mass audience, with quality scripts, convincing performances, and a reasonably authentic *Mickey Spillane* 'feel.'"

Airing on Tuesdays at 8:30 P.M. Central Time, *That Hammer Guy* was sponsored by *Esquire Magazine*, General Mills' Kix cereal, and Camel Cigarettes (a missed opportunity for Lucky Strike, Hammer's favorite smoke in the novels). Produced in New York at WOR radio, it starred

Larry Haines as Mike and Jan Miner as Velda. Haines, a two-time Tony nominee, would play Stu Bergman on television's *Search for Tomorrow* for thirty-five years and win two daytime Emmys. Miner was best known for her twenty-seven-year role as Madge the Manicurist in the Palmolive dishwashing campaign, a feat a certain future Lite Beer pitchman might have appreciated.

Scripts were frequently by Ed Adamson, who had written radio episodes of *The Shadow* and *The Thin Man* (and on television would create *Wanted: Dead or Alive* and the period private-eye series *Banyon*); and Richard Lewis, who on radio directed *The Falcon* and *Murder and Mr. Malone* (and would produce the 1954 *Mike Hammer* pilot starring Brian Keith and written/directed by Blake Edwards).

About midway through the run, *That Hammer Guy* moved to the West Coast where the new multimillion-dollar KHJ Mutual facilities awaited. Actor George Petrie briefly played Hammer until movie tough guy Ted De Corsia took over. De Corsia—whose credits included *Lady from Shanghai* (1947) and *The Naked City* (1948)—holds the rarefied honor of being the only actor ever to portray both Mike Hammer and Pat Chambers (he subbed on an episode for Bart Burns, the regular Chambers in the Darren McGavin–starring late '50s TV series). De Corsia also appears as a "fed" in the film adaptation of Spillane's *The Delta Factor* (1970).

The Golden Age radio website considers Haines more faithful to Spillane, capturing the writer's "own comparatively soft-spoken, yet direct and chilling delivery"; but feels De Corsia makes a perfect "hard-boiled, hard-bitten, and highly cynical gumshoe of the era."

In 1951, Spillane had written both *The Long Wait* and *Kiss Me, Deadly*, the latter the first mystery to make the top ten on the *New York Times* Best Seller list. But 1952 was filled not only with Mike Hammer licensing opportunities and TV guest shots for his creator, but a blinding flurry of backroom editorial maneuvering.

In late September 1950, Marc Jaffe at Signet indicated he was about to return the manuscript of *For Whom the Gods Would Destroy*. But Fawcett Publications circulation manager Allan Adams wrote Spillane in July '51, saying, "It is my personal feeling the manuscript should be published." And in mid-October of that year, Jaffe still had a version of the manuscript in New York.

At any rate, Jaffe wrote Mickey saying he'd "hold it until you come in and if there's anything to talk about we'll have the copy right here at hand."

The next week generated numerous phone calls as Jaffe detailed in a letter of October 25. "Dutton has [*For Whom the Gods Would Destroy*] pretty firmly set in their plans for '52," he told the writer. "You mentioned to Victor and me that you wanted to do a good deal of re-writing on the book—particularly since your style has changed so much in the past two or three years."

Jaffe boasted that Signet was planning to do a December mailing of sixty thousand postcards to book dealers ("a terrific deal") promoting Spillane. He closed with "Very best regards to Mary Ann and the kids, and to Charlie [Wells]."

During this period Spillane was as hot as any fiction writer would ever be. Victor Weybright wrote John Edmondson at Dutton saying, "We estimate that, with three books for 1952, the total printings in the year can hardly fail to be less than eight million, and might well exceed ten million. These staggering figures represent the most phenomenal author-property extant in the paper-bound field."

Concurrently, Spillane now had Scott Meredith as a secondary literary agent, shopping around material not contractually bound to Dutton/NAL, with whom Spillane's agreement ran for five years—1947/48 through 1953. (The exact dates cannot be determined from Spillane's copies because many business documents were destroyed in a mid-1950s attic fire in Newburgh.) The contract was amended in 1951, creating another five-year period that would expire December 27, 1956. The new agreement eliminated a compulsory renewal feature and provided Spillane a $2,000 payment not to be applied against royalties. An ambiguous portion referred to "works of Spillane which are written under an assumed name or under the name of another person," likely a reference to his friends Charlie Wells and Earle Basinsky.

No evidence exists that Spillane ever did more than mentor and provide heavy editing to the "satellite" writers, despite rumors that he may have rewritten or even written entirely Charlie Wells's books.

By early August 1952, Wells had lived with the Spillanes for several years. But now, Weybright noted in his August 9 NAL Inter-Office Memo, Wells had been "banished from the Pickwick Studios [the Little Bohemia artist's building] and has returned to Mississippi so it doesn't look as though we shall be plagued with any more Wells manuscripts." Dave Gerrity said Wells, who had dated Mary Ann back home, had gotten too familiar with Mrs. Spillane and was sent packing by Mr. Spillane.

The night before, Mickey—accompanied by Joe Gill—visited Victor Weybright at the publisher's apartment, arriving at nine o'clock and staying four hours. Spillane promised within another week "to have the new book [no name or description included] in hand so that Dutton can schedule it in January [1953] and we [NAL] in June [1953]."

Weybright continued: "I think [Spillane's] main mission was to leave a manuscript ["Everybody's Watching Me"] for *Collier's* with Scott Meredith, his special agent," whose messenger had arrived at ten o'clock as Spillane arranged. Mickey also informed Weybright that he had been "seeing a great deal of Roger Fawcett," who was urging him to write for *True* magazine.

Frustrated, Weybright wrote, "It is impossible to pin Mickey down, anyway, in the presence of his colleagues such as Joe Gill, since Mickey likes to show off too much under such circumstances."

In an August 16 memo, Weybright noted receiving phone calls from both Meredith and Spillane about a possible *Mickey Spillane Mystery Magazine*, to be "produced and distributed by the St. John's people, who are distributed by American News Co."

"I took absolute exception to any such proposal," Weybright informed his staff, "as violating the Dutton and NAL contract with Mickey."

Weybright considered this "a serious and critical affair, that we and Dutton should take strong measures to prevent the St. John's people from exploiting what has been created."

Mickey Spillane Mystery Magazine, without Mickey's participation, would become *Manhunt*, the long-running digest pulp considered by many a natural successor to *Black Mask*. When, for reasons unknown, *Collier's* declined to use Spillane's short novel, "Everybody's Watching Me," it became a four-part serial in the first four issues of *Manhunt*, January through April 1953.

The idea of a Spillane mystery magazine re-emerged in June 1953, when Alex L. Hillman, publisher of *Pageant* magazine, proposed *The Mickey Spillane Mystery Book*, for which he offered the writer $25,000 a year. Weybright considered this "peanuts" and "a scavenger operation," reminding Edmonson at Dutton that "the *Ellery Queen Mystery Magazine* practically killed the Ellery Queen books." The offer was "an insult to your, our and Mickey's intelligence."

On Saturday, November 15, Weybright visited Spillane to discourage him from writing short fiction for lower-end magazines. It could damage his reputation and income, Weybright insisted; he singled out a Spillane short story in *Cavalier* ("Together We Kill," January 1953 issue, which had hit newsstands in October).

Spillane said he regretted selling "Everybody's Watching Me" to *Manhunt* for $10,000, but had since been offered a $100,000 advance by another party in the book market. Mickey seems to have been angling for a better deal with NAL/Dutton.

The publisher also reported Spillane's annoyance with some of his media coverage. In particular, Mary Ann disliked the *Life* magazine article, although she was happier with the *True* piece.

The real purpose of Weybright's visit was to motivate their author to deliver more material on his existing contract. But talk of the next Mike Hammer, *Tonight I Die*, took second place to a novel Mickey wanted to talk about, which he implied was either written or well under way—*Legion Five*, about Caesar's army.

A few days later, Weybright wrote Spillane that it "was very reassuring to hear your firm statement that you are not going to permit more of your short stuff to be published—especially in St. John's, Fawcett, or wood-pulp magazines. . . . I look forward to seeing you on Wednesday, and to reading both of the manuscripts which you are about to deliver."

What those two manuscripts might be is unknown, but one could be *Legion Five* (either lost or never written).

The publisher then asked, "Are you sure you don't want to touch up *Whom the Gods Destroy* for 1953 publication?"

Weybright closed his letter on a congratulatory note: "It sure is nice to see *Kiss Me, Deadly* in the *New York Times* best-selling list these days. It means you're an author, as well as a writer, and that you were very wise not to get involved in the pure pulp field of dime-novels marked up to twenty-five cents."

The latter refers to the line of original paperback novels their mutual associate Roscoe Fawcett had so successfully launched to tap into the Spillane-style market. Mickey often provided Fawcett (and got paid for) blurbs for Gold Medal's original paperbacks, including John D. MacDonald ("I wish I had written this!") and Peter Rabe ("This guy is good!"). Naturally enough, the Dutton and Signet editorial teams were less than thrilled.

Weybright's concerns were well founded. After all, *I, the Jury* was reprinted eight times in 1949; again in 1950; nine times in 1951; and as of May 1952 was in its twenty-first printing. Spillane's seven novels had, thus far, sold thirteen million copies.

But what would Mickey Spillane's publisher have said if he'd been told it would be almost a decade between *Kiss Me, Deadly* and the next Mike Hammer novel?

TOP LEFT: Mickey, actress Bettye Ackerman, and Jack Stang shoot the Mike Hammer test film in Newburgh. TOP RIGHT: Stang as Hammer. BOTTOM: Biff Elliot as Mike Hammer with Margaret Sheridan as Velda in *I, the Jury* (1953); the Christmas tree denotes the ironic Yuletide setting for a grim detective noir.

CHAPTER ELEVEN

SPILLANE THE JURY

Mickey Spillane lost little time getting disenchanted with Victor Saville. The producer, oozing English politeness and Hollywood bonhomie, brushed away any efforts by Hammer's creator to write the *I, the Jury* script himself. But the producer did express a willingness to consider casting Jack Stang in the lead role—the twenty-nine-year-old Newburgh cop who was part of the Little Bohemia gang and Mickey's idea of the perfect screen Mike Hammer.

Jack was "one of the group of Marines that went onto a Pacific island," Spillane remembered, "and they went in with one-hundred-and-twenty guys and there were four left when they came out. Jack was one of the four. And he was a tough man, physically, mentally and able to accomplish anything he wanted to do. . . . I always wanted this guy to be in the movies to play the part."

Yet despite assuring Spillane the Newburgh cop was in serious consideration, Saville announced he was launching a talent hunt for the perfect actor to portray Mike.

"Marlon Brando is the closest," the producer told the press. "But he's played Shakespeare, so would he be interested?" Letters were pouring in "recommending actors for the role. They mention Robert Mitchum the most. Humphrey Bogart and Alan Ladd, too."

Asked by United Press reporter Aline Mosby why he bought the rights to the Hammer novels, Saville said a woman in New York had suggested he read a Spillane story.

Replying in "his cultured, British voice," the producer said, "I thought, 'You mean people read this?'"

Not a ringing endorsement of the property.

Saville went on: "I bought the series because I didn't want to be bored in making movies these days. Besides, you have to have an added something in a film now."

The producer pledged the trademark sex and violence would not be "censored out of the sizzling celluloid version," and promised to murder as many people on-screen as Spillane did on the printed page.

"And as for sex," Saville said, "you will notice that Hammer approaches sex, but he usually postpones it to a later date. Nothing censorable about that."

With the search for a screen Mike Hammer under way, Spillane pushed ever harder for Jack Stang. Several men's adventure magazines did articles on Mickey and his pal, who *Focus* described as "rock-jawed, ice-eyed, with a face made of sidewalk cement." When Stang looked at you, Spillane said, it was with a "snarl that fades into a cold smile. . . . Mike Hammer in the flesh."

When the writer offered to shoot his own screen test of Stang for Saville's consideration, the producer encouraged it. Helped line up a crew.

Filming on *I, the Jury* was due to start in March and it was February already—Mickey was working against the clock mounting his $1,500 screen test, which he would direct himself in the posh Green Room of the Hotel Newburgh. George Wilson was back to design and build the set. An audience of one hundred or so had been invited to watch, and help stoke media coverage.

"We had good people on that thing, who later became stars," Spillane recalled. Future comedy legend Jonathan Winters played a hobo and Bettye Ackerman—a South Carolina girl who later played Dr. Maggie Graham on ABC-TV's *Ben Casey*—was the femme fatale.

"Those of us who were there," said a writer covering the shoot for the July 1953 issue of *Male* magazine, "stood spellbound as one of the toughest characters of the 20th Century came to life before our eyes. And for the test, Mickey wrote his own script—a five-minute miniature Spillane novel."

The screen test—lost to time, though the script survives—had Hammer solving fourteen murders, shooting a bad guy in an alley, and strangling (as *Focus* put it) "a no good dame and [flipping] a butt on her back."

As had been the case with *Kiss Me, Deadly*, the new godly versions of Hammer and Spillane seemed a lot like the old ungodly ones.

After the test wrapped, Stang "ripped off his trench coat, wiped his brow, and bee-lined for the bar." There he had a shot of rye with a drop of crème de menthe, which "cuts the rye and sweetens the breath," the cop explained.

Saville and United Artists execs had assured Spillane they would "run through the film" the next day and if he got the "all right sign," Stang would "most probably star in *I, the Jury*."

But in the meantime, Hollywood columnist Louella Parsons reported that little-known TV actor Biff Elliot had topped hundreds of contestants for the prized role of Mike Hammer. *Foto-rama* magazine reported in its November 1953 issue that Elliot had won out over "some 500 rugged applicants," describing the winner as square-jawed and good-looking, a Golden Gloves boxer whose previous jobs had included disc jockey and infantryman (he had seen action in Italy).

Spillane assured the local Newburgh paper that Victor Saville had viewed Stang's screen test with great enthusiasm. But the producer told Mickey his friend needed to "undertake extensive coaching and grooming for future leading roles." Stang would play Hammer in the subsequent Saville pictures, the writer confidently asserted.

Soon the twenty-nine-year-old traffic cop was on leave from the police department and "California-bound with his wife Carmella and two junior Stangs." Newburgh Police Chief John Mullarky had "no hard feelings" at the possibility of losing a star cop: "Jack's a real killer. He'd give his own mother a ticket."

Jack Stang may have looked the part, but it was Victor Saville who proved as cold as Mike Hammer. The producer's reward to Stang for making the Hollywood trip was to give Newburgh's finest a silent bit as a poolroom tough in a fleeting few seconds with Biff Elliot's Hammer.

Stinging from the scam his producer had pulled, Spillane—with Stang at his side—nonetheless made nice on set, posing for pictures, sitting in front of a 35mm camera, chatting with Saville and director/writer Harry Essex, sharing drinks with stars Elliot and Peggie Castle, even going through a buffet line with Stang, where the lovely blonde star served them turkey—or was that crow?

Shooting began as promised in March of 1953 at Samuel Goldwyn Studios on Santa Monica Boulevard in Hollywood, with no location shooting in Mike Hammer's emblematic New York. On rigorously controlled sets, *I, the Jury* was photographed in the Dunning 3D black-and-white process, taking advantage of the Three Dimension craze that was part of the film industry's counterattack on television.

The Hackard Building where Hammer keeps his office was represented on film by the Bradbury Building (at Broadway and West Third Street in downtown Los Angeles), a structure known for the ornate ironwork of its atrium of walkways, stairways, and elevators. A true icon of film noir, the Bradbury Building appears in numerous crime films, including *The Unfaithful* (1947), *Shockproof* (1949), *D.O.A.* (1949), and *Marlowe* (1969, from Raymond Chandler's *The Little Sister*, 1949).

The historic building also turns ups in such TV private-eye series as *77 Sunset Strip* (1963, season six only), *Banyon* (1972, created by *That Hammer Guy's* Ed Adamson), and *City of Angels* (1976, based on the 1946 Roy Huggins novel, *The Double Take*, which is—dizzyingly—also the basis of *77 Sunset Strip*).

For a film with such a poor reputation—based primarily on how little it has been seen in decades, and the rarity of film festival 3D presentations—*I, the Jury* boasts stellar noir credentials, starting of course with the Spillane source novel.

Film noir expert Eddie Muller cites "John Alton's glorious black and white cinematography in three dimensions" as the highlight of the film.

Alton had won an Academy Award for cinematography on *An American in Paris* (1951), but black-and-white was his specialty. This most celebrated of film noir cinematographers once said memorably, "The most interesting things in the world happen at night. Of course, lighting, and light in itself, is a mystery!"

Saville chose prolific screenwriter Harry Essex to write and direct, his first time in the latter role. Though Essex would helm only three more films, two of which were low-budget 1970s horror features, his scriptwriting for noir films included *The Killer That Stalked New York* (1950), *Kansas City Confidential* (1952), and (additional dialogue) *He Walked by Night* (1948). He also wrote the noirish 3D horror classic *The Creature from the Black Lagoon* (1954).

I, the Jury greatly benefits from its Franz Waxman score, a masterpiece of melancholy, discordant, off-kilter jazz. Waxman's score is arguably the finest of any Spillane film, and among the finest of any private-eye noir. While no soundtrack has been issued, Waxman's mini-suite of *I, the Jury* themes—"Three Sketches: Nostalgia, Song, Blues"—is featured on the *Crime in the Streets* LP and CD.

The cast is brimming with significant noir players, including Preston Foster (*Kansas City Confidential*, 1952) as Captain Pat Chambers, Elisha Cook, Jr. (*The Maltese Falcon*, 1941) as beekeeper Bobo, Margaret Sheridan (*The Thing from Another World*, 1951) as Velda, and John Qualen (*Casablanca*, 1942) as Dr. Vickers.

Tall, green-eyed Peggie Castle became the actress most identified with Mickey Spillane films, embodying *I, the Jury*'s Charlotte Manning to perfection with a unique mix of sleepy sexuality and keen intelligence. A year later she would appear as the aptly named Venus in Saville's follow-up, *The Long Wait*.

The other memorable "Spillane dolls" in *I, the Jury* (or "dames" as various male-oriented, low-end periodicals would call them in photo spreads) are the Seitz Twins, Tani and Dran, who bring the sexy Bellamy sisters to life—identical but for a strategic strawberry birthmark. Mary Anderson, continuing a long film (and TV) career, and Frances Osborne, primarily a television performer, played respectively the ill-fated Eileen Vickers and Jack Williams's fiancée, Myrna, in non-glamour-girl fashion, adding to a gritty feel that permeates the film.

But what about Biff Elliot as Mike Hammer? Spillane himself, stung by the rejection of his hometown choice, expressed immediate dissatisfaction that grew to something like contempt over the years. Reviewers at the time often found Elliot lacking or at best serviceable, as have many latter-day noir buffs.

"Mike Hammer is a cartoon character like Superman," an eighty-six-year-old Elliot said in 2010. "I am not Superman. I'm an actor. . . . I took a cartoon character and turned him into a flesh-and-blood human being similar to what Mickey Spillane was. It's impossible to please a writer who's writing, without knowing it, his own autobiography."

The ex-boxer actor was reluctantly burdened with padded shoulders, particularly for his camel hair trench coat. He might not have wanted to make a Superman-style character out of Mike Hammer, but when the private eye stomps down dark, rain-slick streets like a good-guy Frankenstein monster, the effect is at once absurd and appropriate.

In retrospect, Elliot's performance seems first rate. He portrays Mike Hammer as an emotional hothead who can be as tough as he is tender. That he is a little smaller than a reader may have imagined Hammer only makes him seem less a bully. He fights hard and loves hard, and may not be as smart as most movie private eyes, which gives him a nice everyman quality, in tune with the novels.

Of all four Saville films, *I, the Jury* captures best the look and flavor of the books—fun and tough and sexy, with dialogue that crackles. What had disappointed moviegoers at the time, however, remains disappointing: most overtly sexual aspects of the plot—a dance studio may or may not be a brothel, several characters may or may not be homosexual—became incoherent due to censorship issues, and the famous striptease finale reduces lovely Peggie Castle's disrobing to . . . taking off her shoes.

Correspondence in the file on the film in the Motion Picture Association of America/Production Code Collection at the Academy of Motion

Picture Arts and Sciences library confirms the many problems the MPAA censors had with the screenplay. The MPAA urged Saville to change George Kalecki's illegal business from drug trafficking (he didn't), and also wanted Hammer to shoot Charlotte Manning in self-defense (he sort of did).

When *I, the Jury* opened in 3D at the Criterion Theatre in New York City on August 21, 1953, the film pulled in $10,000 the first day, a non-holiday box-office record. Though casually described by many as a box-office flop, Mike Hammer's film debut brought in a gross of $1.4 million in the United States and Canada, putting it in the top twenty grossing films of 1953.

Of course, Saville likely thought a hot property like Mickey Spillane's Mike Hammer would do better, and it certainly would have if the 3D craze hadn't begun to founder. The film was released to most theaters in a "flat" format.

Seen that way on TV, the film rarely indicates its 3D origins. Only occasionally do objects and people come out of the screen at the viewer, notably the notorious "back scratcher" moment when one of the come-hither Seitz twins extends that implement toward the viewer. But 3D theatrical screenings reveal Alton's intention to pull the audience deeper within the images, creating a greater sense of reality and not using the process for gimmicky effects.

I, the Jury begins with its most dramatic display of the 3D effect. One-armed Jack Williams—prosthetic arm draped over a chair—is shot by an off-screen assailant. Jack, on the floor now, crawls toward camera, reaching his remaining arm toward the viewer as he attempts to reach the chair where his police revolver is slung. That chair is slowly pulled back, tauntingly, sadistically, while the Franz Waxman score underlines the tragedy with pounding brass, invoking Spillane's trademark italics.

In the wake of what he saw as Saville's betrayal of himself and Stang, Spillane would eventually go public about his displeasure with the film. Elliot was too small, he'd say, though his chief complaints were with the Essex script and such details as a revolver being substituted for Mike

Hammer's trademark .45. He howled about Hammer recovering a perfectly formed spent slug from a brick wall, and moaned about his hero getting knocked out with a wooden coat hanger. Spillane also griped that Biff was "left-handed and had a Boston accent."

Further, he found director/screenwriter Harry Essex obnoxious and disrespectful. Talking to *Vanity Fair* in 2003, he mocked Essex: "[He said] 'I'm going to teach Mickey Spillane how to write.' But he didn't know how to tell a story!"

Yet Spillane was intensely involved with the promotion of the film's initial release. He attended the world premiere in Norfolk, Virginia. He went on the road presenting and hyping the film at theaters, making appearances with Biff Elliot, who at that time was expected to portray Hammer in all the upcoming films (Saville had signed the Boston actor to a multiple-picture deal). Together, Spillane and the screen Mike Hammer dropped by veteran hospitals. Both Spillane and bit player Stang made live appearances at a Newburgh movie house.

During the shoot, Spillane and Elliot became friends, and while the writer remained critical of his new pal having been cast as Hammer, he made sure to underscore this opinion with another: "Biff is a damn good actor," and on several occasions intended to use Elliot in film and TV projects himself.

During the production, he and Elliot had gotten to know each other when they both stayed at the Chateau Marmont.

"We're in the elevator," Spillane told *Vanity Fair*'s Cliff Rothman. "Biff has on white pants and a white shirt. Greta Garbo comes in the elevator, thinks he's a bellboy, and says, 'Would you mind getting my car?' She hands him her keys. Not missing a beat, Biff says, 'Yes, ma'am, right away.' She gives him a dollar and gets out of the elevator."

Which was just what Mike Hammer would have done, Spillane told Rothman with a laugh.

Supporting the film's release, Signet's movie tie-in edition of *I, the Jury* included back-cover photos from the movie version, labeled: MICKEY SPILLANE IN HOLLYWOOD.

"Mickey Spillane's bestselling mysteries," cover copy proclaimed, "can now be seen in exciting 3D motion pictures produced by Victor Saville and released by United Artists."

This indicates Saville's intention to use the 3D process for all four Spillane novels he'd acquired. But the 3D fad fizzled before any subsequent Spillane films could be similarly shot.

The 3D gimmick had seemed a perfect way to exploit the curvy dames and fist-in-your face violence that were assumed to be the secret of Mike Hammer's—and Mickey Spillane's—success. But no gimmick could convey the relationship that existed between readers and Spillane's unconventional, even unbalanced, antihero.

Seldom has a narrator been more effectively used as a point of identification for readers, establishing a personal connection that became an elusive element in screen adaptations. Much as the Hammer paperback book covers emphasized reader identification by never showing the detective's face, shots in the 1953 film mimic those cover poses. So do production stills and movie posters (which show Peggie Castle in a nightgown or about to unbutton her blouse, neither of which are in the film itself).

Director/writer Harry Essex transfers the first-person style of the novels to the film by way of voice-over narration, a common element in film noir of the forties. Voice-over has often been a postproduction attempt to help an audience find its way through an opaque narrative.

I, the Jury on film might fairly be accused of a convoluted narrative, and the use of voice-over is one of its strengths, the language vivid, personal, and appropriately Spillane in tone: "Remember what I promised you? No matter who it turned out to be, Jack, I'd get the killer."

The screenplay is surprisingly faithful to the novel's plot, though at times lapsing into incoherence, due to the necessity of censoring out or at least softening drug and prostitution references. Essex builds a sense of tension and paranoia—Hammer peeks around corners, looking behind him as he prowls these mean, oddly empty city streets.

A common complaint about Spillane's work is the supposed misogyny of the Hammer novels; the ending of *I, the Jury*, both novel and film, has a lot to do with that misconception. Yet the two major female characters are portrayed not as sex kittens but as at least Hammer's equal. Peggie Castle's Charlotte is well educated, an author, a psychiatrist, treated with deference and even adoration by the detective. Velda is Hammer's partner and perhaps lover, and when her office sanctuary is stormed by thugs, she holds her own; watching Hammer's merciless counterattack with cool contempt for the invaders, actress Sheridan sanctions her savior's sadism with a toss of her hair.

Peggie Castle's smoldering performance is compromised only by her final striptease, the scene readers were dying to see how Hollywood would bring it off; but audiences were left with the disappointment of it essentially being skipped. While the famous violent punchline—"It was easy"—is retained, the sexy buildup is not.

On-screen, Mike's voice-over continues: "There was only one more thing to do—order a basket, a real pretty one. And wait for Pat. He had his killer and I had my memories."

Of the Saville-produced films, *I, the Jury* is the only one set in Hammer's signature New York. From its California sound stages, *I, the Jury* manages to recreate the surrealistic, even nightmarish urban landscape through which Mike Hammer moves. The substitution of an LA landmark—the Bradbury Building—for Hammer's Hackard Building provides a baroque backdrop for Mickey Spillane's fever-dream Manhattan.

All of this was lost on Mickey Spillane, outraged by the sham screen-test Saville put him through, embarrassed for his friend Jack Stang (and himself), and disgusted with the disrespect shown him by Essex.

In 1998, Spillane reflected on his first Hollywood experience. "Saville was the producer on *Goodbye, Mr. Chips*, a great picture," he said. "I thought . . . that Hollywood would think enough of a book that sold a lot of copies that they would make a good picture out of it. Now, all Saville wanted to do was buy my name and my character. He wanted to make a big picture fast, *The Silver Chalice*. It fell on its face and it couldn't have happened to a nicer guy. Because Saville loused up those pictures so badly just to make money, now I suddenly saw the greed in these Hollywood characters. That's why I'm very careful when I deal with Hollywood."

For five years Mike Hammer would be tied up by the option clause in the Saville contract. The writer couldn't take his most valuable asset to another studio to make a picture more to his liking.

But he had another asset he could market to Hollywood.

Mickey Spillane.

And someone he'd met there whom he could trust.

John Wayne.

TOP: Mickey Spillane as himself, but invoking Mike Hammer, is clearly the star of the *Ring of Fear* poster art. BOTTOM: Peggie Castle and Anthony Quinn in the surrealistic climax of the *The Long Wait*, a non-Mike Hammer Spillane adaptation.

CHAPTER TWELVE

WRITING JAG

Bestselling mystery writer Mickey Spillane and Hollywood superstar John Wayne—both of whom despised Communism in a somewhat unsophisticated way—were a natural match. Hobnobbing on the wings of celebrity, Mickey Spillane got to know Wayne and others in Hollywood's "solid Republican contingent" (as *Vanity Fair* put it), including James Stewart: "He was a flier, so was I. Nice guy."

Few other actors impressed him, though—Errol Flynn was "strange"—and he didn't enjoy being around actors in general. "Everything is an act," he said.

Wayne, however, was an exception.

"A very nice man," Spillane said in 1998. "Nice to people, didn't do nasty things."

Unlike Victor Saville.

In 1952, Wayne had gone into business with producer Robert Fellows as Wayne-Fellows Productions, and the two were riding high in 1953 with hits like *Island in the Sky* and *Hondo,* with *The High and the Mighty* in the works for '54.

Fellows had been in the movie business since talkies came in, having risen from gopher to assistant director, production manager to associate producer, and from there to full-fledged producer. He worked on several of Wayne's films and the star was heard to say, "What Bob doesn't know about this business isn't worth knowing."

According to Wayne biographer Scott Eyman, similar backgrounds as movie journeymen were what drew the actor to the producer. "Wayne had an innate distrust of the artiste," Eyman writes, which was an element that Wayne and Spillane had in common as well.

Wayne-Fellows acquired an office building off Sunset Boulevard at 1022 Palm Avenue. The company's story editor, Tom Kane, described how their office became a hangout for the actor's cronies, many of them spongers dating back to Duke Wayne's early Hollywood days. Spillane would certainly have understood how a successful guy might find himself surrounded by less prosperous old pals who could use the occasional handout.

Mickey joined this "boy's club," hanging around Wayne-Fellows "kibitzing," but refreshingly not with his hand out. In his unpublished memoir (quoted by Eyman), Kane describes Spillane as a "crude, bumptious hack" who "had gotten lucky with Mike Hammer." Wayne had a different opinion of his new friend.

Possibly Kane was offended by Mickey deriding the Hemingway, Faulkner, and Dos Passos titles lining the Wayne-Fellows shelves.

"Those guys are bums," the mystery writer said, playing the typical Spillane card of outrageousness. He reeled off his sales figures and summed it up: "I've sold more than all those guys put together."

But even by Kane/Eyman's calculation, Spillane was at least "half-joking."

Often Spillane would take lunch with Wayne, Fellows, and in-house screenwriter James Edward Grant at the nearby Cock'n Bull on Sunset. Grant—an outgoing alcoholic ex-newspaperman who'd written for the slicks and pulps before scaling Hollywood—had made a career out of being Wayne's rewrite man. Mickey would stop at a Jaguar dealership to gawk at the XK-160 in the window—at $5,500, a grand more than "the best Cadillac on the road"—before heading into the restaurant with Wayne and company.

Surely as they dined and ate (and drank) their lunch, the writer would have shared with the others what he considered Victor Saville's unethical and unscrupulous conduct. The so-polite producer had even informed Mickey that their contract precluded him selling not only original

Hammer material to any other studio but non-Hammer Spillane stories, as well—right up to the end of the five-year period.

But Spillane had an idea for himself and Stang. Mike Hammer's daddy was a celebrity now, after numerous TV appearances, countless magazine and newspaper articles, and those .38-lugging, muscle-shirt pictures on the backs of tens of millions of softcover editions. So what if Mickey couldn't write a book or movie script for a Hollywood sale? Nothing was preventing him from appearing *in* a movie.

Grant, who had bombed out as a director once already—Wayne had to step in anonymously for him on *Angel and the Badman* (1947)—had somehow convinced Duke to let him make a circus picture, *Ring of Fear* (1954), with Pat O'Brien and lion tamer Clyde Beatty already signed. When he found out Mickey "wanted to be a movie star" (according to Eyman), Grant took him up on it.

Grant's son Colin told biographer Eyman, "My father wasn't really a director and he would have been the first to tell you. DeMille's *The Greatest Show on Earth* had made a fortune, and my dad thought he could make a fortune with another circus movie. I don't think Duke wanted to make it at all."

In November of 1953, Spillane and Jack Stang found themselves in Deming, New Mexico, on the set of *Ring of Fear* as its second-billed star and a featured player respectively—the writer playing his celebrity self, brought in to solve some murders under the big top, and Stang as . . . Jack Stang—"hotshot copper out of New York," undercover as a magazine writer. Spillane was receiving $2,500 per week for "not less than ten consecutive weeks" (Stang's recompense is unknown).

A flimsy script that somehow had required three writers—actor and Wayne crony Paul Fix, British novelist and screenwriter Philip MacDonald, and Grant himself—had been designed to use circus acts to show off the new wide-screen Cinemascope process, which had largely been developed to combat 3D.

Spillane couldn't have been happier—he'd found a way to take revenge on Saville, who was shooting *The Long Wait*, and bask in an enthusiasm he'd had since childhood. ("I was one guy who had his cake and ate it, too. . . . I just about ran away and joined the circus. . . .")

In an article about making the film ("Sawdust in My Shoes") for the 1957 Clyde Beatty Circus program book, Spillane wrote, "For a month and a half I lived under the big top with some of the finest people I ever met. I got sawdust in my shoes and the tawny animal smell in my nostrils . . . for a little while I was part of this world of clowns and acrobats and people whose life was centered around these three rings under the white top."

What Spillane didn't mention in his sunny making-of piece was director/writer Grant's on-set conduct.

"You can't write and drink," Spillane said in 1998. "I watched this go on and I said this movie is falling apart. And it did. I watched it fall down. And what came out was such a hodgepodge, it was terrible."

Indeed, Grant delivered a film that was both over-budget and deemed unfit for release.

Bob Fellows said, "We felt by using James Edward Grant we would get a good script and a good job of direction for bargain prices—we got neither."

Grant's defense to Wayne was pitiful: "The picture may be bad but it is not nearly as bad as Bob has convinced you."

Wayne accused his friend of drinking on the job and had the liquor bills from Phoenix, where much of the film had been shot, to prove it.

As letters and phone calls flew frantically, Spillane was brought into the loop.

"Duke and Bob said, 'We're going to lose all our money,'" Spillane told *Vanity Fair* in 2003. Already back in Little Bohemia, he told Wayne and Fellows over the phone he knew exactly where the problems were and what outtakes could be used to minimize reshoots. But rewriting and reshoots would absolutely be needed to save the picture.

Wayne and Fellows flew Mickey back to Los Angeles and installed him in a bungalow at the Beverly Hills Hotel. Arriving on a Thursday, the writer worked in an office at Wayne-Fellows headquarters. Sunday afternoon, in-house assistant director (and soon to be director) Andrew McLaglen—son of actor Victor McLaglen—found Spillane lounging at the Beverly Hills Hotel and asked how the script was coming along.

"Finished," Spillane said.

Thinking Spillane meant he was done for the day, McLaglen asked, "When will you finish?"

"I told you. I'm finished."

He'd done the entire rewrite in two and a half days.

A frantic scramble to find a secretary to type up the pages followed, while Mickey slipped away and caught a plane back to Newburgh. He knew he would be needed for the reshoots but that wouldn't be for a while—the Clyde Beatty circus would have to be reassembled on location, the actors resecured, and much more.

In the meantime, Wayne and Fellows were trying to find him.

"They called every boarding house, every hospital, every saloon," Spillane recalled. "Well, I don't hang around those places. And finally Bob says, 'Let's try Newburgh!'"

Getting Spillane on the phone, Fellows asked, "What are you doing there?"

"What am I going to do in Hollywood?" Spillane asked.

"Get out here!"

To direct Spillane's rewrites, Wayne enlisted William Wellman, who had just helmed *The High and the Mighty* (1954), which would earn him his third Academy Award nomination for Best Director. Fellows estimated another $115,908 dollars would be piled onto the $700,000 already spent on this turkey. Duke got "Wild Bill" to come aboard in exchange for ten percent of the profits, should there be any.

Wayne biographer Eyman says, "Wellman sailed in with a writer," but—perhaps because he was no fan of Spillane—doesn't name who that writer was. Spillane's personal copy of the screenplay, heavily marked up and sporting a rainbow of yellow, pink, and blue replacement pages, reveals just how the mystery writer helped Wellman make "a facsimile of a silk purse out of a genuine sow's ear."

The front half of the screenplay is a ninety-six-page document with half a dozen pages of on-set rewrites by Spillane already inserted before the actual rewrite began. Further, Spillane has marked up and rewritten the dialogue for most of his scenes when originally shot. Following the shooting script comes Spillane's rewrite labeled

"RING OF FEAR"

SUPPLEMENTAL SCRIPT

for a shoot to begin December 22, 1954. The supplemental script runs forty-seven pages, just over half the length of the original shooting script, indicating just how extensive a redo this was.

Spillane had never written a screenplay before and, at one point, on brittle, browned paper obviously right out of the rewrite man's typewriter, comes the following, in story-treatment form, of mad killer Dublin and a tiger both on the loose with Mickey Spillane and Jack Stang leading the chase:

> *This is the final scene. Here the killer is killed. It is night, in the moody, dangerous area of the train siding. The noise of the chase has been on and in the background you can still hear the urgent commands and shrill answers of the hands searching for the cat. The tempo of the hunt for the madman and the animal is building to a smashing crescendo with the camera hitting Dublin, Spillane, the hands, the cat, Stang . . . all alternately, then suddenly settles to one shot. Dublin makes [it to] an open boxcar . . . tosses a quick look around and climbs in the darkness . . . but not before the camera catches him in one sudden close-up that shows the mocking, triumphal smile on his face that says he's beaten the whole damn pack of them and he's getting away again and this time for good . . . because nobody has spotted him!*
>
> *And this is the fatal mistake . . . because he has been seen! Spillane in a shot close to camera . . . looking toward the boxcar fifty yards off . . . very casual, almost too damn deadly casual. He takes out the gun*

. . . then starts to walk slowly. The kill is only minutes off now. Then
Stang appears out of the darkness and we know he's seen all this too.
Nobody . . . only the audience and these two know the final answer.

Then the walk to the car starts. No[t] hurried. There's no way
out for this guy. But suddenly out of nowhere comes the third party
. . . the tawny hulk of the tiger and for a second Stang and Spillane
freeze. The noise builds up . . . the tiger looks for his escape and then
spots the open boxcar.

Stang sees what's going to happen. He whips out a gun as he goes
to run toward the car . . . but Spillane reaches out wordlessly and
stops him. There's a quick exchange of glances between the two . . .
Stang with the unspoken question and Spillane answering in the
same unspoken negative. Because here is justice . . . final, retributive
justice about to render an accounting.

Spillane's rewrite and Wellman's direction made the film worthy of
release, creating a compelling forty-five-minute crime drama . . . unfortunately
the film is ninety-three minutes. Spillane-written scenes—particularly
prominent in the film's last half hour—make crisp little crackers of pulp
in a soggy sawdust soup.

At its core, *Ring of Fear*—as rewritten, at least—is a decent enough suspense yarn about an escaped psychopath (John Ford regular Sean McClory)
who signs on with Clyde Beatty's circus to take revenge on Beatty and
pursue a now-married former lover/trapeze artist. Unfortunately, the story
is constantly interrupted by flat-footed circus footage designed to show off
the Cinemascope process.

Occasionally, that footage is compelling—Beatty in a cage handling
eight lions at a time still amazes, and a trapeze act thrills. Of course, this
is also a film featuring unfunny clowns, routine acrobats, and sequences
showcasing eight-year-olds eating, a child needing a bathroom waiting
for a line of elephants to pass, Gonzalez-Gonzales doing his Mexican
variation on Willie Best, and three, *count 'em ladies and gentlemen*, three
circus parades.

Spillane enters about twenty-five minutes into the picture, bringing *Ring of Fear* alive with his natural acting style, delivering self-written lines with a Brooklyn cadence. He finds pieces of business—straw to chew, ice cream cones to nibble, fingernails to clean, a fedora to tilt, and is a low-key but always interesting presence. His final showdown with McClory in a claustrophobic trailer brings out the writer's innate Mike Hammer.

Whether it was Wellman who saw the potential in Spillane, or Mickey himself who couldn't keep himself from rising to the occasion, is impossible to know. But as an effort to show off Jack Stang as the perfect screen Mike Hammer, it's Hammer's creator who seems to be the private eye incarnate.

In 1999, Spillane finally conceded Victor Saville's judgment.

"I had the right guy, Jack Stang, a real cop," he told *Crime Time* interviewer Michael Carlson, "only he couldn't act." Elsewhere he admitted, "[Stang] never was able to handle certain types of scenes. . . . He was a cop, that's what he was. Acting isn't in a cop's job unless he's doing an interrogation or something like that—then he can act."

Stang appeared in an episode of *Highway Patrol* in 1955, before returning to Newburgh, where he operated a riverfront bar and grill at Fourth and Front Street.

Ring of Fear serves primarily as a fascinating artifact of Spillane's enormous 1950s celebrity, its female lead—Marian Carr—destined to portray a key role in the next (and crucial) Mike Hammer film, *Kiss Me Deadly*. Her claim to fame may be to have appeared opposite characters named "Mickey Spillane" and "Mike Hammer" in a pair of features likely shot back-to-back.

During the filming of *The Long Wait*, Spillane made no visits to the set and did nothing to help promote the film—his focus, predictably, on *Ring of Fear*. The two films were in release around the same time—*The Long Wait* had its world premiere at Chicago's Essaness Woods Theater on May 18, 1954. The *Chicago Daily News* ran a photo of Peggie Castle, Shawn Smith, and *Playboy* playmate Dolores Donlon, who were at a press luncheon to promote the movie (of the major female roles, only Mary Ellen Kay was absent). The film would open in Los Angeles on May 26.

The Long Wait is the only Spillane film directed by producer Victor Saville himself (although he apparently co-directed *My Gun Is Quick*, 1957, under the joint pseudonym "Phil Victor"). Despite the acceptable box office of *I, the Jury*, Biff Elliot had not scored enough of an impression to be given a second go-round, despite that long-term contract. Saville choosing the only non-Hammer property among the four optioned Spillane novels forestalled the problem of finding a satisfactory screen Mike Hammer.

Little seen in recent years and undervalued by critics of the day, *The Long Wait* is a solid noir beautifully shot by Franz Planer with a workmanlike screenplay by Alan Green and Lesser Samuels, fairly faithful to the source novel, and featuring Anthony Quinn as Johnny McBride in the actor's first leading-man role after years of strong support work. The Mario Castelnuovo-Tedesco score, however, does little for the film, showcasing a syrupy opening-credits ballad, "Once," written by Harold Spina and Bob Russell.

Two recurring noir elements are combined in *The Long Wait*—the amnesiac hero and the corrupt small town. In search of his memory and a killer, Quinn is a tough guy who displays occasional impulsive violence, much in the Spillane manner. The actor's Johnny McBride is a hothead who obviously has the capacity to be guilty of the murder that he is accused of having committed and is trying to solve.

Spillane's central plot device—one of four "dames" is McBride's onetime girlfriend, her appearance transformed by makeup, hair dye, and cosmetic surgery—sets the stage for an array of pinup lovelies to appear along the amnesiac's path. They are attired in almost absurdly alluring apparel, and would be the focus of the PR campaign that sparked another round of photo spreads in male-oriented magazines.

Distinguished Charles Coburn is the banker who aids his disgraced former clerk, and Gene Evans (a regular of director Sam Fuller's) is the evocatively named Servo, a grinning, sinister casino boss. He and literal heavy Bruno VeSota are a pair of grotesque hoods who might have jumped off the page of a Spillane novel. Lawrence Dobkin (who would direct Darren McGavin in *Mike Hammer* TV episodes) is the doctor who gives McBride an amnesia diagnosis, while Jay Adler is a comically deadpan, long-in-the-tooth bellboy. McBride appears to bed all four "suspects," thanks to Saville's suggestive dissolves.

The film's violent, expressionistic finale is its low-lit highlight. Director Saville gave much of the credit to Russian-born art director Boris Leven, who designed the "escapologist scene," making extensive use of storyboards.

"I directed the scene matching the camera to the drawings, shot for shot," Saville said, "eighty-seven [setups] in one day."

In an "abandoned power station," Peggie Castle's Venus is sprawled helpless on the floor of a nebulous space where shadows are pierced by a spotlight that finds the beautiful bound blonde. McBride fails to rescue her, instead getting bludgeoned by VeSota and roped into a chair. Gene Evans cruelly urges Venus to crawl across the cement expanse to earn a final kiss from the hero who has failed her. Castle slithers seductively toward McBride and sadistic Evans tosses a table at her, just one more sharp-edged abstract shape in a chamber of shadows and shafts and pools of light, shared in skewed camera angles. Spillane's nightmare landscape has been made both real and unreal, in one of the two strongest sequences in any of the films, topped only by the fiery ending of *Kiss Me Deadly* to come.

While a reappraisal by noir enthusiasts is overdue, *The Long Wait* is admittedly burdened by the entertaining but silly gimmick of McBride seeking to clear his name by kissing and sleeping with the suspects. Still, it's difficult not to see Anthony Quinn as the Mike Hammer who got away.

Only a little over a month separated the release of *The Long Wait* (May 26, 1954) and *Ring of Fear* (July 2). Box-office returns were respectable for both, however, with neither enough of a hit for Spillane's revenge against Saville to be considered a success or failure. *The Long Wait* grossed about $100,000 more than *I, the Jury*, Biff Elliot and Tony Quinn essentially fighting to a draw. According to Eyman, after Wellman (and Spillane) "fixed" *Ring of Fear*, it "actually made money."

Spillane hadn't received payment for his rewrite—he hadn't asked for any. "I'd already been paid to do the show," he told Rothman.

But of course his contract with Saville precluded him from doing the rewrite at all, much less getting paid for it. Even taking a screen credit would have meant Saville taking Mickey to court.

"One day I'm sitting in my house in Newburgh," the writer said years later. "It's snowing. I look out the window, and there's a beautiful white Jaguar."

The sports car had been shipped by Wayne from England and delivered to Spillane's door.

"And it had a big red ribbon wrapped around it," Spillane recalled, standing next to the gleaming white Jag forty-one years later, "with a card that said, 'Thanks, Duke.'"

TOP LEFT: *Mickey Spillane's Mike Hammer Story* featured a radio playlet, with the writer playing Hammer for the first time, and dramatic themes prefiguring Henry Mancini's *Peter Gunn*. TOP RIGHT: Actor Brian Keith appeared as Hammer in a 1954 TV pilot written and directed by Blake Edwards, creator of *Peter Gunn*; initially given a green light, the project was rejected by the head of the network due to Spillane's notorious reputation. BOTTOM: After a strong start, the Mike Hammer comic strip, drawn by Spillane's comic-book crony Ed Robbins, ran into censorship trouble.

CHAPTER THIRTEEN
THREE BLOODY HAMMERS

S peculation about the "Spillane silence," the so-called drought or "long wait" for a new novel from America's bestselling writer—in particular a Mike Hammer mystery—has continued for years, even to this day. Imagine Stephen King at the peak of his early popularity—after *The Stand*, perhaps—just deciding to take a decade or so off.

The assumption has been that the impetus was Mickey Spillane's religious conversion—that ever since the most controversial author in America had become a Jehovah's Witness, he'd been crippled by the need to avoid the very elements of sex and violence for which he'd become famous. And infamous.

At least a kernel of truth was in that, as a sales promotion executive handling Spillane's record album, *Mickey Spillane's Mike Hammer Story*, discovered the hard way.

"I blew up at that damn idiotic copy 'Love—Beauty—Violence,'" Spillane raged in a November 10, 1954, letter to a Mr. Schwartz of Columbia Records. "I've been avoiding that 'violence' angle for two years even to the point of restricting copy on my books. . . . No more of this . . . or I'll belt this whole thing out the window."

But the latest Hammer, *Kiss Me, Deadly*, had hewed to the previous recipe, stopping short only of Mike consummating any romantic liaisons he encountered along the way. And *Ring of Fear*, largely due to Spillane's rewrites, continued the established approach as well, from the skimpily attired beauty who asks "Mickey Spillane" if he is married and is told, "Slips my mind at the moment," to the psycho killer who is mauled to death by a tiger.

While Spillane was undoubtedly walking a tightrope between his old commercial appeal and his new religious beliefs, he had not abandoned Mike Hammer at all. He felt frustratingly constrained, however, by the terms of the Victor Saville contract.

Somewhat ironically, Saville found himself unexpectedly constrained, too, when he bumped up against a deal Spillane had made prior to theirs. When acquiring the rights to do Mike Hammer on the radio, Richard Lewis—almost as an afterthought—had done the same for television, still in its relative infancy. This barred the producer of *I, the Jury*, who was currently in preproduction with *Kiss Me Deadly*, from licensing his Hammer films to TV after their theatrical runs.

Lewis was friendly with Spillane, describing their relationship in an Archive of American Television interview as "good friends . . . beer-drinking friends." Whether he and Mickey got together on this is unknown (though likely), but the man behind *That Hammer Guy* arranged with Saville to allow the eventual release of the Spillane feature films to television in return for a sum large enough to fund a Mike Hammer TV pilot.

The radio producer had never done television before, and in looking for a writer, he landed on young Blake Edwards, the creator and frequent scripter of radio's *Richard Diamond, Private Detective* (1949–53), which had starred the screen's first Philip Marlowe, Dick Powell (David Janssen would later play Diamond on TV). Edwards also wanted to direct, and Lewis—who already had a top crew lined up—followed a hunch and took a chance with him.

Together they took a chance on Brian Keith, who had carved out a modest name on Broadway and on television. They screen-tested him and felt Keith "was just wonderful . . . couldn't have been better." Lewis set out to make a film that didn't emphasize the Spillane sex and violence, but would be "just a tough, hard, good melodrama."

The pilot retained a genuine Spillane flavor, however, and Keith made a rugged, interesting, if low-key Hammer. The actor would become a minor movie star (*Run of the Arrow*, 1957; *Parent Trap*, 1961) and major TV star

(*Family Affair*, 1966-71; Stephen Cannell's *Hardcastle and McCormick*, 1983-86). In a busy career, Keith also portrayed another well-known fictional PI in the short-lived *Archer* (1975), based on the Ross Macdonald novels.

Keith's Hammer seems to channel Brando somewhat, shifting between shouting and mumbling, and his broad-shouldered build makes him a bully when he gets tough with a gangster's moll who falls for him fast (it's a half-hour show). He and Pat Chambers are more adversaries than friends, and Mike carries a revolver. Hammer's fedora and trench coat go unseen, and Velda is missing in action.

Nonetheless, Edwards sticks to the Spillane playbook: Hammer's newsie pal is killed and Mike is enraged; Chambers scolds the shamus for taking the law in his own hands; the private eye beats people up and people beat him up; a doll who digs him gets bumped off; and Hammer dispatches bad guys like he's delivering the mail. The soundtrack is strictly library cues; the jazzy Mancini music of the groundbreaking, Spillane-influenced *Peter Gunn* is four years and a lifetime away. But voice-over narration helps keep the viewer in Hammer's world: "The city was quiet and the sharp wind blowing off the river smelled like rain." Other narration is more refried *Richard Diamond*—Hammer says coming around after a beating is "like wading through an acre of glue."

But the assessment of producer Lewis seems apt: "It's a smart, sharp half hour," surprisingly tough, especially a brutal encounter between Hammer and two hoods waiting at his apartment. A brief waterfront scene lends some noir credibility, as does actor Donald Randolph as a mobster who is both smooth and slimy.

Working with MCA-TV, Lewis seemed to have made a sale to CBS—sponsors were already on board for thirty-nine episodes with a time slot waiting. Then William Paley, powerful president of CBS, played traffic cop. He admitted the pilot was good, but refused to have "Mickey Spillane's or Mike Hammer's name on my network."

Lewis said, "Well, our hearts sank—no matter what arguments were put up by MCA, by the advertising agency, even by the sponsors, Paley would not give in . . . because the name 'Spillane' connoted sex and violence."

Paley's self-righteous condemnation of Spillane and Hammer reflected the degree to which the writer had become a literary pariah. In the *New Republic* in 1952, Malcolm Cowley had called Hammer "a dangerous paranoiac, sadist and masochist" and ridiculously suggested Spillane's popularity had led to increased "rapes, mutilations and violent robberies." That same year in the *Saturday Review*, Ben Ray Redman accused Spillane of causing "decline and fall of the whodunit," and in 1954 Christopher La Farge in "Mickey Spillane and his Bloody Hammer," also in the *Saturday Review*, found the writer guilty of "a wholly unadmirable kind of wish-fulfillment on both an immature and a potentially destructive level." Less than glowing coverage of the Spillane phenomenon had appeared in *Time*, *Look*, *Harper's*, *National Parent Teacher*, *New Statesman*, and even *Good Housekeeping*.

A television network, Paley obviously assumed, could hardly buck liberals who considered Spillane and his hero violent fascists, or conservatives who considered them to be promiscuous libertines. After all, nobody liked Spillane, with the exception of tens of millions of readers worldwide.

As for the writer/director of the shot-down pilot, Blake Edwards would, of course, go on to create *Peter Gunn*, a sophisticated, "cool" spin on Mike Hammer that initiated the late 1950s fad for television private eyes. Spillane would always insist the famous music by Henry Mancini for *Peter Gunn* was heavily influenced by themes written by jazz conductor Stan Purdy for the *Mickey Spillane's Mike Hammer Story* album produced in 1954 by Hammer's creator and partially recorded by him in his Little Bohemia studio.

That ten-inch album (also released as two Extended Play mini-albums) was just one of several projects Spillane developed into an attempt to reclaim Mike Hammer. Saville had the source material tied up, both existing Hammer books and any future ones, until the five-year contract ran its course. So Mickey began exploring venues that Saville didn't control.

The ten-inch version of *Mickey Spillane's Mike Hammer Story* had a radio-style playlet on one side—"Tonight, My Love"—and four themes on the other, "Velda," "Oh Mike!," "The Woman," and "The Mike Hammer Theme." When Edward R. Murrow interviewed Spillane on *Person to Person* in the knotty-pine-paneled studio, Mickey gave the disc of the Hammer theme a spin, interrupting his own interview ("Ominous," was Murrow's one-word review). Elaborate recording equipment was arrayed on Spillane's desk where you would expect to see a typewriter.

Spillane's evocative six-page, two-act script has Hammer rescuing—twice—a young woman terrorized by a hulking thug on a rainy Manhattan street. The woman is played by Bettye Ackerman (who had appeared as the femme fatale in the Stang test film) and Hammer is brought to life by Spillane himself, in a brooding, whispery performance that underscores the intended poetry of his prose.

"New York," Hammer says. "A strange city. Big . . . alive . . . pretty hard when it wants to be . . . and sometimes soft. Yeah, a strange city, where even stranger things happen. . . ."

Hammer speaks to us, one to one, intimately.

"It starts on a street corner off the Main Stem where the lights are gaudy come-ons and when you listen you can hear the sucker music over the traffic. But not many are listening. Me . . . that's my job . . . to listen and to look. So I heard the music . . . and saw . . . her."

After the bad guy has been blasted by Hammer's .45, the detective asks the damsel in distress her name. And the surprise ending this time isn't flames or gunfire, nor is the big reveal the twisted scarred torso of a beautiful woman or the sex of a woman who isn't a woman at all . . . but one word: *"Velda."*

The musical themes scoring the radio playlet are given their full performance on side two (the 45 rpm Extended Play versions have the story on one disc, the themes on the other)—full-throated big-band jazz, alternately romantic and melodramatic.

Purdy had worked with the likes of Duke Ellington, Bucky Pizzarelli, Lou Mecca, and Maynard Ferguson; later he conducted and arranged studio orchestras for well-known jazz and dance-band musicians, as well as New York Philharmonic string players. Purdy's jazzy take on private-eye music seems to be the missing link, and the impetus, for what followed in Mancini's *Peter Gunn* TV score and those of his talented followers—Pete Rugolo (*Richard Diamond, Private Detective*), Nelson Riddle (*The Untouchables*),

John Williams (*Checkmate*), Elmer Bernstein (*Staccato*), and of course Skip Martin (*Mickey Spillane's Mike Hammer*).

Having written and directed the *Mike Hammer* TV pilot, it's probable Edwards was aware of Spillane's jazz-scored *Hammer* LP released that same year. Purdy's themes had also made it into *Ring of Fear*; exactly how is unknown, but the pathway had to be Spillane.

One thing is undeniable: the way station in the pop cultural transition from Mike Hammer to James Bond is Peter Gunn, and the driving soundtracks of the Bond films—especially the signature theme—would not have existed without Henry Mancini's guitar-driven, big-band "Peter Gunn Theme."

For his album cover, Spillane commissioned George Wilson to paint a boldly modernistic cover with a green-highlighted naked beauty in foreground right, her mouth a scarlet slash, looking toward us with hooded eyes; she's in a sensual clinch with a hunkered-over man whose face is buried in her neck while a photographic figure of Mike Hammer in background left watches. This Hammer is casting a cartoony black shadow and is outlined in red, and portrayed by Jack Stang, cigarette dangling, holding the trademark .45. The image is one of many studio shots that capture Stang as Hammer, just as Spillane envisioned him.

Among the publicity photos for the LP is a shot of Spillane seated at his desk with an array of recording equipment surrounding him. He is directing two actors standing at microphones—Bettye Ackerman and Jack Stang, both smiling over a script.

The significance of this is poignant: Jack Stang may be Mike Hammer on the album cover, but the voice on the record is Mickey Spillane's. Did he record Stang as Hammer and replace him? Or had the *Ring of Fear* performances finally spelled out which of the two men was the real Mike Hammer?

Victor Saville could not block Mike Hammer or his creator from returning to where they began: the comics. For Spillane, it was like going home—he would be working with Funnies, Inc., artist Ed Robbins, and Mike Hammer would finally be appearing in his originally intended medium.

The plan had been for Spillane to write the Sunday page continuity and Joe Gill to write a separate daily continuity—dailies doing one story and Sundays another was a common practice with newspaper story strips of the era. Ed Robbins would handle both pencils and inks, and George Wilson would do the lettering. The latter's tenure was brief, however, and at times Robbins—his workload on a seven-day a week strip was crushing—would reach out for art assistance and/or lettering from other Funnies, Inc., veterans, including Art Gates and Bob Butts.

Rather than approach big-time syndicates like King Features or the Chicago Tribune/New York News, Spillane remained loyal to his friends, and his comics roots. He went with Funnies, Inc., packager Jerry Iger's small Phoenix Features Syndicate, started years before with the great Will Eisner, creator of *The Spirit*. Writer Ruth Roche, another veteran of the Iger shop, edited the strip, which ran from April 1953 to March 1954.

Two of three lengthy Sunday continuities, "The Sudden Trap" and "Comes Murder," are solely Spillane's work; early on, he began working with Ed Robbins on the daily continuities.

"Six weeks into the first story," Robbins recalled in 1975, "Gill dropped out of sight, leaving me with an unfinished script."

Robbins—never intended to be a writer on the strip—picked up the story line out of necessity. After the first Gill/Robbins story, the daily scripting became a collaboration between Robbins and Spillane, the latter providing synopses, sometimes over the phone. The Sunday continuities were given titles by Spillane, incorporated into the *From the Files of . . . Mike Hammer* logo. The daily stories were untitled at their initial appearance, but were given titles in subsequent reprint volumes.

"Comes Murder," the first Sunday page continuity by Spillane, retains bold characterization and vivid dialogue typical of the novels. A variation on a frequently quoted Mike Hammer line ("I never smack dames . . . I usually kick 'em") appeared here seven years prior to its appearance in *The Girl Hunters* (1962); in "Comes Murder," it sets up the punch line. Though Hammer is not seeking revenge, other typical Spillane elements are present—Velda is kidnapped, and rescued, and a violent final confrontation leaves Hammer seriously wounded.

Though the second Spillane Sunday continuity, "The Sudden Trap," focuses on revenge, the avenger is not Mike Hammer but a beautiful young woman whom the PI winds up aiding. Spillane uses a second-person narration typical of the acclaimed but controversial EC comics of the same period; radio's *That Hammer Guy*, running concurrently with the strip, also utilized second-person narration. In "Trap," Spillane and Robbins risk a provocative cliff-hanger that depicts Hammer and a beautiful woman embracing, the partial silhouette of a brass bed looming.

The Spillane/Robbins collaborations on daily continuities are generally first-rate, reflecting the visually oriented writing of both. Robbins's continuation of the Joe Gill story "Half Blonde" improves on Gill's opening weeks, which capture much of Spillane/Hammer but are copy heavy and often try too hard to be tough.

The use in "Half Blonde" of the Pandora's box legend, as a nickname for the trunk of children's playthings in which incriminating papers are hidden, prefigures the atomic climax of the then un-filmed cinematic version of Spillane's novel *Kiss Me, Deadly*. Both this comics story and "The Veiled Woman" (in the November 1952 issue of *Fantastic*) appear to have influenced A. I. Bezzerides, the screenwriter of *Kiss Me Deadly*, though both are among the handful of Spillane-bylined stories Spillane did not write.

The other daily continuities maintain a high standard. "The Bandaged Woman" is a solid Hammer tale with some snappy dialogue ("Heel meets heel, Mr. Hammer!") and evocative narration ("My shadow was in a hurry going across the courtyard, and I moved to catch up with it before someone else did").

"The Child" features some of artist Robbins's most understated, effective storytelling, particularly in a silent fight sequence at a lake cabin. "Christmas Story," in which a shoplifting Santa finds redemption, is reminiscent of Spillane's O. Henry–style "The Pickpocket" (*Manhunt*, December 1954). In "Another Lonely Night," Hammer feels betrayed by Pat Chambers, their final conflict prefiguring *The Girl Hunters*. The dark waterfront shoot-out finale shows Robbins at his chiaroscuro best.

The final daily story, "Adam and Cain," finds a fearful Mike Hammer shaken by what he considers to be a new streak of cowardice. In an Old

Testament resonance, Adam and Cain are father and son—an evil old man (foreshadowing Sonny Motley in *The Snake*) and his equally evil heir. This story also served as the loose basis for Dave Gerrity's *Dragon Hunt* (Signet, 1967).

"The Dark City" is the final Sunday continuity, the first (and only) sequence written by Robbins, Hammer again rescuing a damsel in distress. The suicide ending is one Spillane used more than once, which indicates he probably had a hand in at least the plotting.

Robbins took credit (or blame) for the cliff-hanger panel of January 24, 1954, in which Hammer bursts into a room where a lovely woman, her dress ripped and her undergarments showing, is tied to a bed. She is in the process of being tortured by a thug holding a lighted cigarette to her bare foot.

Gerrity remembered being shocked by the panel, and telling Robbins shortly after, "Ed, you've proven the pen is mightier than the sword—you've done something nobody else has been able to do: kill Mike Hammer."

Robbins wrote in a 1975 letter, "[T]he panel . . . brought screams of disapproval from some readers, and cancellation by some newspapers. Notably the *New York Mirror.* This single page, and in fact panel, resulted in the discontinuance of the strip."

And yet "The Dark City" remains among the best Mike Hammer stories in the strip's short but impressive run, the comic-strip continuity certainly most like the novels.

Perhaps he "killed" Mike Hammer, but artist Ed Robbins is nonetheless the unsung hero of *From the Files of . . . Mike Hammer.* The abrupt cancellation of the strip—a strip that, while not carried by a big list of papers, was clearly a hit, seen in a number of major markets—came as a bitter disappointment to Robbins, who left the field, except for very occasional forays at Gold Key, Dell, and DC.

Robbins recalled burning the last, unpublished original *Hammer* Sunday page in a backyard fire—standing there, watching smoke rise, taking his glorious future as a syndicated comic-strip artist with it.

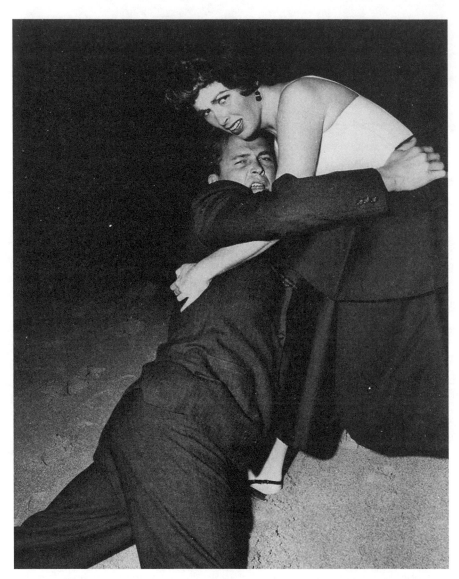

Ralph Meeker as Mike Hammer and Maxine Cooper as Velda in the shocking, restored ending of Robert Aldrich and A. I. Bezzerides's *Kiss Me Deadly* (1955).

CHAPTER FOURTEEN
DEADLY KISS ME

In 1955, in what had to feel like the last blow, the final indignity, the latest Mike Hammer movie from Victor Saville's Parklane Pictures had made a "bedroom dick" out of Mickey Spillane's hero, working divorce cases with Velda as his "woo bait," a "stinker" to FBI agents, interested only in "what's in it for me."

Spillane walked out on the film at his local Newburgh theater, and only returned for a second, complete viewing when people kept asking him what was in the box Mike Hammer was searching for. This struck him as baffling nonsense, because anyone who'd read *Kiss Me, Deadly* knew it was a stash of valuable illegal narcotics!

Of course, in 1974, director Robert Aldrich reaffirmed a claim he and his screenwriter had often made—that he and A. I. Bezzerides "took the title and threw the book away." That highly inaccurate assertion was often echoed by the likes of film noir–influenced author Barry Gifford, who said in the documentary *The Long Haul of A. I. Bezzerides* (2005), "All they used was the title."

In the same documentary, the screenwriter himself was somewhat more measured: "I wrote my version of everything." This is in line with what many, if not most, screenwriters do in adapting a novel to film. But "Buzz" Bezzerides also said, "I read the book and thought it was awful."

Spillane was in the documentary too. His take on Bezzerides's script was, "It was bad, it was terrible."

Both these fine writers were wrong.

So are many of the myths about the film, most of which were generated by Aldrich and Bezzerides. The latter claimed to drop the illegal narcotics angle because he wanted to do something with atomic energy, then very much in the news.

"I made it a nuclear device," Bezzerides said. Not "a cardboard box of dope."

By 1956, Aldrich was bragging to François Truffaut that he had exposed Mike Hammer as an "anti-democratic spirit . . . a cynical and fascistic private eye" whom he personally viewed with "utter contempt and loathing." In 1973, getting high-flown about it, the director told John Calendo at *Andy Warhol's Interview* he had intended to demonstrate "a basic significance in our political framework that we thought rather important in those McCarthy times: that the ends did not justify the means."

Take Aldrich and Bezzerides at face value at your own risk. In September 1954, the director had submitted either an earlier draft of the screenplay or the novel itself to the Production Code Administration. The PCA response had been pointed, as an interoffice memo reported.

"[T]his story was basically unacceptable under the requirements of the Production Code. . . . [T]he basic prop used as motivation for the overall murder melodrama was one of narcotics. This, of course, is in complete violation of present Code regulations and . . . we could not approve any treatment whatsoever of the illegal drug traffic."

In short, the central plot device of drugs had to be changed to something else.

Even more objectionable was the "portrayal of Mike Hammer, private detective, as a cold-blooded murderer whose numerous killings are completely justified. His taking of the law into his own hands and successfully bringing the criminals to 'justice' by killing them, is in complete violation of the Code."

Aldrich displayed reluctance to abandon the "dope" plot, but assured the PCA he could overcome the "numerous items of brutality and sex-suggestiveness" the Code required eliminated.

Despite his misgivings, in November 1954 Aldrich submitted to the PCA a draft by Bezzerides that removed "the narcotics complication" and did its best to "marry the Spillane property with a morality that states justice is not to be found in a self-appointed one man vigilante." With the exception of a few action, dialogue, and costuming details, and a few minor alterations, a Production Code seal was awarded rather perfunctorily.

Aldrich slipped up somewhat, however, in an article he wrote (or at least lent his byline to) for the *New York Herald Tribune*, with the outrageous title, "You Can't Hang Up the Meat Hook."

In it, Aldrich assured one and all that *Kiss Me Deadly* on-screen would "keep faith with 60 million Mickey Spillane readers" with "action, violence and suspense in good taste." Violence, he said, was justified in his films because "such phases of human behavior can be neither ignored nor removed from any true pictorial account of the emotions of two-legged animals."

By way of example, he described a scene from his forthcoming Mike Hammer thriller:

> *The camera focuses first on the helpless girl and her antagonists. The situation leading up to this moment of torture is well established and is a logical development of the plot. Hands are then laid on the victim, and from that moment the suspense is maintained, the violence high-keyed and the horror spotlighted through the sound effects, focusing the camera in a series of close shots, on her feet, her hands, shadows on the wall and similar devices.*

Much of what viewers perceived of this scene, Aldrich wrote, "will be the product of their own thinking."

Immediately, *Kiss Me Deadly* was in hot water with the Legion of Decency, who upon screening the film demanded thirty cuts, changes, and deletions. On May 5, the film was classified B—suitable for adults, who were warned "this film tends to glorify taking the law into one's own hands . . . it contains excessive brutality and suggestiveness in costuming, dialogue, and situations."

The fuss caused a delay of a month in the film's release.

The left-leaning Aldrich and Bezzerides found the pulp-style fiction of the conservative Spillane distasteful—but not distasteful enough to turn down the opportunity to make a film from a hugely successful novel. The ends may not have justified the means on-screen, but behind the scenes in Hollywood, it justified a fat paycheck.

Kiss Me Deadly (minus Spillane's characteristic comma) is a coldly terrifying vision of mid-twentieth-century America, a bizarre, enigmatic look at the McCarthy era and the atomic paranoia to come. Simultaneously, it is an undeniably hypocritical and exploitative attack on the character and author of the source material by the director and screenwriter. In an outcome as surprising as a Spillane socko finish, however, Aldrich and Bezzerides managed to capture on film the dark magic of Spillane's feverdream storytelling at the point of Mike Hammer's popular peak.

"*Kiss Me Deadly* is unquestionably the great *noir* film of the Fifties," according to critics Elliot Lavin and Bob Stephens. "Robert Aldrich's film relentlessly focuses on a world at the brink of madness." By the 1960s, Jean-Luc Godard and François Truffaut "were citing *Kiss Me Deadly* as the one American film most responsible for influencing the French New Wave."

Despite all the praise screenwriter Bezzerides justifiably receives, the film's plot and most characters carry over from Spillane, from the startling girl-in-the-headlights opening to the bomb in Hammer's bad-guy-gifted replacement car, from the key in Christina's stomach to the shocking Carl Evello kill at the beach cottage. The strong, first-person identification is gone, however, no Philip Marlowe–style voice-over here—this is not Spillane's interior view, but Hammer seen from without. And from that perspective, the view is disturbing.

The major difference is the "Great What's-It" everyone is after—the atomic "device" Bezzerides substituted for drugs at the PCA's urging. The film's reputation is so tied to this nuclear MacGuffin that many have bought Aldrich's "we threw the book away" boast. Still, the film's fiery climax remains a variation of the novel's fiery climax.

The opening credits roll backward from the bottom of the screen (starting with VICTOR)—

DEADLY"

"KISS ME

SPILLANE'S

MICKEY

PRESENTS

SAVILLE

VICTOR

—the viewer riding behind Hammer, making him initially the faceless hero of the paperback covers. Composer Frank De Vol sneaks in and Nat King Cole sings "I'd Rather Have the Blues" on the radio, accompanied by hitchhiker Christina's heavy, orgasmic panting. Mike Hammer's delirious, nighttime dreamworld is already enveloping us. Rivaling Franz Waxman's *I, the Jury*, De Vol's score is percussive, punchy, discordant—had he heard Purdy's themes too?—as abrupt piano figures often add tension and anxiety.

A modern, soulless Los Angeles replaces Spillane's rainy, gritty Manhattan—it seems twenty years after Essex's *I, the Jury*, not two. Occasionally, Aldrich visits the baroque Bunker Hill area (largely gone now), bringing a more traditional noir feel. Unlike Spillane's rumpled private eye, this Hammer is something of a clotheshorse, his digs ultramodern, including a newfangled answering machine.

Yet even the most minor characters retain the names Spillane gave them, though Captain Pat Chambers of Homicide is now the condescending Pat Murphy. Wesley Addy's Murphy is a smug, probably alcoholic representative of officialdom who somehow seems to be Hammer's friend. Mike constantly helps himself to Pat's cigarettes, which ultimately will allow Murphy to spot the atomic burn on Hammer's wrist. And Pat, who has a key to Hammer's apartment, helps himself to his pal's liquor cart.

Despite an emphasis on Hammer's divorce work—he refuses such cases in the novels—it's clear this isn't the first time the detective has gone off on a vendetta-fueled murder investigation.

"You want to get even for what happened to Christina, don't you?" Hammer says to Lily Carver. "See what I can do."

Pat (perhaps for the Production Code's benefit) says, "You'd like to take [the law] into your own hands. But when you do that, you might as well be living in a jungle."

Still, Pat also says of Mike with reluctant admiration, "He can sniff out information like nobody I ever saw."

Finally, though, Pat is fed up with his friend, who can "go to hell." This feels as if—as was the case with the novel—it might be the final Hammer story, that both Pat and Velda have had enough of Hammer's offhand, egotistical, outlaw methods. Pat's last scene seems the kiss-off.

But unlike Pat, Velda won't ever let Mike down. Her loyalty and her love for him run as deep as in the novels. She is not the pistol-packing PI of the books, but a reluctant accomplice in Hammer's schemes; and she is her man's conscience as he pursues nameless villains.

"'They'. . . a wonderful word," she says, wearily arch. "And who are 'they'?"

Ralph Meeker as Hammer is smooth, ruggedly handsome, and strangely aloof. The Actors Studio–bred Broadway actor had just won the Critics' Circle Award for *Picnic*, and had taken over for Marlon Brando in *A Streetcar Named Desire*. When Meeker's Hammer meets Christina, he's cool and cocksure, qualities that arise again later, but for a while Hammer is shaken, having nearly gotten killed.

Meeker makes a convincing, even frightening tough guy, but the "Spillane Dames" Aldrich assembles are not your typical sex kittens. With the exception of Marian Carr, the three actresses are attractive if unusual in looks, carriage, and personality.

Cloris Leachman—in her film debut—is indelible in her brief turn as ill-fated Christina Bailey, who taunts Hammer: "You have only one, real, lasting love . . . you." Much later, when she is rolled out on a morgue slab, it's unsettling and sadly moving.

Maxine Cooper as Velda has a catlike quality, her lips ripe with sensual possibility even as her lidded eyes harbor regret. Gaby Rodgers, a stage actress in a rare screen appearance, displays an unconventional appeal as Lily Carver, birdlike one moment, childlike the next, bedroom sultry one moment, terrified victim the next. Yet her final transition into deadly femme fatale seems both credible and inevitable.

The only traditionally Hollywood-beautiful "dame" is Marian Carr from *Ring of Fear*, playing mob boss Carl Evello's half sister, Friday, a nymphomaniac draped in a low-rent Marilyn Monroe impression. Hammer plays along, grants her a couple of kisses, but when the detective goes off snooping, her brother—apparently referring to his sister's warm welcome of their adversary—asks, "Are you kidding?" Without a trace of Marilyn, she replies, "Why not?"

Hammer shows little interest in the attractive "dolls," save for some cagey chemistry between him and Christina. Even so, he asks Christina sarcastically, "You always go around with no clothes on?" Later, when Lily kisses him, he seems unmoved, saying, "Okay. You made your point."

Then there's Velda. Despite using her to approach men to gain information—a distortion of her role in the books—Hammer obviously cares about her. He wakes in the hospital and smiles and says, "You're never around when I need ya."

"You never need me when I'm around," she answers.

Early on, Pat revokes Hammer's private investigator license and yanks his gun permit. Hammer never touches a firearm in the movie. Aldrich rarely shows Hammer engaging in physical violence, but suggests he has unusual martial arts skills that can immobilize and even kill. Hammer becomes an almost supernatural force.

"I figure it's a good thing to speak a lot of languages," Hammer tells Evello. "Any country you go to, you can take care of yourself."

The most violent confrontation starts with Hammer calmly continuing to stroll along the sidewalk between attacks by a knife-wielding thug. Finally, he punches the assailant, knocking him down several long flights of cement stairs, likely to the man's death. This rates a smirk out of Hammer, who continues along.

He slams the coroner's hand in a drawer when the little man keeps demanding more cash, and slaps a health-club clerk who snobbishly huffs at a bribe. Yet Hammer is not sadistic—he's just not fooling around. Later he shows concern for the clerk, after the dangerous atomic container turns up in a locker.

When he visits Christina's apartment, Hammer helps an elderly fellow with a heavy trunk, showing him respect and even warmth. Even when Hammer snaps a Caruso record in two, to get cooperation out of a down-on-his-luck opera singer, he does so out of single-mindedness, not mean-ness. Leaving, he compliments the opera singer on what the old boy is listening to: "It's a lovely record."

Ernest Laszlo's cinematography—on a film shot in a mere twenty-two days—stuns and amazes. In a brilliant display of sustained narrative filmmaking, a three-minute continuous shot in a boxing gym starts on a punching bag and follows a fighter to the exit stairs to pick up an ascending Hammer, tracking the detective for a talk with Eddie Yeager (Juano Hernandez), then over to the phone for a call to Pat Murphy. Aldrich and art director William Glasgow pepper frames with Xs ironically invoking both Xs of death and the Xs signifying kisses at the close of a love letter.

A particularly striking camera setup shows Velda in her ballet/exercise room only to reveal, as Hammer enters, she had been a reflection on a wall of mirrors. Not as flashy but also effective is the uninterrupted master shot of Hammer questioning truck driver Harvey Wallace (Strother Martin), the camera pushing in on the fine character actor in a snippet of a scene that conveys his distress over accidentally killing a man.

Despite Aldrich's assertions to the contrary, his Mike Hammer is pri-marily a positive character. Irritated or not, Mike gives Christina a ride, helps her through a roadblock, and puts himself at risk with the law. When the Interstate Crime Commission interrogates him (he barely acknowledges them), they come off as self-righteous and patronizing. So does Pat Murphy, who ultimately seems not to care about Velda's fate. Hammer hangs out with the outsiders and outcasts of society, Greeks like Nick, persons of color like Eddie Yeager at the gym and Mike's friends at the Pigalle jazz club.

Critics have pointed out the detective is surrounded by art he can't comprehend, and it *is* a nice irony that hard-boiled Hammer must solve the mystery by interpreting a poem. Yet the private eye's pad is rife with modern art, as seen at Christina's place, and Velda's, even at William Mist's gallery. Hammer switches on Christina's radio and classical music plays—more art he doesn't understand? No, because when Hammer turns his radio on at home, it's already tuned to the same classical station.

Hammer moves through the first half hour like a keyed-up sleepwalker, edging down his apartment-house hallway in full-on paranoia. Nick, his mechanic pal, asks, "Are you all right, Mike?" Hammer, with an odd smile, says, "I don't know. Maybe not."

Nick has risen from his grease pit as if from the grave he'll soon inhabit: "Hey, look, Sammy, my friend just returned from the grave! Like Lazarus."

Indeed, Hammer "dies" twice in the film—and maybe a third time, by radiation poisoning—though after Christ-figure Christina's death, it's Hammer who's resurrected. As the film and investigation proceed, Mike returns gradually to his old cocky, self-absorbed self.

After locating the atomic canister, getting burned by it and then beaten by Evello's goons, with Velda kidnapped because of him, Hammer looks small, defeated. This man so careful about his appearance now is disheveled, and for the first time, a character other than Hammer is given the dominant high angle in an over-the-shoulder two-shot.

Pat delivers his chilling speech softly: "Now listen, Mike. Listen carefully. They're harmless words, just a bunch of letters scrambled together. But their meaning is very important. Try to understand what they mean. Manhattan Project. Los Alamos. Trinity."

Alarmed, Hammer hands the locker key over to his now scornful friend.

Yet once again, like Lazarus, he rises, reappearing in a beautiful suit, hair perfect, confidence personified, a force of nature. Screw the atomic box—he's going to find Velda. He's Mike Hammer again. Both Mickey Spillane's *and* Bezzerides's/Aldrich's.

Earlier, Hammer had one short scene with Dr. Soberin, the mastermind of the piece, when the PI is briefly captured. Soberin speaks to Mike poetically: "As the world becomes more primitive, its treasures become more fabulous."

Actor Albert Dekker is on-screen in a single sequence, at the beach house, where his mistress, Lily Carver, pays no heed to his high-flown rejection of her charms. She also ignores his dying warning: "As if I were Cerberus, barking with all his heads, at the gate of hell . . . don't . . . open . . . the box."

When Lily Carver does open that hissing box to reveal its priceless, deadly radioactive substance, she is overwhelmed by flames, as is the beach house. The wounded Hammer rescues Velda, who rescues him, guiding him down the beach-house stairs toward the ocean to stand in its waves and witness in Lot's Wife horror an explosion whose end-of-the-world significance is emphasized by a faint superimposition of a mushroom cloud.

In 1955, *Kiss Me Deadly* was number five on the *Cahiers du Cinéma* list of the ten best films of the year. It made over a million dollars at the box office, very good for a film with a $400,000 budget, but less than the previous two Spillane films. Within the film's first month of release, Senator Estes Kefauver's Subcommittee to Investigate Juvenile Delinquency cited *Kiss Me Deadly* "for its excessive violence and dubious morality."

Ironically, producer Victor Saville didn't understand his own production. "This opus has become a cult film," he said. "I cannot say why—I never completely understood our finished screenplay and my confusion was still there when we ran the completed film."

Plenty of others have understood *Kiss Me Deadly*. Aldrich and Bezzerides, nudged by the Production Code, meant to represent through Mike Hammer the baser aspects of man in general, and America in particular. Similarly, the villain Dr. Soberin (Albert Dekker) stands for the intellectuals of the species turned decadent, his dialogue riddled with literary and mythological references, his manner oozing culture. The conflict between these two opposite types—the brutish Hammer/Meeker and the cultured Soberin/Dekker—brings global destruction, figuratively and perhaps literally, in *Kiss Me Deadly*.

Only Christina—"crucified" at the start, and the sole female who doesn't receive Hammer's deadly kiss—indicates any alternative for apocalypse. She and Velda are the only small hopes for humankind Aldrich and Bezzerides offer.

Spillane, on the other hand, offers a hero. And despite their best efforts, so do Aldrich and Bezzerides—Mike Hammer may be flawed, but he's still the best man in the shabby world they posit.

A few years after the movie came out, two writers bumped into each other in a restaurant in Hollywood. Buzz Bezzerides said he could tell Mickey Spillane didn't like him. Back in the day, Mike Hammer's creator had supposedly said that the next time he was in town, he was going to find Bezzerides and punch him in the nose; but that didn't come to pass.

In 2003, toward the end of both their lives, the two now elderly writers were guests at the same vintage paperback collector's show in California, separated by a wall. Efforts to get them together for a photo and an overdue handshake failed because those who staged the event did not want to disrupt the lines of fans seeking autographs from both. Spillane cheerfully signed *Kiss Me Deadly* movie material and Bezzerides had no problem signing copies of the original Mike Hammer novel. Yet the wall between them remained.

Nonetheless, they are fated to be together for as long as the film they had instigated stays around—which should be at least until the nuclear apocalypse. After all, in 1999, *Kiss Me Deadly* was selected for preservation in the United States National Film Registry by the Library of Congress, deemed as being "culturally, historically or aesthetically significant."

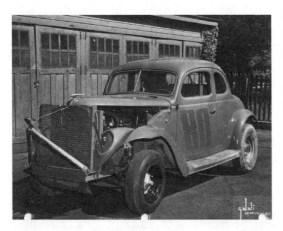

During his self-imposed lay-off from writing Mike Hammer novels, Mickey engaged in numerous macho pursuits, including flying, stock-car racing, and joining his cop pal Harold Cooke in busting the moonshine racketeers (Cooke shown here in photo taken by Spillane).

CHAPTER FIFTEEN

MACHO MAN

M ickey Spillane got his revenge without a gun. Without even lifting
a finger.

Victor Saville's *The Silver Chalice*, a $4.5 million Biblical epic built on
the successes of the first two Spillane films, was released in December
1954; it had an acclaimed score by *I, the Jury*'s Franz Waxman and a
badly panned screenplay by *The Long Wait*'s Lesser Samuels. The *New
York Times* called it "a cumbersome and sometimes creaking vehicle,"
and the *New Yorker* said its new young star had "the emotional fervor
of a Putnam Division conductor announcing local stops." It would lose
money at the box office, Saville's directing career effectively over.

Carla Valderrama in *This Was Hollywood* calls *The Silver Chalice* "so
hilariously bad it nearly derailed the career of one of Hollywood's greatest
stars before it even began." In January 1963, that now-established superstar bought ads in Los Angeles papers reading: "Paul Newman apologizes
every night this week—Channel 9."

"[Saville] fell flat on his face," Spillane said in 1998. "And it couldn't
have happened to a nicer guy."

In the meantime, Saville's next disposable Spillane picture was about
to become "a big cult thing in France," as Spillane put it (unintentionally

echoing Saville), as *Kiss Me Deadly* began on its long road to film noir glory.

By 1955, Mickey Spillane's attempts to keep his version of Mike Hammer alive, and the Spillane/Hammer brand strong, had largely failed. The radio show had done well, but radio dramas were fading, and Richard Lewis's attempt to transfer *That Hammer Guy* to television—as *Dragnet* and *Gunsmoke* had successfully managed—got shot down by William Paley at CBS.

The Mike Hammer comic strip, consigned to a minor syndicate run by old cronies from Spillane's comic-book days, had done modestly well until that one panel mingled sex and violence in a way that got the strip cancelled. *Ring of Fear* had been a moderate success, but Spillane's starring role was viewed as a stunt and generated no further film roles, just the occasional TV variety-show offer. And the Mike Hammer record album? An oddity racking up puny sales compared to Signet's ongoing reprints of Spillane paperbacks.

Now a second Mike Hammer film, *Kiss Me Deadly*, was in the theaters, presenting a distorted version of his detective hero, and Spillane was getting the blame.

As Australian film historian Richard Maltby put it, "Advertising and promotional material consistently identified Spillane as the movie's author, and featured his name far more prominently than those of any of the cast and crew: one tag-line used on a number of advertisements called [*Kiss Me Deadly*] 'Mickey Spillane's latest H-bomb!'"

Due to "their extraordinary successes and excesses," Maltby said, Spillane's novels had become symbols of the decline of mass culture. Unlike his fellow Signet author Erskine Caldwell, however, Spillane had never had a book banned; but Mike Hammer and his creator remained "the focal point of liberal elite anxiety."

Though he had not published a new book in three years, Spillane was under attack by the state of Illinois, West Germany, and the Catholic Church, among others. *Look* magazine dismissed him as an "author of two-bit dreadfuls," and Philip Wylie in the February 1955 *Good House-keeping* called Spillane "a man who stands in contempt of humanity."

NAL publisher Victor Weybright got to know his author early on, visiting Little Bohemia, which he described in his 1966 memoir *The Making of a Publisher*, as "practically a one-room cement-block cottage . . . primitive in its conveniences." He was rather charmed by the way Spillane spent his money "on automobiles and firearms," and they burned through five or ten dollars' worth of ammo shooting tin cans before they settled down for a chat.

At this early meeting, Spillane predicted an output of "three or four books a year which, selling by the millions, would enrich us all." At the time, this seemed a reasonable assumption; but after the first seven novels, Spillane "did not write another book for eight or nine years." Weybright saw this as a result of money pouring in from film deals and book royalties, making work unnecessary. But Mickey was happy to visit chain stores and wholesalers to autograph paperbacks, boosting sales "to a fantastic level."

The publisher sensed that the mystery writer's freak-show celebrity and his reputation as "the exponent of sex and sadism" had worn Spillane down, at the same time making him vulnerable to censors.

Weybright began a defensive campaign, publicizing a course on existentialism at William and Mary College that made Mickey Spillane required reading. To Catholic critics, Weybright emphasized *One Lonely Night* and Hammer's "bloody annihilation of a sinister and godless Communist conspiracy in New York." He challenged *Saturday Review*'s literary editor, Charles Rolo—an early champion of Raymond Chandler—to write a piece comparing Georges Simenon, Europe's current bestselling crime writer, to his American counterpart.

Rolo came up with an interesting thesis—Simenon "represented the fatalistic European Catholic with a genuine and compassionate understanding of human frailty," while Spillane "was an Old Testament writer . . . an exponent of an eye-for-an-eye and tooth-for-a-tooth" approach. Mike

Hammer's creator provided readers with a vicarious catharsis for their aggressive tendencies, and Spillane's themes were in line with folklore and the Brothers Grimm.

The article appeared in both *New World Writing* and *Town and Country*, with Simenon and Spillane pictured together.

Then the publisher threw a cocktail party for Spillane, Erskine Caldwell, and Kathleen Winsor—bestselling Signet authors under Catholic attack. Spillane considered Caldwell, author of *God's Little Acre* and *Tobacco Road*, his big competition; the two knew each other well enough for Spillane to call him "Skinny." The author of the seminal bodice-burster *Forever Amber* "was a nice lady, very tall, very nice," Spillane said, "but she was a wallflower, really. I could look at her and say, 'Everything came out of her imagination for sure.'"

"I invited a handful of literary Catholic priests," Weybright recalled of this cocktail-party summit meeting of his most controversial authors, "since it was the Jansenist Catholics who were the most active instigators of censorship."

When Spillane wandered off with the priests, an apprehensive Weybright followed "to see what sort of row might be developing." Instead, he found the writer in a deep theological debate with the clergy, challenging them to offer up Biblical justification of purgatory.

"After that," Weybright said, "there was no sustained religious or social criticism of Mickey Spillane or his work."

Spillane wondered if he'd gone too far, however, writing Weybright, "I never expected to be invited anyplace again after the set-to with the members of the cloth, but they started it and I'm mighty well up on the subject." He expected to be blacklisted and "Signet'll sell another million copies. Ha."

Speculation that bad reviews and cultural criticism had beaten the writer down, or that his Jehovah's Witness conversion limited his ability to write in his native style, now seems misjudged. Clearly, under the Saville contract, Spillane faced a limited ability to exploit his popular fictional detective, and was waiting out the several years before he and Mike Hammer could do as they pleased.

A third Spillane child arrived in June of 1955—Michael—just as Mickey and Baby were beginning to feel invaded. That one-lane dirt road out front was now two lanes and paved, with tract housing springing up nearby like ugly modern mushrooms. The hangers-on had drifted off and the writing had ground to a stop.

Back in 1953, as part of the Sun Fun Festival in Myrtle Beach, South Carolina, the second annual Miss Carolina pageant was held, with Spillane one of the judges. Was it a coincidence that the same *Life* magazine (June 22, 1952) including the Spillane "Death's Fair-Haired Boy" profile had also featured a piece on Myrtle Beach bathing beauties?

The area had first come to Spillane's attention during the war. "I was flying a P-51 down this way," he told the *Los Angeles Times*, "and saw this enormous sixteen-mile stretch of beach, a grand strand that absolutely fascinated me. There was nothing down there, no big jetties, it was natural. . . ."

He landed at a nearby B-25 base and, despite the plane being fresh off an aircraft factory assembly line, told the mechanic, "Find something wrong with it, would ya?"

The guy did and Spillane got a long beach weekend out of it. He told himself, "After the war, I'm comin' back here. . . ."

And finally he did return—for the 1953 Sun Fun Festival and the tough job of judging a beauty contest. But a kid in trouble on a raft caught the veteran bodyguard's attention and he saved the boy. This got the celebrity hero invited back as a judge for the following year too.

On that trip, Mickey wandered down to nearby Murrells Inlet and found (as Dave Gerrity wrote): "Fishing boats. Quiet nights. Long sun-filled days for the kids to grow up in."

The Spillane family vacationed there a few summers and, finally, in 1955, Mickey returned to judge bathing beauties again. He was poking around the back roads with a pal when he spotted a white house at the end of a dirt road with a "FOR SALE" sign in the yard.

"I asked the neighbor across the street if the house was really for sale," he said in *Coast* magazine in 1985, "and he told me they wanted $15,000 for it."

Mickey had found a second secluded house on a dirt road—eight miles south from Myrtle Beach.

Spillane told Gerrity, "I bought the house from out in the middle of the road. Never even looked inside. "We packed up the kids and left Newburgh."

Murrells Inlet was a place where he could kick back and live. At first, though, he didn't fit in—he was just another "damn Yankee," getting challenged to fistfights in bars. When he'd had enough insults—and drinks—Spillane would rise to the occasion. But as he came to know Myrtle Beach and the Inlet better, he grew more cautious, saying, "If you want trouble, it's easy to find."

With the reprint money rolling in, he might write an article or novella now and then, just keeping his hand in, but mostly it was just play, play, play. Womanizing was not his style, as his friend Bob Curran made clear. Instead he got his bucket list out of the way early.

Mickey Spillane was a guy with enough money to take on all the hobbies and macho pursuits he'd ever dreamed of—flying with the Air Force reserve, scuba diving for Spanish treasure in the Florida Keys, racing stock cars on dirt tracks, and traveling with Clyde Beatty's circus and Ringling Brothers, too, getting shot out of a cannon.

"You're sittin' on a thing like a bicycle seat in there," he recalled in 1998. "It's compressed air that throws you out—*shooom!* And there's no impact to it. Now the boom that goes with it, it's all eyewash."

On summertime circus sojourns, Mickey also performed on a trampoline. He'd brought one back with him to Newburgh and took it along to Murrells Inlet, at a time when trampolines were seen only in circus acts.

Not wishing to play into Victor Saville's hands, he stopped writing about Mike Hammer and instead concentrated on other protagonists, cops and criminals both, never a private eye; like Ernest Hemingway in "Death in the Afternoon," he often wrote about himself. During this period, the raw power of the young artist developed into the mature craftsmanship of a seasoned professional.

The writer in whom Victor Weybright had seen a primitive but "genuine talent" took his well-known byline to the men's adventure magazines where old Funnies, Inc., buddies toiled, and his name wasn't an embarrassment.

He had already contributed several stories to the digest *Manhunt*, including the *Collier's* castoff, "Everybody's Watching Me" (January through April 1953), a dry run for *The Deep* (1961); "The Girl Behind the Hedge" (October 1953), a twist-ending tale about a ruthless millionaire worshipping a beauty from afar; and "The Pickpocket" (December 1954), another O. Henry–influenced yarn with a decidedly non-Hammer-style protagonist in its reformed pickpocket who uses his skill to save the woman he loves. *Manhunt* reprinted these numerous times.

Spillane had already—sort of—appeared in another digest-sized magazine, *Fantastic* (November 1952). Editor Howard Browne, author of the Paul Pine mysteries and later a top television writer, said that after Mickey missed his deadline, "The Veiled Woman"—the heavily promoted first science-fiction story by Mike Hammer's creator—had been hurriedly ghosted by Browne, working from an outline by Spillane, who looked the other way and cashed the check.

Writing almost exclusively for his editor friend Bob Curran at *Cavalier*—a magazine that split the difference between the nonfiction-oriented *True* and the men's adventure "sweat mags"—Spillane produced a handful of fiction pieces between 1956 and 1961, mostly novelettes. These, if nothing else, demonstrated his tough, lusty style had not been blunted by the Jehovah's Witnesses.

"Tomorrow I Die!" (February 1956) might best be described as Spillane combining *The Petrified Forest*'s hostage situation with *The Maltese Falcon*'s corpulent villain and boyish "gunsel." The surprise ending, as was often the case, has to do with the protagonist's identity.

"Stand Up and Die!" (June 1958) features pilot Mitch Valler, forced to parachute into the hills of an unnamed Southern state. Mining more humor than usual, Spillane has fun with a Dogpatch-style cast including a Daisy Mae and a bully called Billy Bussy. The uranium aspect prefigures two posthumously published works, *Dead Street* (2007) and *The Last Stand* (2018).

Pat Ryan, the protagonist of "Me, Hood!" (July 1959), possibly named for the comic-strip hero in *Terry and the Pirates*, is a former gangster turned undercover cop. For once, the female "bad guy" is sympathetic, and Ryan can't bring himself to be an avenger, with a conclusion suggesting the then still-unpublished *The Twisted Thing*.

"I'll Die Tomorrow" (March 1960) is an inversion of Spillane's standard revenge tale, and the most overtly experimental of his short stories, a rare excursion into third person, showing the writer at ease away from his usual first-person approach.

"The Seven Year Kill" (July 1960) foreshadows *The Girl Hunters*—Phil Rocca, an ex-police-beat reporter who has spent seven years in jail because he was framed, is now a drunken bum. Rocca shows uncharacteristic compassion for a Spillane tough guy in his handling of hoodlum Rhino Massley's daughter, Terry.

"Kick It or Kill" (July 1961) finds Federal Agent Kelly Smith recuperating from gunshot wounds in an upstate New York hamlet where a former government bigwig is getting local girls hooked on dope, using them as playthings in bizarre sadomasochistic orgies. This violent throwback to Hammett's "Nightmare Town" (1924) is also a foreshadowing of Spillane's own *The Body Lovers* (1967).

Cavalier editor Curran coaxed four articles out of Spillane, one on deep-sea diving ("Down, Down for Gold," 1955), two on cars, "Tough, Fast and Beautiful" (September 1955) and "Sports Car Fiesta" (August 1957), and "I Rode with the Hot Rod Moonshiners" (May 1956). In the latter, Spillane writes up his experiences shadowing North Carolina State Highway Patrolman Harold L. Cooke.

Mickey wrote a handful of other articles and essays for lower-end men's adventure magazines. In "You Can't Rock a Stock 'Jock'" (in *Stag*, July 1952), he reveals his budding interest in stock-car racing. Here Spillane comes across as an incurable adrenalin junkie: "[Y]ou have to smell the smoke and hear the screeches firsthand. . . . The colors, the noises, the smells are all part of the thing that explodes from the second the starter goes into his dance until the last heap rolls into the pits."

Spillane is quick to point out he's been "practicing skidding turns on a (local police, please note) *private* back road in a hundred-buck heap I picked up and intend turning into a stock racer for next season."

Eventually his enthusiasm for the sport faded.

"I had the fastest car on the track and I was the worst driver," he admitted years later. "So I started at the rear . . . picking off the cars. . . . We had about twenty accidents that night and I said, 'What am I doing in this place?' Here you're putting your life on the line. . . . I finished third that night and I never raced again."

Another factor may have been a non-stock-car crash in May 1956 when his Jaguar skidded and flipped near Newburgh. He was hospitalized at St. Luke's with a shoulder injury and bruised ribs (and ego). The Jag went for considerable repairs. No article resulted from this adventure.

In "Sports Car Fiesta," Spillane again proves himself a vivid reporter as he and cop buddy Cooke make a thirteen-hundred-mile drive in March to Sebring, Florida, in Mickey's John Wayne–bequeathed Jag.

In "The Enjoyment of Women" (*Man's Magazine*, June 1955), a puff piece about Myrtle Beach's Sun Fun Festival, Mickey is pictured with 1953 Miss South Carolina, Miriam Stevenson. Mickey picks four women as his ideal women: burlesque queen Lilly Christine, fellow circus "human cannonball" Duina Zacchini, actress Lisa Ferraday (*Rancho Notorious*, 1952), and Mrs. Mickey Spillane, about whom her husband says, "[Y]ou can look with surprise on the completeness of this woman and wonder how come you were so lucky or so smart to snag her out of the pack. Yeah, this one I enjoy most. Even more than when I married her."

The couple's fourth child, Caroline, was born in 1957, not long before the move to Murrells Inlet, where before long the marriage suffered on two fronts. First, Mickey was smoking again, against the Jehovah's Witness decree; and he was doing some two-fisted drinking—alcohol in moderation was okay, but drunkenness was a serious offense in the church. Though her husband had encouraged her into the faith, Mary Ann seemed to be the one taking it more seriously.

Mickey was always off gallivanting from one macho pursuit to another, calling it work (articles needed writing, right?) when clearly it was play . . . sometimes dangerous play. Researching "I Rode With the Hot Rod Moonshiners," Spillane joined his friend Harold Cooke and various Alcohol Tax Unit men in pursuit of bootleggers with stills in the hills and runners in hot rods carting "white whiskey" along narrow mountain roads.

Spillane wrote vividly of hiking a "narrow and torturous" trail at night to a "still that looked like a fat over-sized scarecrow with short, chubby arms and a mandarin hat . . . [the] peculiar odor of mash, whiskey and kerosene mingling with the freshness of the woods," a stream used by the moonshiners running "hard against the rocks."

The lawbreakers were gone, but their operation was quickly wired up with dynamite. The kibitzer was asked, "You want to blow it?"

Grinning, Spillane nodded and "leaned hard on the plunger and winced, waiting to get rocked off my feet." But the explosion was just "one big, muffled thud and a slow, heavy throated rattle, like a great dump truck slowly disgorging a load of scrap."

Such raids, with the operators often getting away in the woods upon hearing the lawmen's approach, meant "a long walk of chiggers, and dirt down your back" with little to show for it. Road pursuits were faster and more exciting.

Cooke showed Spillane several examples of their pursuit vehicles, all confiscated from the moonshine runners: a patrol car with the proper markings and a shortwave was "a big Olds 88" with "a hot one under the hood" and "a rear end geared up for high speed . . . sitting light on the shocks . . . beefed up [to] cream a turn when it had to."

Spillane was also shown a device called a "wampus," a heavy, steel-studded belt that when "tossed on the road and a car screams over it" would wind up around the axle, "metal tearing like cheesecloth." The moonshine runners had their own wampuses and also were known to fling roofing nails on the road to discourage pursuing cop cars.

On a stakeout outside a roadhouse, Spillane and Cooke spotted a guy pulling in with an obvious heavy load of white-lightning cases.

"Whatever signal system he set up was a good one and he was in gear almost as soon as we were," Spillane wrote. "He dragged that heap . . . back on the highway and was over a hundred before he dropped it into high. There was a mile stretch before the hill country and the hundred yards between us got bigger with every second. All we could hope for was to stay close enough so we wouldn't lose him before he reached the hills."

The car ahead threw on a pair of rear-mounted blinding spotlights, hitting Cooke and Spillane with twenty-thousand candlepower. "And," Spillane said, "if ever you've had a flash bulb popped in your face you know how it can work." He certainly did: the mad killer in *Ring of Fear* had done just that to him!

After Cooke almost hit the shoulder, the highway patrolman suggested they try again tomorrow.

"[B]ut there was no tomorrow for our tricky friend," Spillane reported. "He killed himself taking a turn too fast four miles away from where we dropped him. He thought we were still back there. A whole week later you could still smell the place where he cracked up."

Spillane accompanied Cooke on numerous other raids, including "a 1,500 job . . . [w]e dumped the mash and blew the guts out of a lovely hunk of machinery," a stakeout going after "the biggest outfit working in the Carolinas," and a roadblock where fists and a nightstick flew.

The *Cavalier* article was the only time Spillane ever detailed a time when he worked side by side with police.

"On the bootleg booze yarn," he wrote Saville (of all people), "I got shot in Baltimore while photo-ing a 37,000 dollar haul"—white whiskey (moonshine) from North Carolina and Virginia in Domino sugar cartons en route to New York, Philadelphia, and Washington, DC.

"It's a bottle refill service and great story," Spillane wrote, "if anybody will believe it. . . ."

This appears to be the federal work he assisted on, which he teased about in his short-lived weekly column, "Mickey Spillane Writes" for the *Greensboro Daily News*, January 8, 1956.

"Federal teams are doing some tight work in the cities," he wrote, "trying to run down the source of the bootleg that's been pouring into the gin mills. It's a bottle refill setup and gives tavern owners who have been working close to the breaking point, a big margin of profit. The racketeers haven't even got a bite on this one yet. . . . It's all being run very business-like by a group of personable newcomers."

Those personable newcomers were apparently responsible for the two gunshot wounds and one stab wound Spillane received assisting the Bureau of Internal Revenue's Alcohol and Tobacco Tax Division. Other undercover work included helping out Jack Stang in the Newburgh area, but that was just the beginning.

Asked what his undercover identity had been, he said, deadpan, "Mickey Spillane."

The writer went as himself into seedy joints under dangerous circumstances, rooting out information for police and the FBI. Supposedly he was picking up color and background info for his novels, which due to his notoriety and the nature of his fiction got him admitted just about anywhere, unquestioned. In the 1950s and '60s, this undercover work for which he took police tactical training took him to New York, Las Vegas, Los Angeles, and Washington, DC, gathering intel for local authorities and federal agencies. Drug rings and organized crime were the targets, his moonshine adventures a small part of it.

He was having a good, dangerous time, no question; but Baby was having none of it. A breakup was brewing. They separated, and would divorce in 1963.

When asked to comment, Spillane would only shrug. No excuses, he told his friend Gerrity. "Whoever knows exactly why?" he asked. "Mistakes are made. Looking back doesn't change things."

At the time of the divorce, his old editor friend Curran said in *Saga*, Mickey Spillane was no longer a member of the Witnesses or any formal religious group.

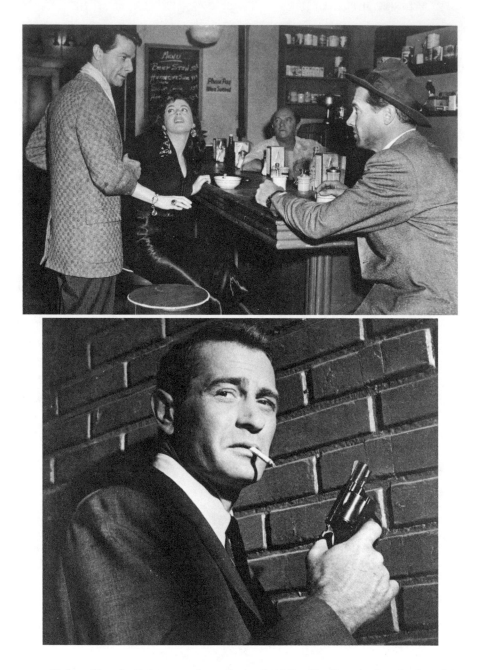

TOP: Robert Bray bulls his way through the final Saville film, the low-budget *My Gun Is Quick* (1957), ending the film series on a dismal note. BOTTOM: Darren McGavin as a tough, affable Hammer in the syndicated TV series *Mickey Spillane's Mike Hammer* (1958–1960) revitalizes and helps restore the character's popularity.

CHAPTER SIXTEEN

IF I HAD A HAMMER

As his contract with Mickey Spillane ran out, Victor Saville managed to squeeze one last drop of life from Mike Hammer in a low-budget big-screen adaptation of *My Gun Is Quick*, doomed from its inception to the drive-in circuit.

Released in August 1957, the film stars Robert Bray as Hammer, giving him an "introducing" credit despite sixty previous films going back over a decade, when he'd been promoted by RKO Pictures as the next Gary Cooper.

Bray certainly fit the bill as a towering, rugged Mike Hammer, closer to Jack Stang physically than either Biff Elliot or Ralph Meeker. Unfortunately, the most notable characteristic of the actor's performance in *My Gun Is Quick* is a tendency to shout. With better direction, Bray might have made a solid Hammer; here he seems a humorless, short-fused, thick-headed lout. In support, pros like Whitney Blake and Donald Randolph—so good in the Blake Edwards pilot—appear to have been left to their own devices under an apparently indifferent hand.

"I felt sad for the actors," Spillane said, adding, "[Bray] didn't ever hit big stardom, but you know he was a competent actor. He was caught in the wrong vehicle."

Director "Phil Victor" was two men—Saville himself and film editor George White. *Evergreen*, Saville's autobiography, has nothing to say about *My Gun Is Quick*, omitting it from his filmography.

In an interview, actor Darren McGavin refers to two pilots having been shot prior to his Hammer series, one being the Blake Edwards effort. With a cast and crew largely drawn from television—including co-scripters Richard Powell and Richard Collins—*My Gun Is Quick* may have started out as the other TV pilot film.

The two directors could mean White directed a one-hour pilot and Saville came in to bring the running time up with a few new scenes for a feature release. Saville had been the executive producer of the Blake Edwards 1954 pilot and might have worked out a deal with rights-owner Richard Lewis, although radio's *Hammer* producer goes unmentioned in the credits. Possibly White was fired after a bad start, with seasoned director Saville stepping in—one sequence late in the film has enough style to be the work of the director of *The Long Wait*.

Under the credits, in a location-shot opening, the camera tracks along as Bray's Hammer trudges past sleazy movie houses and burlesque joints, as jazzy music pounds out the promise of danger and violence. This is the best the film will get out of composer Marlin Skilles—veteran of *Bowery Boys* and other lower-grade B-movie entries—who soon settles into clichéd "Mickey Mouse" scoring, spelling the action out as if the audience needs help to follow scenes they had seen a thousand times before, and better.

As in *Kiss Me Deadly*, the Bunker Hill area depicts the seamier side of Los Angeles, again filling in for Mike Hammer's Manhattan. But this is not the modern-looking Robert Aldrich version of LA, rather the crummy nightclubs and rundown apartment houses of a sprawling, unglamorous metropolis.

Hammer is a weary urban traveler in a battered fedora, though his suit is pressed, and he packs a revolver, not Spillane's trademark .45 automatic. Velda (Pamela Duncan) and Pat Chambers (Booth Colman) are present but simplistically portrayed. Frequent Mike and

Pat scenes have Hammer yelling at Chambers and Chambers yelling at Hammer.

Pat raves, "You've got thoughts in that scrambled brain of yours that could make the track nice and muddy." In a phone conversation, Mike—for once not yelling at his police contact—advises him, "You might want to pick up a butler type . . . called Lou or Louie if you prefer." Such stilted lines receive the stilted readings they deserve.

But Saville had written Spillane that more of the mystery writer's dialogue would be used in *My Gun Is Quick* than in previous adaptations. And the opening ten minutes do hew close to the novel, if ham-handedly staged and performed. Then suddenly Spillane's bestseller is exchanged for a road company production of *The Maltese Falcon*, including a Brigid O'Shaughnessy wannabe and a skinny variation on Casper Gutman. Sam Spade's black-enameled bird has become "the Venacci jewels."

Saville again cited a Production Code objection—prostitution—for this clumsy revision; but the murder victim Hammer is avenging in the film remains a prostitute, so once more the producer proves himself cynically manipulative with his famous source writer.

Of the requisite Spillane "dames," Red, the hooker victim, is competently played by attractive, waiflike Jan Chaney, while dark-haired B-movie queen Pamela Duncan as Velda mostly strikes pinup poses in Hammer's shabby office. Pat Donahue's Dione makes a believable barroom pickup and Gina Core's Maria a heart-of-gold stripper, her pretty features hard-looking in possibly intentionally harsh lighting. Neither is exactly beautiful, appropriate denizens of Hammer's after-dark world of flophouses, greasy spoons, and strip joints.

Blonde Whitney Blake makes an effective Charlotte-like femme fatale, though burdened by clumsy expository monologues as she glides around in seductive attire—white short shorts, a snug swimsuit, and a baby-doll teddy. "Nancy Williams" (a character not in the book) lives in a bland, dockside bungalow, a location making possible ludicrous scenes in which Mike Hammer plays motorboat skipper. After much crawling through the sleazy side of the city, Hammer—in a pullover sport shirt produced out of thin air—is suddenly a sailor spouting nautical terms, skilled in cabin cruiser repair.

My Gun Is Quick provides the audience nap time with what is perhaps the most boring car chase in movie history. After going down the *Kiss Me Deadly* Bunker Hill cement staircase, Hammer spots a murder suspect and follows him by car, leaving the gritty side of LA behind to take the freeway on a tedious five-minute tail job. If the film indeed began as a TV pilot, this could well be feature-film padding.

A group of dialogue-free villains are unintentionally hilarious French sailors in striped shirts and stocking caps or berets, stopping short only of baguettes under their arms. Effete Colonel Holloway (also not in the novel), bookended by a brunette and blonde on either arm, announces that a strip club is the perfect place to be "gay," chewing scenery right up to his all too familiar, finally-the-jewels-are-mine death scene.

One strong sequence, late in the film, suggests the seasoned hand of Saville. Wanted for questioning, Hammer goes to the seaside bungalow, which by night finally takes on a noir ambiance. After sneaking past police, he leaps to the roof and onto a balcony where, through the window, he sees Pat in the living room below with Nancy and the diamond cutter. Butler Lou (Louie if you prefer) is dead on the floor, crime-scene protocol in full sway, flashbulbs strobing. Hammer watches as the diamond cutter has a heart attack and Nancy goes into hysterics for the benefit of Pat, who goes upstairs to a hideaway in the brick wall, from which the missing jewels are now missing. On the balcony, Hammer is on one side of the frame, outside, while Pat is on the other, inside, looking out. It's an impressive piece of wordless storytelling.

Fights in the film are adequately staged, as is a climactic confrontation with the French sailors on the pier, where Hammer clashes with a hook-handed thug. But the showdown on the little "yacht" between Hammer and femme fatale Nancy is—it should come as no surprise—more warmed-up *The Maltese Falcon* and *I, the Jury* leftovers. No bad-girl execution, though—sailor Mike merely heads to shore to hand her over in the most disappointing finish of any Spillane film, TV episodes included.

While Saville had been halfheartedly mounting his feeble final Hammer film, Spillane—though publishing little—had been busy. He'd penned a Western screenplay at John Wayne's request, *The Saga of Cali York*, a film of which kept threatening to happen. He wrote a screen treatment for Mickey Rooney—"The Duke Alexander," a modern-day comic variation on *The Prisoner of Zenda*. Nothing came of it.

For comedian Milton Berle he wrote *The Night I Died*, a one-hour TV teleplay (possibly a reworking of the lost, unfinished Hammer novel, *Tonight I Die*). Berle had been dabbling at the time in dramatic roles. In "Mickey Spillane Writes" in the *Greensboro Daily News*, May 13, 1956, Spillane said of Berle, "You might not believe it, but he's got a fine sense of subtlety and a dramatic quality that has never been brought out in the open."

But the teleplay—based on an unproduced Mike Hammer radio script with the hero renamed "the Mick"—may not have been intended for Berle to star in, but to produce with an actor named Spillane in the lead.

Mickey had given interviews to the Newburgh News about his plans to film television shows and motion pictures in his home area. He spoke of construction of a studio and of his own desire to act. The latter was reflected in his efforts to narrate *That Hammer Guy* on the radio.

Previously Mickey had been set to star as "Irish" in "The Big Run" for the anthology series *Suspense*, the television version of the Golden Age radio show. The episode, scripted by Spillane, was in serious pre-production, including storyboards and sets designed by old pal George Wilson. Jonathan ("Johnny") Winters was again cast and so were both Biff Elliot and Jack Stang. The extensive existing materials even include a "Presentation Date": March 2, 1954.

But "The Big Run"—about an innocent fugitive aboard a train reuniting with a childhood love (prefiguring the 1961 Spillane novel, *The Deep*)—appears never to have aired. Never to have been produced. Did Victor Saville step in and apply the kibosh?

The column for the *Greensboro News* ran from January 1 until about June 1956, bylined Newburgh, New York, when Spillane had one foot in South Carolina and the other in New York. The columns were heavily geared toward Manhattan and Spillane's wishful-thinking theory that New York City was replacing Hollywood as the center of filmmaking. He spoke occasionally of his own ambition to make films there; an original screenplay of his, he says, "will be done the way I want to see it done."

Now and then, throughout the decade, Spillane would start a Hammer novel, intending to finish it, and then set it aside until the Saville contract elapsed; but these never got past a few chapters and perhaps the ending (one of these false starts became the posthumous *Murder Never Knocks*, 2016, another *The Will to Kill*, 2017). He was making more steady progress with *The Deep*, a non-Hammer crime novel he'd been working on for five years—not the usual few weeks or months.

In 1956, he began seriously kicking around TV projects with his *Ring of Fear* producer Bob Fellows, who had recently broken off with John Wayne. Fellows had lost half his interest in the Wayne-Fellows films in a messy divorce. But the producer still owned ten percent of the net income from the company's pictures in excess of $2.34 million, as well as control of Anita Ekberg's contract and several scripts, including Burt Kennedy's *The Tall T* (1957), the classic Budd Boetticher/Randolph Scott Western based on an Elmore Leonard story. Fellows also had a film in the works based on Spillane favorite Fredric Brown's novel *The Screaming Mimi*; it would be released in 1958.

That same year, anticipating the reversion of Saville's Hammer film rights, Spillane began work on a *One Lonely Night* screenplay, which he appears to have finished (it is lost, however). He wrote Fellows in May: "This letter is to guarantee you first refusal of the motion picture rights to the book *One Lonely Night* and to the latest E. P. Dutton release, which at this writing, is as yet untitled," apparently *The Deep*.

Starting in 1956, Fellows and Spillane came up with something called, variously, *Mickey Spillane Presents*, *Murder by Spillane*, and *I, Spillane*. In Spillane's files, "The Punk"—another hour-long telefilm script—may be a pilot for a version of the proposed series.

Also involved was a young LAPD cop turned TV writer, Gene Roddenberry, who had written episodes of *Dragnet*, *Bat Masterson*, and *Have Gun, Will Travel*—the latter an idea Spillane claimed to have created but was stolen from him.

That wasn't any fault of hired-hand Roddenberry, whom Spillane spoke of glowingly in his *Goldsboro Daily News* column.

"Out Hollywood way, where you're nothing if you're unknown," Mickey wrote, never mentioning Roddenberry by name, "the hottest writing talent in TV . . . was just nominated for a TV 'Emmy' and if he makes it, he's going to shock the shoes off all the pen-pushing idiots by coming on the stage in his working clothes. He's a Los Angeles police officer." How Roddenberry and Spillane became friends is unknown; but well before the Murrells Inlet move, the TV writer was already spending time at Little Bohemia on New York trips. In one letter, Roddenberry talks of arriving with tortillas, hoping the Spillanes know how to make tacos; their mutual correspondence finds them remembering each other to their respective family members.

The future *Star Trek* creator and his new friend developed *Murder by Spillane* in a format similar to *Alfred Hitchcock Presents*. Roddenberry felt confident the show had a real future—he had interest already brewing, and was turning investors away. He worried only that Spillane's identification with "blood, sex and gore" might be a problem—TV execs were always looking for an excuse to say no.

In 1957, the show was announced as *Mickey Spillane Presents*, to be produced by actor Sam Jaffe, the husband of Bettye Ackerman, who had been part of both the Stang test film and the *Mike Hammer's Mickey Spillane* record album. According to Lee Goldberg's definitive *Unsold*

Television Pilots: 1955–1989, *Murder by Spillane* (apparently the same show) would showcase a different fictional detective each week, not exclusively created by Spillane.

Roddenberry may or may not have been part of this iteration, and it's unclear whether a pilot film was ever shot. In any case, Spillane would have hosted, which indicates his growing post–*Ring of Fear* interest in performing.

But the post-Saville sale of Mike Hammer to MCA/Revue for television seems to have short-circuited *Mickey Spillane Presents*. With Mike Hammer finally under his control again, Spillane was back in business.

Mickey Spillane's Mike Hammer debuted on January 7, 1958, the "fastest-selling film series in MCA's ten years of syndication"; soon it would be the highest-rated syndicated mystery series nationally. Seventy-eight episodes would appear in a two-season run through September 1959, staying in syndication well beyond that.

What did the critics think? *TV Guide* said it "could easily be the worst show on TV." Viewed decades later, the black-and-white series has much to offer, starting with Darren McGavin's star-making performance.

Having already made a mark on stage (*The Rainmaker*, 1954) and screen (*The Man With the Golden Arm*, 1955), McGavin bore a strong physical resemblance to Mickey Spillane and, like Hammer's creator, had an easy masculinity minus the bulk of Stang or Bray, as well the charisma and wry humor neither had . . . just right for the intimate medium of television.

Initially, Spillane was annoyed with the choice. After a screening of the pilot, he asked an MCA executive, "How come you picked such a little guy to play Mike Hammer?"

When he was told you couldn't have a big guy going around hitting people, Mickey responded, "Yeah? How about Marshal Dillon in *Gunsmoke*? He belts a lot of people around. And he's not small."

Spillane also wanted to know why McGavin was carrying a .38, not a .45. Much to his displeasure, he was told, "A .45 is so cumbersome."

Yet Mickey soon came around to liking McGavin, in part because the actor "knew how to wear the hat."

"He was great," Spillane said in 1968. "[H]e played it with humor. . . . For TV, it was a good concept. For a half hour in black-and-white, it came across."

Despite the infusion of humor, many episodes deliver typical Spillane vengeance-driven fare, often pitting Hammer at odds with his pal Captain Pat Chambers (Bart Burns), the only other recurring character. Frequent gunfire turns Manhattan into a new Wild West, and an unending stream of consenting cuties distracts Hammer between bone-crunching brannigans. The notion that McGavin's Hammer is too sunny is belied by how little mercy he shows the bad guys—he's easily as ruthless as Mike on the printed page.

In *Kiss Me Deadly*, Ralph Meeker heartlessly snaps a collectible opera record in half to make a witness talk; in the TV episode "To Bury a Friend," Darren McGavin wrecks one collectible clock after another to pry a faker out of a wheelchair, without losing viewer sympathy or support. The actor makes the difference.

Chambers is featured only occasionally, and—possibly a budgetary consideration—Hammer often talks with Pat on the phone with only Mike heard. Yet Hammer's relationship with Chambers is among its best screen depictions. McGavin and Burns—one of the jurors in the original Studio One version of *Twelve Angry Men*—enjoy a strong screen chemistry.

Velda is mentioned in the pilot, but never again, much less seen—Hammer's very spare office has no reception area. As with the Blake Edwards pilot, a half-hour version of *Mike Hammer* doesn't seem able to accommodate Velda.

Writers of scripts and source stories on *Mike Hammer* include such pulp luminaries as Evan Hunter, Robert Turner, Stephen Marlowe, Richard Deming, Bill S. Ballinger, James Gunn, and, most frequently, Frank Kane. Ken Pettus—as "Steven Thornley," identified by TV scholar Stephen Bowie—had an impressive small-screen career, including scripts for *Mission: Impossible*, *Hawaii Five-O*, and *The Big Valley* (created by A. I. Bezzerides).

Directors included Boris Sagal, serial director William Witney, and Richard Irving, whom some sources credit as the series' unbilled producer, while others suspect *That Hammer Guy*'s Richard Lewis.

Original music by Dave Kahn alternates with generic dramatic "library" music. Following the success of Mancini's *Peter Gunn* album for RCA, orchestrator Skip Martin recorded *The Music from Mickey Spillane's Mike Hammer*, also for RCA, using Kahn material written specifically for the album, some of which made its way into the second season. The LP includes liner notes credited to (but not written by) Mickey Spillane.

The stirring yet melancholy theme, "Riff Blues" by Kahn, swells over the Manhattan opening and closing credits of each episode. Melvyn Leonard shares Kahn's credit but the composer—in an interview with Hollywood music expert Jon Burlingame—insists Leonard's credit was "designed to capture composer royalties for the publisher."

Premiering as it did in January 1958, *Mickey Spillane's Mike Hammer*—and *Perry Mason*, which debuted in September 1957—initiated the late 1950s/early '60s private-eye boom on American TV. Blake Edwards's *Peter Gunn* first appeared on September 22, 1958, and *77 Sunset Strip* on October 10, 1958; these two series caught fire, but *Mike Hammer* and *Perry Mason* lit the fuse.

Mini-films noir, *Hammer* episodes showcase fluid photography, long-take master shots, and skillful integration of New York B-unit work woven into Hollywood-produced studio principal photography. Working cannily within its budget of under $50,000 per episode, the filmmakers cultivate a gritty Manhattan of low-end apartments, seedy burlesque houses, and shoddy offices.

The series was shot at Universal Studios and at the ancient Republic Studios back lot, where *My Gun Is Quick* had filmed the year before. Framed starving-artist paintings on dingy apartment walls in *Quick* turn up more than once on *Hammer*.

In the seventy-eight episodes, fifty-some people are killed, and almost as many are wounded. Violent intimidation is commonplace, fistfights frequent, occasional scenes of torture no surprise. Sympathetic characters sometimes don't make it out of an episode alive.

The common denominator of the private eye's cases is money: a guy named Lonzi runs a scam investment racket; a beauty contest winner is swindled out of fifty bucks; a drifter dies for less than a C-note; a businessman is blackmailed over a $500 gambling debt. Not big money by twenty-first-century standards, but death always comes cheap in Mike Hammer's world, though the price for murder is high.

Mike Hammer rides the middle ground between society's lowest and highest levels. Now and then he takes a job for the rich and visits their lavish estates. More often he shuttles between cramped, cheaply furnished apartments and struggling businesses, dealing with people who have lost hope, caught up in drab existences and, too often, loveless marriages. The rich in Hammer's world seem as miserable as the poor, and rob and kill just as often. It's a bleak place where money is more the disease than the cure, and entering it is made worthwhile only by the amiable company of McGavin's Mike Hammer.

Darren McGavin starred in several subsequent series, including *Riverboat* (filmed concurrently with the second season of *Mickey Spillane's Mike Hammer*), *The Outsider* (a PI series from *77 Sunset Strip* creator Roy Huggins), and the cult favorite *Kolchak: the Night Stalker* (initially a top-rated TV movie co-starring Ralph Meeker). McGavin's enduring legacy, however, is his role as Ralphie's "Old Man" in *A Christmas Story* (1983).

Mickey Spillane's Mike Hammer featured such stars-to-be as Robert Vaughn (*The Man from U.N.C.L.E.*), Lorne Greene (*Bonanza*), and DeForest Kelley (*Star Trek*). Notable Hammer "dolls" include Angie Dickinson, Sue Ann Langdon, Nita Talbot, Lisa Gaye, Diane Brewster, Fay Spain, Marion Ross, Bethel Leslie, Ruta Lee, Abby Dalton, Allison Hayes, and Yvette Vickers. Peggie Castle—Charlotte Manning herself—re-enters Mike Hammer's sphere in "The Big Drop," as does Whitney Blake, in the pilot, "Just Around the Coroner."

B-movie beauty queens aside, the series hinges on McGavin, who gives Mike Hammer a new affability, spoofing the material slightly while not losing its hard edge. In a 1994 *Scarlet Street* interview with Richard Valley, McGavin said MCA was unhappy with early episodes, feeling the actor was making fun of the material.

"I'm not making fun of it," McGavin insisted. "I'm just treating it in a lighter manner."

When they threatened to replace him, McGavin said, "I got a farm in upstate New York, and I'm really very happy there. I don't wanna do this the way you wanna do it. Let's just call it quits today, and you can hire somebody else to do it."

When he was reminded he was under contract, the actor told Universal's top executive, Lew Wasserman, "We have a contract for me to say the words that are put on the paper. I don't want anybody telling me how to do it."

MCA was on the spot—they had set a record assembling sponsors for the series, which was already airing. They caved.

"After that," McGavin said, "they left us alone, and we went ahead and made them—and they were instantly successful."

The two-year run of *Mickey Spillane's Mike Hammer* strengthened the brand Saville had weakened. But the new TV money was making Spillane lazy, some friends claimed. One said, "He's goofing off."

Finally, the writer got a draft of *The Deep* done and sent it to Victor Weybright, only to get bogged down in editorial requests. Henry Adams reported, "He fools around with his gun collection, tinkers with his hot rods," tumbled on his trampoline, assembled an elaborate hi-fi set-up. He liked classical music, Wagner particularly.

Alone now in the Myrtle Beach house, his kids and their mom living elsewhere in the area, Spillane let his mail pile up, sorting through for checks, then burning the rest, unread. He answered the phone grudgingly or not at all—once, according to Adams, even took a shot at it.

He must have missed, because eventually the increasing demands on him seemed to get through—before long, Mickey Spillane had the finishing touches on *The Deep* and re-upped with Signet/Dutton.

And maybe it was time to write a Mike Hammer novel.

Spillane back in Manhattan, in Mike Hammer mode, 1961.

CHAPTER SEVENTEEN

COMEBACK TRAIL

No statement from Spillane like the one announcing his initial affiliation with the Jehovah's Witnesses accompanied his break with the church. Nor did the Witnesses make any public statement regarding Spillane's having been "disfellowshipped," their form of excommunication.

Though he and Mary Ann would not divorce till 1963, Spillane's use of tobacco, his more than moderate use of alcohol, and his continued military service put him at odds with the church. He would, after all, soon be a Colonel in the United States Air Force Reserve, part of the 354th Tactical Fighter Wing at Myrtle Beach Air Force Base.

As he began to write and publish novels again, Spillane needed to "beat the publicity drum," as his old editor pal Bob Curran put it. Living by himself in his beachfront house in Murrells Inlet, where some still viewed him as a "damn Yankee," he perhaps got restless. Mike Hammer may have been a misanthropic introvert, but his creator was an extrovert who liked having people around.

Dealing with publishers and promotion took Spillane to New York City more often than when he'd lived in Newburgh fifty-some miles away. Curran described a typical Spillane visit—sometimes accompanied by a "stand-up guy" or two from Newburgh—making the Manhattan rounds.

The day before his arrival, Spillane calls Curran—then Mickey's editor at *Cavalier*—to set up a lunch date, which Curran does gladly. But the next day Curran doesn't bother cancelling a previous commitment, knowing that Spillane will "get into all sorts of involvements just getting across town."

He hears from Spillane around four P.M., no mention of the missed lunch date, and is summoned to P. J. Moriarty's at Sixth Avenue in the fifties. Curran waits till five and takes along a fellow editor who has business with Spillane, though taking "a dim personal view of the Spillane phenomenon." When the two editors arrive, the restaurant's bar is empty but for two pals of the writer gabbing with owner P. J., and Spillane himself at the bar chatting up the bartender. Without missing a beat, Mickey pulls the new arrivals into a small-talk session.

Curran, noting that Spillane's abilities as a raconteur are perhaps second only to Casey Stengel's, finds Mickey saying, "Remember those little circles of candy they used to have on the long rolls of paper when we were kids? Remember how you couldn't get them off without getting paper on the bottom? What did they call those things anyway?"

That gets everybody thinking about their childhood as the drinks flow. Curran sees this as "a typical Spillane maneuver against which there is no defense," but the writer doesn't have to work at it—like the drinks, the nostalgia flows too. Before long the place is filling up, United Press columnist Hal Boyle and some friends on Spillane's left, Hy Gardner on his right.

After a while, Curran slips away, unnoticed, to catch a basketball game at nearby Madison Square Garden. At the half, he returns to the restaurant's bar, his absence apparently unnoticed, joins in for a few rounds, then returns to the Garden for the second half. When he gets back to the bar again, the crowd is thinning and Mickey is on the move. The writer and his two buddies, with Curran in tow, start "the Grand Tour"—the Gaslight Club in the Village, an East Side advertising hangout to see Rocky Marciano, then an old buddy's pizzeria, and finally a posh joint catering to (and over-charging) celebrities, where the employees are not, typically, terribly impressed by famous clientele. But Spillane is different—several bartenders want autographs.

"Off we go again," Curran recalled, and—after "a few more courtesy calls"—the editor and his writer finally get some business done over beers.

Curran's last dim memory is Mickey arm wrestling all takers. The editor doesn't even consider joining in, well aware that any who take the challenge will be "drinking leftie for the next two days."

Mickey Spillane was back in Manhattan—not living there, just owning it.

In 1961, his non-Hammer *The Deep* was published, and in the fall of '62, the first Hammer in a decade: *The Girl Hunters*. Over a stein of beer, the writer predicted to Curran, "There's going to be a new Spillane wave—only bigger than the first one."

The period beginning in 1961 did represent a second tide of Spillane titles, including four Hammer thrillers—ten novels in all, four more than the first wave. Sales were excellent. By 1970, *The Deep* and *The Girl Hunters* had sold four million copies each in the USA, matching all but *I, the Jury* and *The Big Kill* at five million.

But a seismic shift had quietly begun rumbling in 1958, started by Victor Weybright—unintentionally aided and abetted by Spillane.

"On the basis of no demonstrable logic," Weybright recalled in his auto-biography, he had taken "the plunge on Ian Fleming just as I had earlier on Mickey Spillane."

James Bond had been a bust in its American reprint editions from Popular Library and Pocket Books. The industry opinion was that Fleming and Bond were "too British." But at the time, it had been half a dozen years since a new Spillane manuscript, and Spillane even refused to resubmit *For Whom the Gods Would Destroy*. The publisher saw in Fleming a potential methadone for Mickey's heroin.

After all, *Casino Royale* (1953), Bond's debut, was an espionage twist on *I, the Jury*, with similar scandalous sex and sadistic violence. Weybright assigned frequent Spillane cover artist Baryé Phillips to the Fleming titles, with Signet's first Bond reprint, *From Russia With Love*, bearing *Time* magazine's sneering imprimatur—"Mickey Spillane in gentleman's clothing."

"Bond's a killer," notes Benjamin Welton in *Artistic License Renewed*, a Bond literary magazine, ". . . a 'blunt instrument' of London. In sum, Fleming's original Bond is a kindred spirit of Mike Hammer, and this fact has been noted by no less of an authority than Italian academic and novelist Umberto Eco."

If Spillane had even noticed Fleming, he probably wasn't worried—didn't he have a new Mike Hammer movie in the works with Bob Fellow producing? And a big announcement to make about who would be playing Mike Hammer. . . .

After a nine-year absence as a novelist, Spillane returned with *The Deep* and explored a soon-to-be recurring theme of his—the return of a tough guy (known only as "Deep") after unexplained time away, a less than subtle metaphor for his own literary hiatus. Its otherwise nameless hero appears to be a criminal but, in another ending reserved for the last word, is not.

Years before in the old neighborhood, two young hoods had flipped a coin for control of their territory. Buddy Bennett won the toss and Deep left town a loser. The street denizens assumed he'd gone elsewhere on his dark path. But years later, after Bennett's murder, he returns to the same corrupt stretch. He meets hoods old and new, warring over the territory Bennett controlled, and lets it be known he'll avenge his old friend and take over. Along the way he and his childhood sweetheart, Helen Tate, reconnect.

Deep concludes the only person who actually hated both Bennett and himself was Roscoe, Helen's half brother, whom he is forced to kill. This convinces Helen that Deep has remained a criminal: "You're one of them, Deep. . . ." With the police closing in, Helen thinks it's too late for them. Then Deep shows her his badge as a police lieutenant.

While Anthony Boucher of the *New York Times* granted *The Deep* was "occasionally effective," the writer's old foe complained rather hypocritically about the lack of sex and violence, describing it as "a degeneration into morality." And, despite the novel's big sales, some readers felt (as Curran noted) "Spillane without Hammer wasn't Spillane."

This time it wouldn't be a long wait. In another metaphor for Spillane's crime-fiction comeback, Mike Hammer returns in *The Girl Hunters* (1962). He's found "in the gutter" by a pair of cops sent to fetch him for Captain Pat Chambers, who has nothing but contempt for his "old buddy" since Hammer, years ago, sent Velda out on a case from which she never returned.

The loss of Velda has been too much for Hammer; he's become a helpless, hopeless drunk.

But a dying FBI agent reveals that, for the past seven years, Velda has been behind the Iron Curtain. She's back in the USA now, but in hiding, hunted by the Dragon, a KGB assassin. A trail of corpses leads a suddenly sober but weakened Hammer to a farmhouse where he and the Dragon battle in a roundhouse free-for-all as violent as anything in early Spillane. Hammer has promised his FBI contact he won't kill the Dragon. Knowing a thing or two about metaphors himself, Mike Hammer uses a "twenty-penny nail and a ball peen hammer" to nail the unconscious brute's hand to the floor.

Hammer informs murdered Senator Knapp's widow, Laura, that her husband's killer, the Dragon, is a team—"tooth and nail." As for dragons, Hammer says, "Today, I'm St. George." While Laura takes a shower at the pool—lending the conclusion a Charlotte-like naked femme fatale—Mike stuffs her shotgun's barrels into the dirt, having earlier described in grue-some detail what would happen in the case of soil-induced blowback. He leaves the booby-trapped weapon as a test, turning his back as he walks away, hearing behind him "the unearthly roar as she pulled both triggers at once."

The Girl Hunters marks a strong return for Hammer and his creator, who uses dialogue as the novel's engine, doles out the sex and violence effectively, and makes Velda a major presence in a novel in which she does not appear—a remarkably bold narrative stunt.

Mike and Velda have their reunion in *The Snake* (1964), rather unbeliev-ably (even in Spillane's world) being thrust immediately into a new case. For once Hammer is not seeking revenge—he is trying to protect a young woman Velda had befriended while in hiding. Somebody is trying to kill pretty little "Lolita-type" Sue, possibly her politician father—his daughter holds the key to his closet full of skeletons. Meanwhile, rumbles in the underworld suggest someone is putting together a new mob, funded by big money that may come from a long-ago robbery in which recently released old-timer Sonny Motley was involved.

Elderly Sonny is the underworld's potential new Mr. Big. He confronts Hammer and Velda on a bucolic hillside near the thirty-year-old getaway car, whose double-crossed driver, Blackie Conley, sits mummified behind the wheel. With three million in cash in that car waiting for Sonny, Hammer taunts him into opening its door, and as Conley's corpse turns to dust on exposure to the air, the rifle in the corpse's hand fires and kills Sonny. Mike and Velda walk away hand in hand for a long overdue consummation "up there on the hill [where] the grass was soft."

The Snake received the best reviews of a Hammer novel to date, Boucher calling it "almost certainly Mike Hammer's best case . . . ending with the damnedest last-second rescue in history." A complex tale efficiently told, lean and tough, *The Snake* nonetheless lacks the revenge-driven rage that propels the best Hammer novels.

When Victor Weybright announced his early retirement at age sixty-six, Spillane gave him *For Whom the Gods Would Destroy* to publish as a farewell gift—one that cost Signet "a bundle," the writer said. Mickey's only copy of his final version had nearly been destroyed in the Newburgh attic fire, leaving the last page or so scorched and unreadable, requiring Spillane to restore them as best he could. When another copy materialized, he claimed his near two-decade memory test came up only a few words off. This follow-up to *I, the Jury* from 1948 was published as *The Twisted Thing* (1966). Spillane likely substituted it when he missed the deadline for the novel that would posthumously be published in 2010 as *The Big Bang* (completed by MAC).

In a delicious slice of irony, Spillane was bestowed his best Anthony Boucher review, the esteemed critic having no idea he was actually reviewing 1948 vintage Spillane: ". . . I suggest [Mike Hammer's creator] is one of the last great storytellers in the pulp tradition, as he amply demonstrates in *The Twisted Thing*. . . . Spillane is a master in compelling you always to read the next page."

In *The Body Lovers* (1967), Mike Hammer discovers the corpse of a young beauty who has been whipped to death, the friend of a sister of a guy Hammer once sent up the river; as a favor, Hammer goes looking for the sister, Greta Service, who may be in danger herself. The bad guys, protected by diplomatic immunity, have been using the girls as playthings in sadomasochistic orgies. Hammer rescues both Greta and Velda from the sex-party mansion and turns on the gas, rigging a booby trap that can be set off by a phone call. When a bystander asks what the hell the explosion was, Hammer replies, "Wrong number."

The ending's black humor, and a right-wing attitude toward the foreign baddies, is typical of Spillane's '60s work. His improved craftsmanship is on full display here in his most underrated novel, whose quality Boucher (and other reviewers) recognized: "It's more than probable that *The Body Lovers* is Mickey Spillane's best book to date. Hardly a touch of excess, self-parody, or moralizing: just a straight, fast, effective private-eye novel. . . ."

In *Survival . . . Zero!* (1970), a world-weary Mike Hammer discovers the slaughtered body of his friend Lippy Sullivan, then does his best to convince Pat Chambers of a lack of interest in the case: "He was a guy I knew, that's all." This almost comic reversal of the first chapter of *I, the Jury* has Spillane toying with the reader. Soon Hammer again sets out to avenge a friend's death.

Still, the tone is different. This is not the intense, driven avenger of the early novels. Hammer's creator may have been no longer aligned with his church, but a Jehovah's Witness sensibility toward the inevitable Armageddon provides a subtext of impending holocaust via germ warfare.

With the end of the world looming, Hammer can't get excited about it: "New York without smog because the factories and incinerators had no one to operate them. No noise except the wind and the rain until trees grew back through the pavement, then there would be leaves to rustle. Abandoned vehicles would rot and blow away as dust, finally blending with the soil again. Even bones would eventually decompose until the remnants of the race were gone completely, their grave markers concrete and steel tombstones hundreds of feet high, the caretakers of the cemetery only the microscopic organisms that wiped them out. Hell, it didn't sound so bad at all. . . ."

The detective foils the foreign agents' plot to unleash a deadly bacterial strain on the world: "Maybe now some of this crappy rivalry between countries will slow down and there will be some sensible cooperation." Instead of shooting them, he says, "At least here you get due process of law. Your own people would kill you the slowest way they know how."

The second-period Hammer novels suffer under the weight of the first six. But in these later works—from *The Girl Hunters* through *Survival . . . Zero!* (note the care of the punctuation)—Spillane is at the top of his craft, and often of his powers, writing vividly and poetically, yet able to deliver blows with either hand.

But why, from 1962 through 1970, did Spillane publish only four Mike Hammer novels in what was his most prolific decade? You could ask Victor Weybright, if he hadn't retired just as his last gamble on a sex-and-violence author paid off. But surely you already know that Ian Fleming, with a major assist from actor Sean Connery, had hijacked Mickey Spillane's high-flying plane.

Spillane recognized that 1960s secret agents had shouldered past private eyes thanks to the kind of big-screen success that Victor Saville hadn't managed for Mike Hammer. This found Mickey trying to play another man's game, creating his own supposed spy, Tiger Mann.

There's something halfhearted about the way Tiger Mann is just Mike Hammer under a name even its bearer calls "ridiculous." Though he seems only to walk Hammer's Manhattan streets, with none of Bond's exotic locale hopping, Tiger works for a supersecret organization supplying him with money and technology beyond Mike Hammer's reach. His "M" is an ultra-right-wing billionaire, Martin Grady, whose "Group" is his own privately financed personal espionage organization, working for supposedly altruistic, patriotic purposes. Tiger—Grady's top agent—has completed many successful missions but, though still extremely active and virile, knows middle age approaches. In *Day of the Guns* (1964), Tiger pursues a murderer, and a lost love, thinking they are one and the same: Edith Caine and Rondine Lund. At the close of World War II, Tiger and Rondine were OSS agents; although upper-class British by birth, Rondine was a double agent for the Nazis. After making passionate love with Tiger, Rondine shot him and left him for dead.

In a darkened New York nightclub, Tiger sees a beautiful woman with a remarkable resemblance to Rondine, whom the spy promised himself he would kill if he ever found her again. But when Tiger is about to kill Edith, she declares she's the late Rondine's sister. Then Edith kills the real villainess of the piece, tossing a black grenade and blowing her out the window onto the street below.

This first, and best, Tiger Mann adventure, concludes with a "happy ending" variation of *I, the Jury*'s striptease.

As *Bloody Sunrise* (1965) begins, the secret agent, planning to resign, is about to be married. But Tiger is soon called to duty after some suspicious radioactivity is discovered in a ship's cargo. He has no choice but to tell Edith their wedding day must be postponed.

Tiger seeks a top Russian spy who defected for his former lover, an Olympic skier. Soon Ann Lighter, Tiger's fellow Group agent, is dead from a broken neck; an enraged Tiger promises revenge. One agent killing another is not worthy of Mike Hammer–like righteous rage, and Tiger's response feels forced and flat.

In a replay of *One Lonely Night*, Tiger goes to a warehouse where the villain hides. Inside, Edith (subbing for Velda) is a prisoner in a plan to blame Tiger's Group for blowing up Washington, DC, scoring a major coup against the right-wing organization. Tiger agrees to sign a confession, but uses a weaponized trick pen, the resulting explosion thwarting the project.

With death looming, Edith tells Tiger: "I'm not your Rondine, remember? . . . I'm Edith." He is struck by her loyalty and her love. They survive to see the bloody sunrise, but their future remains in question.

In *The Death Dealers* (1965), Teddy Tedesco, a high-level agent for the Group, has uncovered a death plot against Teish El Abin, the King of Selachin, where oil has been discovered. Key Spillane elements abound: the right-wing attitude, sex associated with violence, a revenge motif. Tiger explains to Lily Tornay, an Interpol agent: "When you play with the death dealers you use the only weapon they understand—violence."

Tiger knows that one of his old enemies, Malcolm Turos, is working for the Russians. Turos leaves his "calling card" by using a rope trick on Edith that strangles a victim after a contorted position forces muscle cramps. She is lucky enough to live, but Lily is killed. Tiger's reaction: guilt, and a pledge of revenge.

Tiger wants to make Turos suffer as Lily had: "[I put] the final loop around his neck that would choke him to death long before he was found and nobody would care at all." As he leaves Turos to die, Tiger recycles a Hammer line: "Kismet, buddy." For all the Sturm und Drang, *The Death Dealers*—the only Spillane novel lacking a surprise ending—is a routine effort.

In *The By-Pass Control* (1966), American engineer Louis Agrounsky has helped install an ICBM automatic triggering mechanism while secretly including a bypass system that gives him control of the fate of the USA, and the world. Spillane is not bothering to make any distinction between Mike and Tiger by now, as indicated by the opening line: "The guy was as good as dead and knew it." Tiger faces down a Russian agent, who has murdered three American agents, and shoots him between the eyes.

Camille Hunt, the Personnel Director for Belt-Aire Electronics—a Martin Grady Company directly connected with the ICBM project—is a typical Spillane femme fatale. When they meet, Camille sits in the corner of a darkened office while Tiger studies her framed nude portrait. He knows she's watching but pretending not to; he turns on a light and says, "Hello, spider," and she says, "Hello, fly." It's the novel's best moment.

The search for Agrounsky ends in Leesville, North Carolina, in a rainstorm—Mike Hammer weather. Tiger and an enemy agent battle on a rain-swept beach in bloody confrontation. Later the lady spider has a cold and thoughtlessly uses Tiger's nasal inhaler, rigged with cyanide; Spillane uncomfortably imitates himself in the final line: "She was dead when I reached her and she never heard me say, 'I told you I was the mud-dauber type, spider.'"

Here the series—an undignified, misguided exercise in one major writer following another's lead—sputters out.

Back in 1962, however, with Fleming barely a blip on his radar, Spillane had just put Mike Hammer back on the bestseller lists with *The*

Girl Hunters. At a press conference, he made the big announcement not just about a movie version of the new book, but who was starring as Mike Hammer—Mickey Spillane.

He was asked, "How come *you're* going to play Mike Hammer?"

"What do you mean 'play' Mike Hammer?" he said with a grin. "I *am* Mike Hammer."

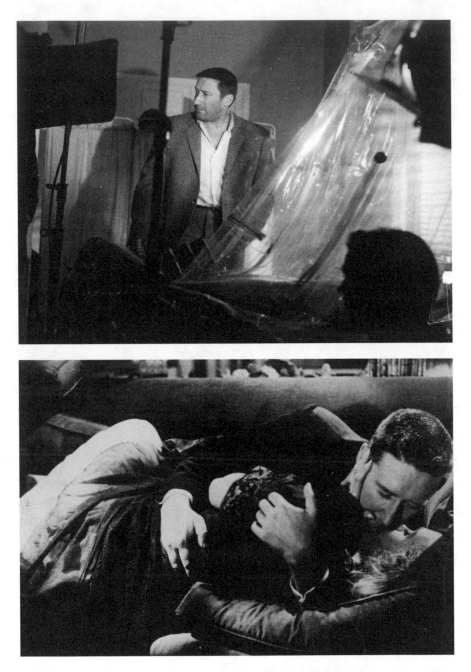

TOP: Mickey as Mike Hammer in *The Girl Hunters* (1963). BOTTOM: Co-starring with Shirley Eaton—soon to be James Bond's "golden girl" in *Goldfinger* (1964)— he co-wrote and co-produced the largely British production.

CHAPTER EIGHTEEN

I, THE ACTOR

In November of 1982, *Cavalier* magazine editor Bob Curran—"walking across 44th Street on the West Side"—bumped into his friend Mickey Spillane outside the Blue Ribbon restaurant. The editor stepped around "a mess of stuff" where some workers were crowded around at the curb, but his attention went to his old pal Mick, whom he had not seen in person for a while.

The greeting Spillane offered up was typically soft-spoken, "very cordial and pleasant with a special personal feeling about it." Nothing in Spillane's manner tipped off the editor that he had stumbled onto the set of *The Girl Hunters*, the "mess of stuff" having been a camera crew and its gear, the crowd just assorted gawkers taking it all in.

Curran was a little embarrassed for being so slow on the uptake—he knew Mickey was going to appear in a film version of his comeback Mike Hammer novel, *The Girl Hunters*. He also was aware that a copy of *Cavalier* with a key clue stuffed inside its pages was making a cameo appearance in the film; the product-placement plug hadn't been the editor's idea but Mickey's own.

When Curran later saw the film and wrote it up in *Cavalier* and then *Saga*, he was surprised—perhaps relieved—to find Spillane's performance was "great" and in "a pretty damn good picture."

The day after the Spillane sighting, the *New York Times* reported the same disturbance at the Blue Ribbon. Customers expecting sauerbraten and Wiener schnitzel (among other German comfort fare) found themselves treated to a side dish of movie-making. *Times* reporter A. H. Weiler spoke to "both the star and scenarist," who happened to be one and the same.

"I play Hammer in this one," Spillane told Weiler, who seemed surprised. The writer somewhat "diffidently" brought up having previously starred in *Ring of Fear*, explaining this new motion picture was "being done independently on various locations here in New York."

From there it would be going to the United Kingdom, the film a co-USA/UK production made under the Eady Plan.

Spillane went on: "Robert Fellows, who is directing and has a fine record as you know, is doing an excellent job here even though the only featured 'actor,' if you can call me that, is me."

Only one other "actor" who had been cast thus far was an amateur—showbiz columnist Hy Gardner, appearing as himself. Four days of Manhattan shooting would include Gardner's *Herald Tribune*, and various buildings on the West Side between Fortieth and Fifty-Third Streets and on Hudson and Beach Streets, plus a police precinct downtown.

"We'll cast more people," Spillane added, "once we get to England. And there's no definite budget—we'll do it as realistically as we can as we go along."

These last few words would be among the most ominous ever to emerge from the mind of Mickey Spillane.

Why was he appearing as Mike Hammer himself this time? Well, people had been telling him for years he looked like Mike Hammer, and maybe *he* should play the character.

"Now," the new screen Hammer said, "I'm going to prove to myself and others that I can do it."

Spillane always claimed it was Fellows's idea for him to star, but *The Girl Hunters* was the culmination of a desire to perform that included everything from trying to narrate *That Hammer Guy* on the radio and playing his hero on the *Mickey Spillane's Mike Hammer* record album, to capering with Milton

Berle on TV and planning to star in the failed "The Big Run" on *Suspense*. Not to mention getting shot out of a cannon at the circus.

"I knew the words because I had written the script," he said of *The Girl Hunters* in 1998. Producer Fellows and director Roy Rowland had taken co-scripting credit, though the dialogue was right out of the book. Mickey had clearly done the heavy lifting, including taking on a producer role. "I was in charge of casting," Spillane recalled with a smile and self-deprecating humor. "So I looked very tall because I wouldn't hire anybody that was any bigger than [me]."

Principal photography took place at MGM's British Studios in Borehamwood, Hertfordshire—"next to Burton and Liz Taylor," Spillane said, who "were making the picture *The V.I.P.s*." The director—not Fellows himself, as Mickey had told the *New York Times*—was Hollywood veteran Roy Rowland (Fellows apparently directed the B-Unit footage in Manhattan).

Rowland made his reputation in the 1930s doing Robert Benchley and Pete Smith shorts, then went on to direct everything from musicals (*Hit the Deck*, 1955) to Westerns (*Gun Glory*, 1957), from films with child star Margaret O'Brien (*Our Vines Have Tender Grapes*, 1945) to the Dr. Seuss extravaganza *The 5,000 Fingers of Dr. T.* (1953). More pertinent were a handful of films noir: *Scene of the Crime* (1949), *Rogue Cop* (1954), and *Witness to Murder* (1954).

The black-and-white film's credits, rather confusingly, labeled *The Girl Hunters* a Colorama Production, a New York-based firm with Italian roots. Everything but funding would be handled by the newly formed Fellane Productions, the Fellows/Spillane equivalent of Wayne/Fellows.

Was the black-and-white cinematography a conscious throwback to old-school film noir? Hardly.

"We ran out of money," Spillane admitted.

Not being able to shoot in color was a huge frustration to Fellows and Spillane—the first James Bond film, *Dr. No* (1962), had been shot in color, and had already successfully opened in the UK. The Bond picture was receiving considerable pre-release fanfare and financial backing in the USA from United Artists and Eon Productions.

"I licensed rights to some novellas I wrote to my English publishers," Spillane said, "so they could make books out of 'em." He returned from his publisher, Corgi, with his trench-coat pockets "stuffed full of pound notes." Colorama had "stranded" the production in the UK and Spillane "had to pay their bills for them."

"We paid for the movie, we paid for all our expenses," the writer remembered, including the bill at the staid Rembrandt Hotel. He'd never intended the novellas to be collected, but allowing Corgi to do so had bailed out the production; the books were later published in the USA as well, in slightly different form.

"It was nice to be able to do that," Spillane said, "without having to get tied up in the mechanics of Hollywood thinking."

Ironically, this was the short fiction he had written largely to keep his hand in during the years when his contract with Victor Saville had discouraged him from writing any new novels. That these novellas came to underwrite Mickey Spillane's own Mike Hammer film was sweet—and necessary—revenge.

Spillane and Fellows were frustrated by the slower pace of British filmmaking. The unions required teatime at ten o'clock in the morning and three o'clock in the afternoon. Twenty minutes here, twenty minutes there, had Fellane Productions bleeding money they did not have.

Spillane called the crew together and asked them, "Why do you guys have to interrupt us with this teatime business?"

"Oh, sir, that's in our contract," a chosen union representative responded. "We always have our teatime, you know."

"Why don't you have teatime all day? You know, you don't have to do it at just ten and three."

"Oh, all day, sir?"

"Yeah. We'll have tea carts here and you can have it all day long and all the cookies you can eat."

Having made this decision on his own, Spillane explained to Fellows it would cost only an extra fifty or hundred dollars a day to bring tea carts and pastries in that the crew could partake of any time. Fellows thought this was a great idea. And beer was brought in at wrap each day, as well.

When a shoulder holster for Hammer's .45 couldn't be located in London, Spillane sent his stuntman back to the states to bring one over to the UK, as well as a whip for Mickey's amusement.

"Boy," Spillane said, remembering, "it was a beautiful whip—you could crack it like a son of a gun."

But the items had trouble making it through Customs—they suspected the American bringing in such things must be up to no good. Finally, Fellows and Spillane let it be known they needed both the man and the props in a movie being made. Customs relented.

At the hotel, the elderly woman across the hall complained about noise in the evening, mistaking Mickey's whipcracks for gunshots. She was moved to the suite below, where she heard the footsteps of actors rehearsing in the evening and told the front desk that the American above had a horse in his room. She was moved to the top floor.

Back at the Borehamwood studio, Mickey was having a ball working with Shirley Eaton, who played the rather obvious femme fatale, Laura Knapp. She performed many of her scenes in a succession of what one reviewer called "onion-skin" bikinis. For Spillane, however, one fully clothed scene was particularly memorable.

Shirley Eaton recalled it with a smile. "I walk down the stairs, typical love scene of those days really," she said in 1998. "Titillating without being, you know . . . [I'm] in a black negligee, and he's on the sofa. . . ."

She joins her co-star and they begin to kiss, and to recline, in each other's arms.

Spillane said, "As we're getting together on the couch, there's no world out there, just Shirley and me, the camera's comin' closer and closer. Now, when you say 'Cut' on a set, there's instant pandemonium. And everybody gets up, and rushes, runnin' around. The director says, 'Cut!' And nobody moves. He says 'Cut,' and nobody moves. And this little voice way in the background says, 'Throw cold water on 'em!'"

Laughing with the memory, Eaton said, "It was really fascinating to be working with a writer, as he likes me to call him, not an author, and playing his own leading man, and not an actor. Anyway, he was terrific, he was absolutely terrific."

The script was scrupulously faithful to the novel, but one new scene had been had added, involving a tough guy with an ice pick in a bar.

"That was based on something that really happened," Spillane recalled. He had told Roy Rowland about the incident and the director insisted on putting it in the film.

Asked to share the true story behind the scene, Spillane complied:

> *Well, I had to meet a guy on 8th Avenue in New York City. This is a tough area. You get all the prostitutes and rough stuff down that way. And I had to meet this guy, he's a reporter, I was gonna meet him in a saloon. And he'd picked out the place.*
>
> *Now I went in there, I had my Mike Hammer clothes on—you know the black suit and the hat and all that stuff. I didn't have a gun on me. But in my pocket I had a clip of .45s. My gun was in the car that I had parked. So I went in there and I got right on the end of the bar and ordered a beer. And the bartender looked at me very funny.*
>
> *And I looked at the guys in the bar and, boy, they started doin' these things they do in the movies . . . somebody comes in, there's going to be a shoot-out, everybody starts moving chairs over—and there's one guy at the bar there and he was a Spanish lookin' guy, and he had a funny look on him. And I looked at his hands, and he's got an ice pick.*
>
> *Now this goes on a little bit and everything got very quiet. And the bartender moves away from me. And the guy's there and he sticks the ice pick in the bar and he pulls it back and the handle comes off and the pick stays in the bar. Now I know about this trick—what they do, they can stick you with that ice pick, meanwhile their prints are still on there and in the meantime you die of loss of blood, internal bleeding is what you die of. And the doctors don't even know you're stuck.*

So he's talkin' to me now and I could see that something's goin' on down there and the next thing is he's going to approach me. And he's gonna either rob me, he's gonna stick me, or something. . . . In the meantime, my heart's going boom boom boom boom boom. *So I'm fairly calm, I don't want my hand to shake like this. This is a deadly situation. These guys are down there all lookin' at what's happenin'.*

So, I reach in my side pocket and say, 'I just happen to have somethin' here to show you.' I had this .45 clip in my pocket. So I took it out and put it on the bar top, and I flipped that top bullet out with my thumb. Now that's a spring-loaded clip. And it went ping.

The bullet shot about ten feet down the bar and stopped right in front of that guy. Now the sound it made running along the bar was zzzzzzzzzzz. *It stopped right there, just like I had a wire on it. And he's lookin' at that, and everybody saw the bullet go down there, everybody heard that. And I could see this guy lookin' at that bullet.*

Now I have to top this off. I can't just let him look at it. I had to say something so terrible, I scared the dickens out of myself. I looked down there and he looked up at me and I said, 'Eat it.'

Now all these guys could think of was anybody who would have a clip in his hand had to have a gun that's got another clip in it. And anybody who would do a thing like that, will kill ya.

And I'm thinkin' to myself, jeesh, what kind of situation am I in? . . . I feel like my feet are tied up in that barstool, I can't get to that door that fast, and before I could even think my way out of this thing, the guy picked the thing up and looked at it—and swallowed the damn bullet.

And then he ran out the door. And I see all of these heads lookin' this way. They didn't know what to do. So I finished my beer, put my clip in my pocket and looked around and I went out, I got outside and I said, 'Am I nuts?' I went out of my head. I'll never do that again, and I never have. Wild.

Replicated in the film, the sequence is among its most memorable.

The Girl Hunters is admittedly not the best Mike Hammer film—that is an honor that most would agree belongs easily to *Kiss Me Deadly*. But it stands up well next to Harry Essex's *I, the Jury*, and marks the only time the Hammer of the novels makes the trip to the screen without compromise.

The plot is almost willfully absurd—"derivative drivel," the *Newsweek* film reviewer called it, while confessing that "if one checks his brains at the popcorn counter, *The Girl Hunters* is outrageous good fun." Its meager budget does the film no favors, and the pop-cultural ground had certainly shifted under Spillane's feet—can it only be three years since Darren McGavin so credibly walked Manhattan's streets—and the Republic studio soundstages—as a rumpled, noirish Mike Hammer?

Adding insult to injury, Hammer's film comeback would see its greatest American success as a re-release two years past its June 1963 debut, after Shirley Eaton had become the "golden girl" of *Goldfinger* (1964). Paired with *Dr. No*'s Ursula Andress in *Nightmare in the Sun* (1965), *The Girl Hunters* played drive-ins as part of a "Bond girl" double feature. Eaton's presence in *The Girl Hunters* is a sad irony indicating the passing of the popular-culture torch from Hammer to Bond. That the film is a British co-production rubs salt in the wound.

Adding to the illusion of an American-made film are Lloyd Nolan as Federal Agent Arthur Rickerby and (Canadian) Scott Peters as Captain Pat Chambers of Homicide. Nolan had played another popular private eye, Mike Shayne, in a series of Twentieth Century Fox films in the 1940s, while Peters—a friend of Spillane's—was an experienced TV and B-movie actor. A few distracting English accents—notably Eaton's—do intrude; but even with all the B-unit location work, Spillane's Manhattan remains an imaginary one.

Still, the second-unit material proves helpful in setting the scene, even if redundant shots of Hammer walking New York streets, going in and out of buildings, and getting in and out of cabs (and his trench coat), flirt with tedium.

The film follows the novel like Scripture: Mike Hammer is found in the gutter, where he's spent much of his time these past seven years since

Velda's disappearance. He's sent for by Chambers, now filled with hatred for his old "buddy," convinced Mike's negligence caused Velda's death. Chambers, it seems, had been in love with her too. But a badly wounded FBI informant will talk only to Hammer, which Chambers reluctantly allows. Velda is alive, the dying man says, but she's in hiding somewhere in or near New York; and a Russian assassin—the Dragon—is hunting her.

That Spillane transforms quickly from bedraggled derelict into trench-coat-wearing, porkpie-hatted Mike Hammer is not exactly believable, yet it's great fun to see. Mike takes enough time before leaving the hospital to flirt with a curvaceous nurse and make a pact with spook Rickerby, agreeing not to kill the Dragon—the fed wants to watch the assassin die in the electric chair. Hammer goes on his own hunt, running down leads, stumbling onto corpses, dodging a few bullets, and getting sapped (it's a private-eye tradition). Though finding the beloved Velda is his crusade, he allows himself to be seduced by Eaton's Laura Knapp, the widow of a powerful US senator murdered in a home invasion.

Between lively scenes, the film is slowed by Mike gabbing with various middle-aged men, getting puzzle pieces in a manner acceptable in a novel but less so in a film. Hy Gardner is a key exposition carrier, surprisingly stilted and uncomfortable on camera for someone who once had his own TV show.

Hammer's climactic fight scene is a wild, protracted, harrowing cross between *The Perils of Pauline* and a Sam Peckinpah film. A stuntman cleverly doubles Spillane a few times, but mostly the screen-writing star seems to be giving and receiving the brutality himself. The most shocking on-screen moment has Hammer—after resisting the urge to kill his now unconscious foe with an axe—nailing the Russian assassin's hand to the floor . . . after all, he has promised Rickerby to spare the Commie for a ride on Old Sparky, and a promise is a promise.

The most shocking off-screen moment is saved for last—a genuine Spillane "socko" finish. It's the only denouement in a Mike Hammer film that accurately translates to the screen the kind of the sexy, violent, sudden ending that typifies the novels. As a shotgun roars off-camera, Hammer winces at the sight of Laura accidentally blowing her pretty head off trying to kill him.

Yet this is a Mike Hammer who draws his .45 while never shooting anybody—though the potent image of tough-guy Hammer hammering the Dragon's hand to the barn floor makes the point. Spillane relished sharing how the script girl got sick on set during the filming of that scene (the namby-pamby British version substitutes footage of Hammer hammering a clamp around the Dragon's wrist).

Hammer stumbling over gruesome corpses and everybody going on about what a badass he is, or at least used to be, works well enough. But *The Girl Hunters*, however definitive a transfer of Spillane's vision of Hammer to the screen, cannot touch *Kiss Me Deadly*'s willful misrepresentation of the writer's intent, which nonetheless nails the sex, violence, and surrealistic atmosphere of the early Hammer novels.

The Girl Hunters screenplay is a competently crafted if overliteral translation of the novel, despite its unfortunate abundance of expository scenes. (At a 1981 screening, Spillane said he would like to see the film trimmed by ten or fifteen minutes—of course, he also wanted it colorized.) The script avoids the pitfall of overdoing novelistic first-person voice-over—so common in private-eye movies—by using narration only when Mike is musing about the missing Velda or contemplating impending violence.

Rowland's direction is serviceable, but—possibly in an effort to seem less dated—noir trappings are minimal, limited to neons flickering in Hammer's office window, a gritty gin mill, the occasional dark alley. Nicely composed Cinemascope images avoid a TV feel, but somehow there's a British sense to the interiors, and a general lack of the visual panache found in Saville's *I, the Jury*, *The Long Wait*, and *Kiss Me Deadly*.

Spillane claimed to have played some of the solos in the effective if repetitive Philip Green score, having insisted on a trumpet theme for Hammer, not the sublime sax of Waxman's *I, the Jury*, although the McGavin series had a similar theme employing a trumpet as well. The various Stacy Keach TV movies and series of the 1980s and '90s would memorably return to sax for Earle Hagen's "Harlem Nocturne."

In the most outrageous storytelling device of *The Girl Hunters*—movie and novel alike—the "girl" Hammer hunts is never on-screen. A photo with its head torn off leaves the lovely rest of her for the imagination to conjure. The girl hunt ends with the detective heading off to fetch his beloved from hiding.

The Girl Hunters is no *Kiss Me Deadly*—there is only one of those—but it brings its source novel alive with rare fidelity. The savage final fight, the glow of bikini beauty Shirley Eaton, the snappy dialogue right off the page, combine with Spillane's impressive performance to slap a Hammer novel onto the screen in all its pulpy glory.

And Spillane is impressive, all right, commanding every scene with a soft voice and hard eyes, as comfortable on-screen as Robert Mitchum or Lawrence Tierney. In every scene, virtually every frame, he controls the proceedings—even when paired with pros like Lloyd Nolan and Shirley Eaton.

Dr. No and *The Girl Hunters* were released in America just over a month apart in 1963—May 8 and June 12, respectively. They were often reviewed together and *The Girl Hunters*—amusingly, considering Spillane's track record with book reviewers—was at least as warmly received.

A series of Spillane-as-Hammer films was planned to follow *The Girl Hunters*—Spillane wrote *The Snake* with that in mind—but the film's tepid initial release didn't make that possible. And its *Goldfinger*-inspired double-feature run in 1965 wasn't anything but a desperate cash grab.

Private eyes like Mike Hammer were relics of the 1940s and 1950s by that point, made irrelevant by the dazzling gadgets and sophisticated anti-heroics of James Bond—the British answer to Mike Hammer.

TOP: Spillane met his second wife, actress Sherri Malinou, in 1963, at a photo shoot for an image used on *The Girl Hunters* paperback. BOTTOM: Christopher George and Yvette Mimieux in the film version (1970) of Spillane's 1967 novel, *The Delta Factor.* Sherri co-starred.

CHAPTER NINETEEN

POSING

Feature writers for magazines and newspapers, interviewing Mickey Spillane, often wrote their pieces in tongue-in-cheek imitation of his style, or at least of generic hard-boiled prose. This ploy usually resulted only in embarrassment, serving to demonstrate that what Spillane and his fellow "tough guy" fiction writers did wasn't so easy to duplicate or even satirize.

In 1963, Lyn Tornabene, in her regular "Lunch Date With" feature in *Cosmopolitan*, did better than many: "I noticed the dame with [Spillane]: small, lithe, in a red dress, wide-set saucer eyes, pink cheeks. Lolita hair spilled onto her shoulders like melted butter."

Spillane made the introductions. "Hi. I'm Mickey. Meet Sherri. She's Lolita, I'm Humbert Humbert."

The pretty young woman in red blushed.

At lunch in the Mermaid Room of the Park Sheraton, Spillane—sitting next to his protégé—told the journalist that the hotel was where he usually stayed in Manhattan.

"You should have been here last week," he told her. "We staged a brawl."

A pal named Dusty—his stuntman on *The Girl Hunters*—had flipped backward out of a chair and the writer had chased him out of the elegant cocktail lounge.

"Sometimes Sherri and I sit at the bar," he said, more scamp than tough guy, "and Dusty comes in with his whip."

Seemed the whip had made the trip back to the States.

"Sherri lights a cigarette and he snaps it out of her hand." Mickey glanced at Sherri, who giggled. "Everybody jumps, but we just sit there."

Spillane's lunch companion was Sherri Malinou, then appearing off-Broadway in the musical *Riverbend*, in which she'd won excellent reviews in an ingenue role. Earlier that year, Spillane had set up a photo shoot in Manhattan to create a back-cover shot of himself as Hammer with a model who could represent Shirley Eaton on the paperback edition of *The Girl Hunters*. Because the model's face would not be shown, only beautiful legs and flowing blonde hair were required.

The writer wanted to put together a good backlog of promotional photos of himself as his detective, accompanied by a typically sexy Spillane "doll." The session would last at least an hour and involve considerable dramatics.

"The first time I met Mickey," Sherri told *People* magazine in 1976, "I'd never heard of him. I thought he was a gangster."

Sherri came from "a very normal, middle-class family. My father was a doctor. I had led a very sheltered life."

The photo shoot came as a surprise and perhaps a rude awakening. Sherri (formerly Selma) Malinou had gone from high school to modeling, then auditioning for musicals like *All American* and *Riverbend*. Now Spillane was staging "very violent" scenes, "knocking me around and pulling my hair."

The photo session extended to three hours and moved from one Mike Hammer trademark, violence, into another, sex. The strangers wound up necking for the camera. Then the man in his midforties took the young woman of twenty-one to dinner and informed her he intended to marry her, presenting her with his high school ring and saying, "We're engaged."

Spillane never disputed this story, however cooked up for publicity it might sound. He liked to say he ordered up a "leggy blonde" for a photo shoot and forgot to send her back. Quickly he got caught up in the young singer's career. At the luncheon with *Cosmo*'s Tornabene, music arranger Lew Douglas and a record executive (both in Spillane's employ) joined the little party. The mystery writer was gearing up to launch his own record label and had composed a song for *The Green Woman*, the film set to follow *The Snake* into production.

"Wouldn't it be something," Mickey mused, "if my first song became a hit." (It didn't.)

With Sherri off to do an interview, Tornabene accompanied Spillane to a ballroom in the hotel to meet Shirley Eaton, in town promoting the impending release of *The Girl Hunters*. Eaton, the journalist reported, also had "hair that spills onto her shoulders like melted butter."

The buoyant Spillane was riding high on his movie, getting unexpected rave reviews for his acting and renewed attention from the press. He could hardly guess the disappointment ahead, with *The Girl Hunters* getting barely seen. He and Bob Fellows were launching Vassar Records (address: Newburgh, New York) as a label for Sherri Malinou. Its first release—"Follow My Tear Drops" backed with "Besame Mucho"—bore a picture sleeve announcing the artist as "The New 'Spillane Dame,'" although the image Sherri projects on a beach in pedal pushers and a loose top is very fresh and innocent.

Her new mentor took care of the liner notes himself.

"Great things can happen by accident," Spillane wrote. "When Sherri Malinou posed for the back-cover photo of my latest book *The Girl Hunters*, I discovered not only a beautiful model, but one of the greatest voices I ever heard. Now, on top of recording single records and albums for Vassar Records, she'll be featured in my Mike Hammer motion pictures produced by Fellane Productions."

The rather lengthy back-cover notes continued with Spillane charting Malinou's show-business career thus far—dancing on the vaudeville stage since age five, singing on the *Bell Telephone Hour*, *Oldsmobile Show*, *All American* on Broadway, *Riverbend* off. He praised her training and talent, and the "incredible range and calibre" of her voice, "destined to thrill music lovers of all ages."

The single record sank like a stone, likely for the same reason *The Girl Hunters* disappointed at the box office—a lack of decent distribution. But Spillane's enthusiasm for his blonde protégé did not falter. Soon they were sharing an East Fifty-Seventh Street penthouse apartment with a huge terrace.

"I was a virgin when I met Mickey," she told Lillian Roxon at *Esquire* in August 1972. She stayed a virgin for the first year they were together. He refused to "de-virginize her," she said, until they were wed.

"I would have married him right away," she said. "He wanted to, but I was young and kind of liked the idea of living in sin. . . . Mickey told people I was a houseguest."

In November of 1964—having divorced Mary Ann two years before—Mickey married Sherri in Malibu, California.

As half of a celebrity couple, and with her husband's support, Sherri Spillane began a successful run on the musical comedy circuit and in nightclubs. She returned briefly to off-Broadway in *Look Where I'm At!* but made a larger mark with star turns in classic musicals.

She was top billed in *Oklahoma!* and *South Pacific* at the Union Plaza Hotel in Las Vegas, and appeared in civic light-opera productions of *The Wizard of Oz*, *The King and I*, *Bye Bye Birdie*, *Little Me*, *A Funny Thing Happened to Me on the Way to the Forum*, and *Pal Joey* at theaters in Atlantic City, Malibu, Honolulu, Phoenix, Dallas, and more.

Spillane put together a nightclub act for his young wife, called *Mickey Spillane's Noveltease*—"5 ORIGINAL ACTS WITH SHERRI SPILLANE AND COMPANY." With a pop-art poster by old Funnies, Inc., pal Ray Gill, promotional materials announced an "original concept by Mickey Spillane, lavishly staged with productions numbers and solo features from comic book fantasy to ultra sensuality." Promised was "a wild splash of colorful action and original music by Howard Danzinger and Joe Tremaine," two show-business pros.

Whether this extravaganza came to pass or not, Sherri made numerous nitery appearances in Dallas, Miami, New York, and Toronto, among others. Her brassy cabaret "Spillane doll" persona seemed at odds with the sweet ingenue of her musical roles—Laurie in *Oklahoma!*, Nellie in *South Pacific*, even Dorothy in *The Wizard of Oz*.

Perhaps these approaches clashed in a way that prevented her from greater success—certainly it was not for want of effort from her husband or herself. They appeared together on game and panel shows (*The Merv Griffin Show*, *Tattletales*) and she landed a few TV acting roles (*The F.B.I.*, *Policewoman*, *Hello Larry*).

The couple soon developed what *People* called "Their Unusual Stay-Apart Marriage," and *Esquire* termed "a system of 'his' and 'hers' residences." *His* was his house in Murrells Inlet, where Sherri spent as little time as possible. *Hers* was the New York penthouse. When they were together in the latter, his schedule ruled—bedtime after the eleven P.M. news, no travel beyond a three-block radius of their pad. When Spillane was away in South Carolina, his wife was free "to zip all over the city at any hour of the day or night."

Sherri could take in the shows and go to parties with her theater crowd cronies. She and Mickey traveled in "completely different" circles, with the exception of media types like Hy Gardner and his wife, Marilyn, and comedian Joey Adams and his wife, Cindy. Even in that case, her husband seemed to have "no friends under forty." In her nightclub act, she referred to her husband as "the best dressed man of 1941" and kidded his "Rudi of Poland" buzz cut.

Throughout, the couple relentlessly worked at image promotion, also his and hers. Each was a false if fun extension of what the public expected of them: Mickey "the living embodiment" of Mike Hammer and Sherri "a walking reminder" of the fantasy "dames" of her husband's fiction.

In England in 1967—in a photo spread in the inelegantly dubbed *Tit-bits* tabloid—Mickey and his doll, accompanied by his Corgi editor Pat Newman, staged a corny hunt for Jack the Ripper at some of the original murder sites, for a proposed novel Spillane had no intention of writing. Returning to the UK—and the same tabloid—for more promotion in 1973, Sherri posed in a macramé bikini—looking not at all like an ingenue—with Spillane in hat and black suit, looking every titbit of Mike Hammer. This article claimed—not a quote—that Spillane had in the war shot down a Messerschmitt 109, an unlikely event in Greenwood, Mississippi.

Whether Spillane had made that claim himself is unknown, but no other example of such outright lying bravado had been recorded—just the opposite. Even in the tabloid article, when he says he took training from RAF pilots, he is clear that happened stateside.

But during his marriage to Sherri, particularly on his London junkets, he became increasingly boastful and belligerent, taking a stridently macho stance very unlike the private man.

Men Only, a slickly sleazy publication from the notorious Paul Raymond, finds Spillane saying things like, "put two sex maniacs, one male, one female, in a room together—and they're the happiest people in the world."

He was clearly catering both to the magazine's "skin mag" audience and the changing, sexually liberated times.

"If you look at any sexual act," he tells interviewer Angela Carter, "it's the male that's the aggressor. Some animals get very aggressive. Did you ever see two chickens going at it?"

Sherri, at his side through all this, says little. Early on, Carter asks Spillane if Sherri is his "dream girl" and he replies, "Most of the time. When I leave her alone in the kitchen, she's not, because the only thing she can cook is the kitchen. She set it on fire three times."

Here Sherri speaks in her own defense: "You knew that before you married me."

He is similarly frank and outrageously so in a March 1974 *Gallery* interview with Earl Doud. At his most braggadocious, Mickey says he reads one to four books a day; wrote five novels in one year and released them a year at a time; says he can write a book in two weeks (he's slowing down); and confirms that Velda and Mike got "laid" in *The Snake*.

Love Story "stinks," he says, but he likes *Jonathan Livingston Seagull* (Sherri doesn't). Rex Stout is good but dated. Donald Hamilton's Matt Helm books get high marks and of course so does Fredric Brown. He writes the Tiger Mann books (actually he had stopped at this point) because so many readers "hate radicals," which is his word for "liberals."

For once, Mickey's in-Hammer-character ravings go cruelly too far when he contemptuously says of "the poor starving people": "Let them die—then you won't have to feed them anymore." For a guy who hated Dickens, he could paraphrase Ebenezer Scrooge to a tee.

While Spillane had a deep and abiding contempt for Communism—if a fairly simplistic grasp of it—he was known by friends to be the biggest soft touch and most compassionate human they'd ever known. He was often seen settling up at a diner for the tab he was running for guys down on their luck.

"He reached for every check," a friend said, "and gave you a Mike Hammer glare if you tried to beat him to it."

Interviewer Doud sensed that softer side of his irascible subject, writing, "Mickey Spillane is folks. A regular guy. Her loves to quote from the Bible.

He's at home in the '21' Club or Flannigan's bar—but he'd rather drink with you in Flannigan's."

Mickey Spillane and Bob Fellows—despite the producer suffering health problems—had not given up on making movies together, particularly with Sherri eager to up her Hollywood game. They made a deal with a group of Tennessee financiers to establish a motion-picture producing company: "Spillane-Fellows."

Veteran director Tay Garnett—his impressive résumé including both film (*The Postman Always Rings Twice*, 1946) and TV (*The Untouchables*, 1959)—was brought on board by his old friend Fellows. First up would be Mickey's recent novel, *The Delta Factor*.

In 1967, with much fanfare, a new Spillane hero was introduced—Morgan the Raider. As the writer's "answer" to James Bond, Tiger Mann had been somewhat disappointing, selling well but—in an era glutted with spy films—untapped by Hollywood. *The Delta Factor*, Spillane's second attempt to work in the espionage/thriller genre, was extremely well received—Anthony Boucher calling Morgan "Spillane's best creation to date."

Morgan has no first name, and—like Tiger Mann—was once shot by the woman he loved. Named for real-life pirate Sir Henry Morgan, the *Delta Factor*'s protagonist is a swashbuckling throwback to Spillane's boyhood favorites.

A falsely imprisoned Morgan is enlisted to rescue scientist Victor Sable from the Rose Castle, a Caribbean island prison. Promised a reduced prison sentence if he succeeds, he is dropped into the country as a man on the run with no passport; but he also has a new wife and sufficient funds to pay off the corrupt island dictator. His "bride" is government agent Kimberly Stacy, their cover "marriage" not to be consummated.

The rescue of Sable is secondary to Morgan's growing relationship with Kimberly. After rescuing Sable from the Rose Castle, Morgan faces his war buddy, Sal Dekker, who now hates him. Somehow *I, the Jury*'s loyal Jack Williams has become the demented Dekker, his face as disfigured by fire as the torso of the false Lily Carver, and he blames Morgan.

Not anxious to return to prison before clearing himself, Morgan makes his choice: he will jump from the rescue plane and meet Kim later. This is a Spillane hero who does not carry the rage and fire of vengeance of Mike Hammer or even Tiger Mann; but he's every bit as tough, clever, and courageous.

In his autobiography, *Light Your Torches and Pull Up Your Tights*, Tay Garnett writes, "Mickey Spillane and I worked together at his home in South Carolina, turning out a shooting script in about eight weeks." They fashioned a "taut, cops-and-robbers screenplay" with a third-act high-speed car chase over winding mountain roads.

Preproduction started well. Garnett and an associate flew to Nashville and quickly arranged studio space. They cast local talent in secondary roles, then scouted locations for the Rose Castle, coming up with an ideal fortress in Puerto Rico's Morro Castle.

Garnett reported back to Bob Fellows in California, but had to hide his alarm—Fellows looked deathly ill. The director did his best to compensate for his old friend, "doing whatever needed doing," including finding the two leads—Christopher George, who had starred in ABC-TV's *Rat Patrol* (1966), and Yvette Mimieux, the sexy waif from *The Time Machine* (1960).

Then Bob Fellows died of a heart attack.

"I have said many times," Garnett said, "that *The Delta Factor* should have been buried with Bob."

Spillane's grief was heightened by the responsibility of essentially producing the picture himself. Both he and Garnett felt they had lost their best friend in the film business. But *The Delta Factor* limped, or perhaps lurched, into production.

The Puerto Rican mountain range became the real villain of the piece. Garnett needed point of view "vertigo" shots, requiring the cameraman to ride in the stunt car's back seat. The director was in front with stuntman/driver, Roger Creed. The Volkswagen had been reinforced with a roll bar, and its engine "beefed up to equal a Porsche's performance."

The first three hairpin turns proved little problem, just some minor spinning of tires and sliding of wheels. But on the fourth curve, overlooking a forty-five–foot drop over the canyon into the rain forest, the road got spongy and just "seemed to ooze away."

A witness saw the car go end over end, several times, slamming into rock, revolving in space. . . .

The cameraman was thrown clear, the driver, too, though needing forty stitches. Four crew members with mountain-rescue training conveyed the director by stretcher, which a truck pulled up the cliff with a pair of ropes.

The film was completed back in Nashville, Garnett directing from a wheelchair, his right arm in a sling.

The Delta Factor is a moderately entertaining B-movie. Charismatic George makes a strong Morgan, performing with energy and humor. Mimieux as CIA agent Kim Stacy conveys intelligence and provides eye candy in an array of bikinis and lingerie. The climactic rescue of a political prisoner from an "impregnable" castle/prison brings the novel alive, but inconsistent lighting throughout makes for garish visuals and a TV-movie feel.

"The first cut was so bad," Spillane recalled in 1998, "I [had to do] a lot of re-editing. . . . I took out most of the walking shots and got 'em where they were going. We had to do these things to make any sense out of the picture."

Spillane had helped out with editing before. John Wayne and Bob Fellows had taken him into a screening room where William Wellman was having trouble with a scene. Spillane whispered to his friends that he knew what the problem was and Fellows yelled to Wild Bill, "I got a guy here who knows what is wrong."

Mickey suggested the director reverse two shots.

Wellman considered that and said, "Doggoneit, he's right." The film was probably *Lafayette Escadrille* (1958).

On *The Delta Factor,* Spillane took no credit other than the title's possessive "Mickey Spillane's," either for the source novel or the script he co-wrote. Screenwriter Spillane does producer Spillane no favors trying to stay true to the novel when the budget advises otherwise, as when a hurricane threatening the island stays mostly off-screen. The film's meager budget and its tragic production circumstances negated any possibility for a wide-ranging, exotic-locale Spillane film to truly rival James Bond.

Sherri Spillane takes on a major supporting role and a nightclub scene sequence, all so poorly shot, directed, costumed, and choreographed, the talented performer is ill-served.

The failure of the film on both artistic and commercial levels soured Spillane on Morgan the Raider, despite the warm reception reviewers and readers had given the character. The already-announced second Morgan novel, *The Consummata*, would not see publication until 2011 (completed by MAC).

This time Spillane's storytelling skills, including his editing acumen, weren't enough. He would never again get involved in film production.

While the Mike Hammer and Tiger Mann novels of the 1960s had sold over a million copies each, with the solo Morgan the Raider adventure keeping pace, Spillane witnessed an encroachment upon his all-time bestselling domination of doorstop blockbusters from the likes of Harold Robbins and Jacqueline Susann. This competition inspired him to concoct a bigger, more expansive work that would nonetheless be an authentic Mickey Spillane novel.

The Erection Set (1972) is Spillane's modern take on a swashbuckling adventure novel, specifically an updating of *The Count of Monte Cristo* by Dumas. Dogeron Kelly returns to New York after twenty years in Europe to collect a $10,000 inheritance left by his grandfather, Cameron Barrin. Dog hardly needs the money—he's got a suitcase with $2.5 million in it—but he also has a mysterious past and a rascally sense of humor. Said to be illegitimate, he's fighting it out with five siblings over control of Barrin Industries.

Dog connects with Rose Porter, a high-class call girl close to his Air Force buddy Lee Shay. But the real love he meets is businesswoman Sharon Cass, a self-professed proud virgin of thirty-two. Spillane plies his target audience with the sexually explicit scenes that the critics falsely accused him of in the 1950s.

Dog and Lee have dinner in Oliver's Lodge—named for a real restaurant in Murrells Inlet—and Kelly refers to his three-year ordeal by invoking the second Hammer novel: "And whom the gods would destroy they first make mad." Dog tells Sharon he's just a guy who wants to come home.

The Erection Set is a summation of Spillane's body of work, more *Fountainhead* than *Valley of the Dolls*—sexually charged beautiful women, real cops and fake cops, spies, World War II fighter pilots, the drug cartel, the perfidious sycophants of Hollywood and media, all topped off by a world-changing invention. While he uses his signature first person, he boldly breaks the rules with a third-person chapter. The ending is among Spillane's best, combining the dispatching of evil with the staccato rhythms of long-anticipated consummation.

After reading the typescript of *The Erection Set*, Sherri Spillane told her husband she wanted to be naked on the cover.

Lillian Roxon at *Esquire* recorded Mickey responding "gruffly" yet assenting. He didn't think he'd been getting good-looking enough models on his book covers lately anyway.

"So there she is," Roxon wrote, "stripped for action with a gun in her hand and her legs invitingly if modestly parted, decorating a book" with her extended leg riding up the spine.

Spillane's greatest tribute to his wife was also his most outrageous marketing stunt. The book flew up the bestseller lists, but now it was time to take Mario Puzo on.

Unlike any previous Spillane novel, *The Last Cop Out* (1973) is written in third person, with shifting points of view. Gillian Burke, a good cop who's been framed, is out to settle a score with the mob. He's brought back in to the department to deal with an assassin (or group thereof) executing top mobsters; Gill is meant to help curtail the intermob bloodshed before it costs too many innocent lives. The novel utilizes techniques and points of view from Spillane's pulp-novella interlude, tougher and more graphic than his early work in its mix of sex and violence with a touch of genuine sentiment. The revenge killing at the end of the novel is unforgettable.

For this second assault on the bestseller market of the 1970s, Sherri—who had bared her breasts on a book cover, a first in American publishing—now turned her backside to the camera. As he had with *The Erection Set*, Spillane supervised the closed set. The result was another startling, effective, memorable cover, emphasizing Mickey Spillane's uncanny ability to shock. Mickey and Sherri had done it again.

The real surprise ending, however, was that the marriage was just about over.

TOP: In 1976, Mickey made a splash with Lee Meredith as the "Doll" in his long-running series of Lite Beer commercials, spoofing his (and Hammer's) image. BOTTOM LEFT: Kevin Dobson appeared as Hammer in a well-reviewed TV movie, *Margin for Murder* (1981), which did not lead to a series. BOTTOM RIGHT: Armand Assante starred as Mike in a sexy, violent film whose troubled production and distribution woes sank a big-screen Hammer comeback (1982).

CHAPTER TWENTY

HAMMER TIME

A melancholy sax wails in the night as the camera presents a neon-swept street, then finds Mickey Spillane—in full trench-coat regalia—leaning against a lamppost, adjusting the brim of his black-banded, money-green hat.

"I started drinkin' Lite Beer from Miller a couple of years ago," he tells us. "I *started* drinkin' it because I heard it was less filling."

The camera follows his leisurely sidewalk stroll.

"But you know something?" Mickey asks rhetorically. "I kept *on* drinkin' it because it tastes so great."

Mickey lands in front of a bar, its window wearing a Miller Lite neon, happy customers glimpsed in the smoky world within.

"Now I don't care what you guys like about it," he threatens amiably, "as long as you *like* it."

A tall, curvaceous blonde materializes and says breathily, "Hello, Mickey. Got a Lite?"

"Sure, doll," he says and ushers her inside. "What's a nice girl like you doin' in a commercial like this?"

It's a pickup job by the blonde, probably just a one-night stand—a one-night stand that will last eighteen years.

Mickey Spillane's new role as a spokesman for Lite Beer—or "salesman" as he always put it—began with a one-shot spot in 1974 that quickly led to more. And it came along at a good time—he'd been working hard for over a decade, writing book after book and promoting his young wife's showbiz career. Being hired to sell Miller Lite would sell his own product, as well—he'd be gently spoofing his (and Mike Hammer's) persona while keeping himself and his character in the public eye without having to break a sweat at the typewriter.

And he would be performing again, without the time and rigor required of starring in a film—not that anyone was asking.

Ad agency McCann Erickson developed the series of ads for Miller's offshoot brand Lite Beer in 1973. The spots were part of a wave of entertaining commercials transforming TV advertising—witness "That's a spicy meatball!" for Alka-Seltzer and "Where's the beef?" for Wendy's. This campaign was based around two opposing call-and-response groups chanting, "Less filling!" or "Tastes great!" Spillane made a rare non-sports personality—comedian Rodney Dangerfield another—among mostly retired sports figures . . . Ray Nitschke, Ben Davidson, Bubba Smith. *Advertising Age* would come to rate Miller Lite's campaign in its all-time top ten.

"We took Lite beer from Miller," Spillane proudly recalled, "from a beer that wasn't in existence and made the second-highest selling beer in the world."

Spillane appeared in solo and group commercials, perhaps most memorably the 1980 spot—so popular that a frame of it was used on Spillane paperback covers—called "To Be Continued."

In a dark office in the light of a single desk lamp,

Mickey Spillane
Famous Mystery Writer

pounds away with two fingers at his manual typewriter, pork-pie fedora in place, concentration mighty.

"Chapter Nine," Mickey narrates. "I kicked in the door and shouted, 'Freeze!' to the lone figure in the room. Even in the darkness I could see she was the most beautiful woman I ever met. Then I saw the Lite Beer from Miller."

"'It's got a third less calories than regular beer and it's less filling,' she whispered, 'but the best thing is it tastes so great.'"

Mickey pauses in his work. "Suddenly all of the pieces fell into place and I knew I'd come to the end of a long, long road."

He reaches for his bottle of Miller Lite to refill his glass but a bejeweled female hand reaches out and does it for him.

"She poured," Mickey says, smiling, pushing back his hat, "we drank." A wink from Mick. "To be continued. . . ."

A paperback on the desk was difficult to identify, but likely a Spillane title, possibly an edition of *The Last Cop Out*. If so, it would be the first and only time Sherri Spillane appeared in a Miller Lite spot.

There was a new Spillane "doll" in town, after all, and her name was Lee Meredith. The lovely actress who in a leopard bikini so memorably played Ulla in *The Producers* (1967) would be the only female in the regular Miller Lite repertory company. She would co-star with Mickey in all but a handful of his commercials and make public appearances with him as well.

Despite her ten years of being the Spillane doll, playing the role her husband had cultivated for her in nightclubs, newspapers, and magazines, and on TV, radio, and book covers, Sherri had not been cast as Mickey's Miller Lite co-star. Neither she nor he ever spoke in public about this slap in the face, almost certainly a decision in which her husband had no say. Nonetheless, it had to be a blow worse than any in Spillane's world since Charlotte took one in the tummy.

Around this time, Sherri Spillane moved to Hollywood. A few years back, their unusual his-and-hers marriage, him in South Carolina, her in New York, had been mistaken by columnist Earl Wilson for an actual separation.

Now, belatedly, they proved Wilson right.

◆

MAC: *The night before I met Mickey Spillane, I slept almost not at all.*

I'd been approached by the organizers of Bouchercon XII to be the liaison between Mickey and the convention, which was held at the Marc Plaza in Milwaukee ("Beer City Capers"). The convention organizers had approached Miller Brewing about bringing Spillane in as a special guest (at Miller's expense).

The Anthony Boucher Memorial World Mystery Convention is held in the autumn in a different city and is run by a different group of fan volunteers. In recent years, over two thousand of those interested in the crime fiction genre have attended—fans, authors, agents, booksellers, filmmakers, and publishers. Bouchercon is named, of course, for the New York Times *mystery reviewer who had excoriated Spillane in the 1950s, then declared him a pulp-fiction master in the 1960s.*

The irony of that wasn't lost on Spillane—who had somewhat reluctantly accepted, as some in the mystery fiction community had over the years led him to believe that he was something of a pariah among aficionados. Legend had it the Mystery Writers of America had banned him from the organization even though he never tried to join.

Mickey had been my favorite writer since I was thirteen, when I got caught up in the TV private-eye craze of the late 1950s, typified by Peter Gunn *and* 77 Sunset Strip. *Many of those shows had a basis in novels, so* The Thin Man *led me to Dashiell Hammett,* Philip Marlowe *to Raymond Chandler, and* Mickey Spillane's Mike Hammer *to . . .*

The first Spillane novel I read, One Lonely Night, *I purchased at age twelve by assuring the cashier I was sixteen. I had never read anything remotely like it and consumed the other Spillane titles ravenously. Researching Hammett and Chandler, I learned they were revered. But I was flabbergasted to find Mickey Spillane was roundly reviled.*

So I became a defender of the most popular American mystery writer of the twentieth century, starting with letters of complaint to reviewers who attacked him, composing pro-Spillane essays in junior high and high school English classes, and, from around age sixteen, sending my own private eye novels out to publishers who wisely rejected them.

At the University of Iowa, in the Writers Workshop, assigned to write (as part of my thesis) a paper on a major American author, I of course chose Spillane. This suicidal response to the assignment found me stopped in the hall by Seymour Krim, the instructor reviewing the papers. Uh oh. Then he thanked me—"If I have to read one more word about Hemingway or Fitzgerald, I'll scream." As I began having modest success with my own mystery fiction, I published articles and essays that praised Spillane's work. I became known in mystery circles as the "go-to" Spillane guy.

*Now, I had written countless fan letters to Mickey since I was in junior high. I never received a reply until finally in 1973, when my first two novels were published (*Bait Money *and* Blood Money*); I sent them to him and he wrote me a warm letter welcoming me to the business.*

My near-sleepless night came out of a fear of meeting my idol—getting kicked by a much-admired person's feet of clay can be painful. Despite that single warm letter from him, I kept thinking about tales I'd heard about Spillane—how someone had sent him first editions of the initial six Hammer novels for an autograph and he'd shot a bullet through them and returned them unsigned; that an interview going well blew up in Mike Hammer rage when Mickey was questioned about spending the war stateside. . . .

At the con, the organizers took me to Mickey's hotel room and knocked. Mickey answered, looking just like himself, and the con folks introduced themselves and then pointed to me and said, "Mickey, this is Max Collins," and Mickey grinned and said, "Oh, I know Max! We've been corresponding for years."

And I said, "That's right, Mickey—a hundred letters from me and one letter from you!"

He roared with laughter and we were immediate friends.

I interviewed him before the entire convention and we were at ease together and the packed room loved it—their excitement at seeing this living legend of mystery fiction was palpable. At one point he said that writing a novel was like sex—starting slowly and building up to the climax, then you're finished and wait a while before the next go-round. And I said, "But Mickey—ten years?" And the room erupted in laughter and Spillane's grin was endless.

Mickey signed books and chatted with each "customer." I was sitting next to him, signing my own stuff—I was surprised and moved that he considered me a peer.

One evening The Girl Hunters *was screened for the convention's several hundred attendees; the star beamed throughout and would yell a comment at the screen at times. A 1950s episode of* Mickey Spillane's Mike Hammer *was shown and at one point he shouted, "I didn't write that!" He conversed warmly with fans in the restaurant and bar, and discovering that, despite the many attacks on him over the years, he was beloved by mystery fans.*

◆

Jay Bernstein, Hollywood producer, flying to New York for business meetings, walked onto the plane and sitting there in the first-class cabin was Mickey Spillane—as the *Philadelphia Inquirer*'s Margaret Kirk described him, "all squat and crumpled up behind a newspaper, a bulldog of a man wearing a porkpie hat."

Memories flooded through Bernstein—reading *I, the Jury* as a young man "and thinking, this is really fun! This is hot stuff! This is sexy! . . . turning back page corners to mark the best parts." The producer had read every book this author ever wrote.

"I couldn't believe it," he recalled in 1998. "I thought it was a dream."

For Mickey, it was a nightmare. "I was coming home from California," he recalled in 1998, "sittin' there about to go to sleep and [this guy] said, 'She walked toward me, her hips waving a happy hello.'"

Spillane looked up at the smiling fan, hovering over the empty aisle seat, and didn't allow himself to smile. He was dog-tired after days in Los Angeles shooting commercials and signing autographs, hawking Miller Lite. He scowled over the newspaper at the intruder.

"And I think, oh, gee, I got another fan," Spillane remembered, "and he's gonna sit down here and talk to me all night when all I want to do is sleep."

Bernstein says, "'Women stuck to Mike Hammer like lint to a blue serge suit.'"

Not a line from any of the books—something from dust-jacket copy. Still, it was enough to make Mickey smile and nod toward the empty seat.

Bernstein, lugging a fancy mahogany briefcase, sat. Spillane took in that briefcase, an expensive item; this gent had money. The fellow passenger introduced himself.

Spillane recognized the name—Sherri had talked about Bernstein as "a big star maker." Before he became a manager and producer, Jay's public relations firm had represented Tony Bennett, Faye Dunaway, and Brooke Shields. He'd gone on to launch Farrah Fawcett and Suzanne Somers.

The two men chatted for a while. "He was talking nicely," Spillane recalled. "It wasn't that Hollywood crap you usually get."

Bernstein listened to Spillane's tale of woe on how Hollywood had, in his view, consistently messed up Mike Hammer. Sympathetic, Bernstein said if he had the rights, he would do it right—Hammer would have short hair, work in New York, and carry a .45-caliber pistol ("not some sissy .38").

"Okay," Spillane said, going for the surprise ending. "It's yours."

Bernstein could hardly believe it, until Spillane added, "If you screw up, I'll kill you."

"And before we got into New York," Mickey recalled, "I had sold him the rights for $1 to Mike Hammer."

On Thursday evening, October 15, 1981, *Mickey Spillane's Mike Hammer in "Margin for Murder"* aired on CBS-TV. Spillane scarcely involved himself in the production, its screenplay credited to Calvin Clements Jr. and Alex Lucas; but *I, the Jury* provided the obvious inspiration.

Kevin Dobson, second banana Crocker to Telly Savalas on the hit CBS series *Kojak*, appears as an updated Hammer—a Vietnam-vet private eye avenging the death of a fellow "grunt." Dobson split the difference between an amiable regular guy and a violent, seething avenger.

The early '80s TV approach manages no particular noir mood other than what New York locations naturally provide. Hoods and their capos are typical stereotypes, the action adequately staged, the sex and violence diluted; the pace drags and scenes with the victim's grieving mother are uncomfortably over the top.

After Hammer helps the cops collar the bad guys—not taking the personal vengeance he's promised—six endless minutes follow as Hammer plays cute with Velda. Puppies are involved. Such padding could not be more at odds with Spillane's signature sudden endings.

As originally scripted, *Margin for Murder*—originally titled *Death by a Dainty Hand*—went out of its way to make the late Joey De Fellita, disco bouncer, a real if flawed person, worthy of Hammer's revenge. The story included a gruesome murder weapon, a small, steel fist used to beat De Fellita to death, suggesting the killer was female.

The rapport between Charles Hallahan's Pat Chambers and Dobson's Hammer echoes the novels well. To a degree, so does Cindy Pickett's Velda, who is clearly in love with Mike; she even packs a little pistol. But Pickett—a waifish blonde with a pixie cut, reminiscent of Gaby Rodgers in *Kiss Me Deadly*—seems the opposite of Spillane's sultry, raven-haired Amazon.

Although its Hammer indeed wields a .45, *Margin for Murder* does not own up to Mike's anachronistic nature, nor does Dobson—in Spillane terms—wear the hat well. Not that anyone could—it's a feathered, sporty abomination as miscast as Velda. And sadly, the score is a collection of cop-show clichés from the great Nelson Riddle, leaning on *Shaft*-style wah-wah pedal and lifting the Ides of March rock hit "Vehicle," uncredited.

All these shortcomings do not entirely defeat *Margin for Murder*, which was nominated for a Mystery Writers of America "Edgar" as Best Television Feature, made film critic Judith Crist's list of the best TV movies of 1981, and beat out a World's Series play-off game in the ratings.

Dobson displayed a suitable grasp on the character—affable yet believably tough, if not the powerful TV presence of a Brian Keith, Darren McGavin, or Stacy Keach. As a "backdoor pilot," the telefilm suggests a watchable weekly series.

But none developed. Spillane must have suspected Jay Bernstein was a one-shot wonder. Making things worse, a renegade Mike Hammer production was in the works. Without Spillane's blessing or even knowledge, the Victor Saville estate had licensed a remake of *I, the Jury* (and the other three Spillane properties) to writer/director Larry Cohen.

The *New York Times* described Cohen as "a writer and director whose wide-ranging career [includes] mainstream television series, outlandish horror movies featuring killer babies and killer yogurt, slick thrillers and even a few blaxploitation films." The director of cinema's *It's Alive*, the creator of TV's *The Invaders*, Cohen might—under the right circumstances—have been perfect for a Spillane property. But to Spillane, Larry Cohen was Harry Essex redux, the ectoplasmic residue of Victor Saville's ghost.

Spillane, who would receive no direct financial remuneration from the Cohen deal, was understandably irritated by such a production coming just when Bernstein was exploring other options and avenues for Mike

Hammer. He rejected Cohen's overtures soliciting promotional help. And Mickey had read the screenplay and deemed it garbage.

Cohen's *I, the Jury* reflected a minor Spillane revival in the early '80s, spearheaded by the popular Miller Lite commercials. Paperbacks with the Miller Lite "To Be Continued" image and a movie tie-in edition of this new *I, the Jury* appeared just when Spillane's literary output picked up speed in an unlikely way.

In 1979, *The Day the Sea Rolled Back*, reflecting his nautical interests, had unexpectedly won Mickey Spillane a Junior Literary Guild Award. Designed for readers between eight and twelve years of age, the short novel led to renewed media attention for the improbable author of "a kid's book." *The Ship That Never Was* followed in 1982, the second of three "Josh and Larry" novels (a third—*The Shrinking Island*—would be published posthumously in 2022 in a collection of all three).

"There's a lot of schools that now have your books in there," Spillane explained of his unexpected storytelling side trip in 1998. "Kids are a great market. They grow up to be adults, you know."

In November 1980, another unlikely project got media attention when Spillane told the *New York Times* that Mike Hammer would be coming to Broadway soon in *Oh, Mike!*—music by Cy Coleman (*Sweet Charity*), lyrics by Michael Stewart (*Barnum*), and book by . . . Mickey Spillane.

The producer would be another famous Cy—Feuer, who brought *Guys and Dolls* and *How to Succeed in Business Without Really Trying* to Broadway. Feuer wanted to do a musical comedy "based on the jazz of the 1950s" and Mike Hammer seemed perfect source material. When they approached Spillane, Mickey said he'd write the book himself.

Though *Oh, Mike!* never came to fruition, Coleman's *City of Angels*, mining similar territory, came to Broadway in 1989 with no Spillane involvement. None of the fairly wide press coverage of the proposed *Oh, Mike!* noted a previous, similar project. In 1967, working with (or for) actor Charles Tannen, Johnny Mercer wrote nineteen songs for a Spillane-derived musical, "Mike," also never produced. The lyrics are included in *The Complete Lyrics of Johnny Mercer* (2009), and a demo of Mercer singing and playing the songs has circulated among collectors.

By the early 1980s, Spillane had been reinstated as a Jehovah's Witness. He and Sherri were living apart—she had been listed as a "consultant" on *Margin for Murder*—and his bitterness toward her was manifest. When he referred to her, which was rarely, it was as "the Snake"—the Biblical implication clear, but also an odd reminder of the never filmed version of his novel, in which she would have had a starring role.

With his Lite Beer film shoots, print-ad photography sessions, and public appearances livening things up, Mickey had settled into a quiet Southern lifestyle, hanging with writer buddy Dave Gerrity over beers, spending time with his kids, establishing a truce with his ex-wife, driving his Ford pickup (his "Carolina Cadillac"), and avoiding parties, crowds, and bars.

"Nothing happens here," he would tell the curious. "I don't want it to."

◆

Larry Cohen understood that Mike Hammer had spawned James Bond and grasped the potential that carried. His screenplay also updated Mike into a Vietnam vet, yet retained memorable moments from the novel, as when Hammer and Velda, being shadowed, trap the guy in a revolving door. And he included the "It was easy" conclusion in all its nude brutality. But he tossed the original plot aside in favor of post-Watergate paranoia.

The older, more moderate Spillane was offended by the womanizing Hammer of Cohen's screenplay, which opened with the private eye in bed with the wife of a divorce-case client. Even factoring in changing times, such casual immorality lent a hypocritical tinge to Hammer's outrage over his army buddy's murder.

Shooting began on April 22 in Manhattan, with locations to include Harriman State Park and several in Long Island. But after only six days of shooting—much to Spillane's pleasure—Cohen was fired as director and replaced by TV director Richard T. Heffron, the picture a day over schedule and $100,000 over budget.

Heffron delivered a darkly funny, fast-paced, rather nasty action film, driven by a jazzy score from Bill Conti (*Rocky*) and benefitting from the extensive Manhattan location shooting. Armand Assante is among the best screen Hammers, true to the core character like Spillane's middle-aged Mike, young and impulsive like Biff Elliot, as dangerous and mesmerizing as Ralph Meeker. With his hooded-eyed good looks and Brando-esque mumbling, he exhibits a fatalistic outlook that is pure Mike Hammer.

This Hammer's war was not fought on the Pacific front but in God-forsaken Vietnam. This Hammer still smokes Luckies, but also sub-scribes to *Soldier of Fortune*, where Pat Chambers—a wonderful Paul Sorvino—suggests his pal check the classifieds. Hammer thanks him for the job leads.

The aquarium tank in Hammer's office says it all: Hammer cannot keep the fish alive, and after every human death, he discovers another dead fish or two. His secretary, Velda, suggests he try a coyote for a pet.

Though a blonde—the film's Charlotte is the dark-haired, dark-eyed, and stunning Barbara Carrera—Laurene Landon's Velda seems to walk out of Spillane's pages: a statuesque beauty who packs a revolver under her skirt. She backs up Hammer, tossing bullets at baddies, wants to marry her boss but resignedly wipes the lipstick off his face, saying if he cheats after they're married, he'll be strangled.

Kidnapped by a CIA-programmed maniac, Velda is nearly free of her own accord when Hammer finally bursts in. About to pursue the killer, Hammer pauses and says, "You exhaust me," then picks up the chase.

In the final confrontation with Charlotte, Hammer brings along a flower box not with roses in it, but his murdered war buddy's prosthetic arm.

Spillane hated the film, walking out on it. He already hated the script. He admitted Assante was a good actor, but too short: "He wore Italian heels." After all, Mickey had been smart enough not to work with tall actors on *The Girl Hunters*.

Twentieth Century Fox—inheriting the film from bankrupt American Cinema—initially shelved the film, despite a March 1982 *Playboy* cover story touting the nude Carrera. The studio cobbled together a lackluster ad campaign—Assante was not Mike Hammer, but "The Hammer"—and gave the film a limited release.

Hollywood had managed to kill Mike Hammer yet again.

TOP LEFT: Jane and Mickey. TOP RIGHT: Stepdaughter Britt, Jane, and Mickey at his 80th birthday celebration. BOTTOM: Stacy Keach as Mike and Tanya Roberts as Velda (with "Hammerettes") in *Murder Me, Murder You* (1983), the TV movie that launched three series and several more telefilms.

CHAPTER TWENTY-ONE

A CREEK GIRL

The petite brunette with blonde highlights was easily pretty enough to be a Spillane "doll," but somehow she didn't seem a likely candidate.

Jane Rogers grew up "splitting time between Marion County and Murrells Inlet, South Carolina," she says in her charming memoir, *My Life with Mickey* (2014), "always living around the water, trying to stay out of trouble, constantly looking for something fun." She found it, years later, never guessing that the "writer of some type" who lived down the way—with a dock she and her friends used to jump off—would play such an important role in her life.

When they met, Mickey Spillane would say, Jane was on her tricycle. She remembered it differently: "It was on my bicycle with training wheels," she insisted in 1998.

A self-described "Creek girl," she had been runner-up in the 1965 South Carolina pageant—a five-foot-two cutie who had killed with her rendition of "I Ain't Down Yet" from *The Unsinkable Molly Brown*, only to lose to the future wife of Senator Strom Thurmond. She went off to college in New York, studied drama, and in 1982 returned to stay with her parents. She was divorced with two daughters—Lisa and Britt.

Jane Spillane: *My best friend from Connecticut came down to help with the move. She was a Spillane fan and wanted his autograph. Because I still*

knew him from his days down here, I took her over to Mickey's house. That
day, Max Allan Collins was there, no surprise because he was Mickey's close
friend and fellow writer, and we all got to talking. Mickey was a com-
plete gentleman and signed anything he could while Max just sat back and
smiled.

This was the first conversation between the adult Jane and the much
older Mickey, and one topic covered was how neither of them intended
ever to get married again.

Jane Spillane: . . . *[B]ut I assure you Mickey changed his tune as soon as I*
walked out the door. Max told me much later, that after we left that day, Mickey
looked right at him and said, "That's little Jane, huh? Ya know what, I'm gonna
marry that woman one day."

Two years later, a few days before the wedding, daughter Lisa filled in
the *Chicago Tribune*'s Patricia Ward Biederman about the couple's unconventional courtship.

"Well," Lisa said, "he picks her up and takes her to the A&P and the
post office. Occasionally, they go to Myrtle Beach to the lumberyard or
to Kroger's." The garbage dump was another destination when he picked
"little Jane" up in his red Ford pickup.

Jane thought this older, friendly neighbor was just being nice. But her
father said, "No, Jane, that guy likes you. No way, nobody does those kind
of things unless they're a little taken." Finally, Mickey asked her out for
dinner—Chinese, his favorite—but invited her daughters along too.

The rough-and-tumble creator of Mickey Spillane was anything but,
asking her father for her hand ("Ask her mother!") and informing his
intended he didn't believe in sex before marriage.

"He told people he had to marry me," Jane said, "because he didn't have
the willpower to fight me off anymore." Indeed, before Mickey brought
her home at ten P.M., the couple indulged in half an hour of "necking" in
the red pickup truck.

With family and a few friends in attendance, they got married "in
front of the fireplace" at Oliver's Lodge, their favorite restaurant, then
"moved out to the big live oak to take pictures next to the view we had

loved for years." It was October 30, "mischief night," but Mickey would say he'd been wed on Halloween, so he could tell journalists he wasn't sure whether Jane was "the trick or the treat." He loved to describe the ceremony as "We do, let's eat."

A belated honeymoon found Jane reverting to childhood and skinny-dipping off their private island only to have a boat cruise by. Rather than duck under water, Jane scrambled onto the beach and hustled back to the house to the yells of men on the boat and her husband's applause and laughter. The same boat and its little crew glided by every honeymoon day, so (Jane recalled) "they must have liked what they saw."

Jane Spillane: *One thing I didn't know before I married him was how he acted at night, something I had to get used to over twenty-three years of marriage. We would be asleep with nothing but silence in the middle of the night when I would be shaken out of nowhere from the rustling of Mickey getting out of bed, throwing on a lamp and grabbing a sticky note to write down ideas. No matter how many ideas occurred to him in the night, he would get up every time, turn on the lamp, and write them down on a sticky note. Then a book would result from his midnight musings. Even after Mickey passed away, we found his ideas in the house and around the property, things Max (Mickey's writing partner, Max Allan Collins) would use to finish the last manuscripts.*

Jane had to get used to the tourists seeking autographs—ironic, considering the autograph-seeking meeting that brought her and Mickey together. The slatted fence around the property didn't stop the fans, nor did the signs on it: STOP and DEAD END.

Behind that fence, the house—whose dock she'd once jumped from with her girlfriends, under the watchful eye of a former lifeguard—was a white-frame oversize bungalow on stilts twenty feet from the water, wherein thrived clams, crab, oysters, and shrimp. A twenty-two-foot fishing skiff—nothing fancy—rested on a trailer, its stern bearing the wing number of Mickey's P-51 Mustang in the war: 819. From here, Mickey and his fishing buddies could "round the point" and go looking for kingfish, marlin, flounder, mackerel, shark. But Mike Hammer's papa only caught what he could eat.

The John Wayne Jag was in the driveway, his Ford "Carolina Cadillac" parked nearby. In the yard was the Shipwreck Bar, assembled around some trees by Spillane and his son Ward; it included a counter and a roof and lights "so soft," Spillane said, "all the girls look beautiful and all the guys look young" when seated there.

Inside, the house was anything but fancy, carpet and linoleum clean but worn, books and magazines everywhere—a reader lived here. Nothing out of the ordinary. But then, as *Chicago Tribune* writer Connie Fletcher put it, "[Y]ou started noticing things: a diving helmet sits next to the fireplace . . . an entire wall of books, hardbound and paperback, in English and 14 foreign languages, all with Spillane's name on the spine. . . . Mounted fish, seashells, skis, snowshoes, guns, toys. . . . The whole place has the feel of a boy's room, crowded with sports gear, pennants, pictures of heroes, mementoes, treasures, dreams."

These were the memories of a man who had settled down, his dreams already come true. He would joke to a journalist that he had four kids— "Five, counting my wife."

His four grown children would visit often, and he was (according to son Michael) "on speaking terms" with their mother. His only complaint about having two teenaged girls in the house was that each had "one ear swollen" from using the telephone, and also the mystery of how the household could run through so much toilet paper.

Jane told Cindi Clemmer of *Myrtle Beach Magazine* in 1986, "People can't believe it, but we have dinner at five o'clock every day and go to bed very early, generally between 9 and 10. We eat seafood, pork chops, meat loaf and—yes—southern fried chicken and gravy and biscuits—that's us, biscuits every night." They put in "his and hers" stoves, her husband known for his pepper steak and Thanksgiving Day feasts, and shared the rambling house with three black cats and an "attack Yorkie." Mickey was always remodeling and building on himself, complaining that, "The guy who built it owned a lumber yard, but he didn't own a level."

Spillane told the *Chicago Tribune*'s Fletcher, "I'm very lucky at my age, to meet a good-looking woman who has everything going for her and who likes the same things I do. That's the really important thing."

The *National Enquirer*, looking for dirt, got this instead from Spillane: "Jane and I have found paradise here in Murrells Inlet. We have everything we want—each other."

Spillane had something else, as well, "to keep the smoke coming out the chimney" (as he put it)—a new *Mike Hammer* television series on CBS.

Some critics found Stacy Keach overqualified to play Hammer, but he became the actor most identified with the role, eclipsing even Spillane himself. Keach's classical training and stage experience, and his many major films, made him an ideal performer to deliver both wry tongue-in-cheek humor and credible toughness. Somewhat surprisingly, Mike Hammer became this fine actor's signature role.

Keach portrayed the private eye in four telefilms and three television series, an accomplishment making *The Guinness Book of Records* for one actor in the same role in multiple series. In a decades-spanning association with the character, he narrated numerous Mike Hammer novels on audio book and appeared in three full-cast radio-style installments of *The New Adventures of Mike Hammer*, the second of which (*The Little Death*) won the Audie for Best Original Work in 2011.

While the Jay Bernstein–produced TV movies vary from excellent to merely adequate, Keach maintained the toughness of the character and the integrity of the source material even when an indifferently written script came along. And his warmly distinctive voice provided narration that set a noir tone even when the scripting stumbled.

Bernstein felt the series had to temper the strong medicine of the original novels—Spillane fan though he was, the producer saw Mike as both anachronistic and politically incorrect, a problem he addressed by playing into it. This Hammer—though a Vietnam veteran—had old-fashioned musical tastes, wore a fedora, and generally seemed a man-out-of-time from the World War II era, the conscience of yesterday unleashed on the 1980s. Of course this is a Jiminy Cricket who sleeps around and occasionally kills those who step across the line.

A loose reworking of *Vengeance Is Mine!*, *Murder Me, Murder You*—airing on April 9, 1983—is the first and best of the Hammer TV movies. Well plotted if hindered by occasionally wince-worthy dialogue, the screenplay fills in Mike's updated past and nicely indicates the bruised idealist beneath the cynical surface.

Charlie's Angels alum Tanya Roberts is Velda—Lindsay Bloom would take over in the series—and frequent movie/TV bad guy Don Stroud is Pat Chambers. Kent Williams as weaselly Deputy DA Lawrence D. Barrington stands in for the parade of similar such political adversaries in the novels.

Roberts is the perhaps the best of all screen Veldas and closest to the source material, projecting savvy, sexual allure, and unstinting loyalty for her boss, even coming to his rescue with a gun in hand. Roberts would go on to star in the 1984 film *Sheena*—a comic-book character dating to Spillane's Funnies, Inc., era. Bloom would do well in the series to follow, but the sexually charged Mike and Velda partnership of the novels is replaced with a brother and sisterly relationship.

Murder Me, Murder You transforms the bluesy big-band standard "Harlem Nocturne" into Mike Hammer's best-known theme. Its composer, Earle Hagen, provides the score for not just this first telefilm, but two Keach series to follow, setting an appropriate noirish tone perfect for location shooting in a snowy, slushy Manhattan.

Voluptuous Delta Burke slyly invokes Marilyn Monroe while Lisa Blount nicely underplays Mike's newly discovered daughter, Michelle. Keach breathes life into some unfortunate lines—"You got giant lizard breath" and "I'm gonna dump these toads in their own burn bag"—and comes off legitimately tough despite the sometimes campy context.

Producer Bernstein said, "I knew when Ronald Reagan got in, Mike Hammer could get on." He plays up to the Silent Majority in a reflective exchange between Mike and Pat at night on a front stoop. "It's about time we stopped bad-mouthing this country," Hammer says, and Pat wholeheartedly agrees.

Yet there's nothing conservative either politically or morally about Keach's Hammer, who complains about what's happened to good old-fashioned American values while bedding beauties, bashing law enforcement officials, and starting bar fights. Hammer even manhandles a pornographer in a film that gives us busty, mud-wrestling babes.

Yet *Murder Me, Murder You* plays off this seemingly hypocritical attitude toward women, as when womanizing Mike Hammer realizes his behavior has driven his daughter into pornography. The parade of willing women includes a lovely transvestite, underscoring the artificial means—cosmetics, hairstyles, padding—a woman might use to attract men. Hammer tells his daughter he can never allow himself to get serious with a woman because of the "pain and guilt" he'd suffer if she were to die in his dangerous world.

Bernstein seems to have taken the wrong message from the TV movie's popularity, going on to litter each series episode with an array of beauties immediately drawn to Mike Hammer. While *Murder Me, Murder You* confronts Hammer's (and its own) double standard, the subsequent series follows a sometimes campy course that Spillane himself privately disliked.

A second Keach telefilm, *More Than Murder*, aired on CBS-TV on January 26, 1984, followed by the first regular one-hour episode of the series on Saturday, January 28, in the usual ten P.M. time slot. The second film plays like a two-part series episode and is inferior to its predecessor.

But Keach already seems to own the role, more comfortable in a fedora of his own choice than a pork-pie hat Spillane had requested. Already, however, the onslaught of Hammerettes (as Keach referred to them) has begun, and a less serious, more arch tone takes over.

While not a ratings blockbuster, *Mickey Spillane's Mike Hammer* lasted for forty-six episodes, eventually leaving CBS in 1987. Though maintaining admirable production values, Bernstein's focus seems more on guest stars and less on good scripts. Some first-rate writers—notably Joe Gores—were hamstrung by the producer's precarious recipe of tough action, sly sex, and camp humor.

What pulls it together is Keach's confident portrayal, an ability to be tough and tender, cruel and kind, leering and romantic. All these qualities were shared both by Stacy Keach's Mike Hammer and Mickey Spillane's.

In April 1984, Keach and his secretary, Deborah Steele, arrived at Heathrow Airport from France after filming *Mistral's Daughter*, a CBS-TV miniseries; sound recording for a Hammer episode was scheduled in London. Both Keach and Steele were arrested for possession of 1.3 ounces of cocaine. Pleading guilty, Keach began an unexpectedly stiff nine-month sentence in December.

The very anti-drug Mickey Spillane stood behind his TV Mike Hammer, suggesting enigmatically that Keach had not been guilty. Spillane may have been kidding himself.

"Let there be no illusions about cocaine," Keach wrote to London's *Daily Express* halfway through his sentence. "Cocaine is a diabolically destructive force which can ultimately ruin not only your physical and mental health but also your career and personal relationships as well."

In 2013, Keach said, "I think subconsciously I was hoping to get caught. . . . As it turns out, looking back, it was the best thing that ever happened to me. It saved my life actually."

CBS-TV issued a statement saying they stood by Keach and planned to carry the series in the fall. Nonetheless, producer Bernstein was required to produce what was essentially his third Hammer pilot. The network wanted to see if the ratings indicated audience forgiveness for a postscandal Keach-as-Hammer.

The Return of Mickey Spillane's Mike Hammer aired on April 18, 1986, five months before the start of the fall TV season. *TV Guide*'s Judith Crist hailed Keach's return as a "stylish, sharp-tongued and sophisticated [TV movie] with a sensational helicopter sequence." Keach and Lauren Hutton shared a chemistry aided by a more age-appropriate pairing than usual.

The New Mike Hammer followed, its first episode airing January 28, 1984, with—according to a Bernstein press release—"no more portrayals of women as bimbos." The promise was halfheartedly kept, and the violence toned down somewhat as well. Keach emerged from scandal unscathed, his Hammer the same affable avenger with self-mocking swagger and genuine charisma, in a show that carries with it the strengths and weaknesses of its TV era. The frustration for fans of both Spillane and Keach is sensing what the actor might have done with a more faithful take on Mike Hammer.

With Mike Hammer on TV again and his Lite Beer commercials going strong, Spillane didn't really need any further publicity. But he got it, when his ex-wife Sherri sued him in Nevada, seeking to raise the $18,000 settlement of their 1983 divorce. She contended her ex-husband had not told her a *Mike Hammer* TV series was ramping up.

In 1983, of course, that wasn't the case. *Margin for Murder* with Dobson had not spawned a series—Sherri was listed as a consultant on the film and was in a position to know—and Keach's *Murder Me, Murder You* similarly would be a TV movie, a backdoor pilot at best.

Sherri described her ex-husband as "an alcoholic, a sexual pervert and a liar," who had encouraged her to have sexual relations with other men. She claimed Spillane had written a note to that effect, to which he said, if so, "I must have been pretty smashed."

But he also said, "If I'm a pervert, I'm a pretty poor pervert. That woman made mention in court that we went together for two years before we got married. And her brother the lawyer wanted to know, 'Was she a virgin?' when we got married. She was. Not the usual way of a pervert. . . ."

People magazine said Judge Leavitt "indicated that Sherri was ill-positioned to cast the first stone." She had lived with actor Michael Standing during the last three years of her marriage to Spillane, and married Standing twenty minutes after the divorce was finalized.

"The court will not pass judgment on morality," the judge said, "but such actions are not those of a caring, faithful, loving spouse."

Sherri took the case to Washington and the Supreme Court, but the justices let the Nevada court decision stand, without comment.

Mickey had a comment: "It was the case of the missing case—a frivolous lawsuit by a former wife trying to get back into my pocket."

The ex–Mrs. Spillane was unaware that her former husband had saved her life shortly after their divorce. Catching singer Julie London's act at the Copa, Spillane—at a table with Hy Gardner—spotted a familiar face.

"This Mafia guy sits through three sets," he told *Vanity Fair*. "I sit through three sets. Hy has gotten up to go to the bathroom. That same night someone is bumped off, and I became the alibi. . . ."

The police pressured Spillane not to corroborate the mob chief's story. "I don't care if he's Adolf Hitler," Spillane told them. "He didn't leave the table."

At a restaurant a few weeks later, a mob flunky said the boss wanted to talk to him.

"Normally," Spillane said, "I'd say, 'Tell him to come over here.'" But not wanting a scene, the writer complied.

The capo said, "You're a good boy."

Spillane said, "First of all, don't call me boy."

The capo let that pass. "You did a good thing. If you ever want anything done, just let me know."

Spillane said, "No thanks," but when his and Sherri's divorce made the news, he was approached in Las Vegas by a stranger who whispered, "The boss is going to bump her off."

"No!" a panicked Spillane blurted. "No! *Don't* bump her off."

Sherri went on to develop the scandal division of the Ruth Webb Talent Agency, becoming a successful agent for such "high-profile, controversial" clients as Tonya Harding, Joey Buttafuoco, Kato Kaelin, and Omarosa.

One last CBS Mike Hammer TV movie with Stacy Keach, *Murder Takes All*, aired May 21, 1989. As an apparent attempt to launch another series of Hammer TV movies, *Murder Takes All* is instead a disappointing finale for Keach's '80s run as Hammer. With Bernstein's usual emphasis on glitz and glamour, the script seems an afterthought. Las Vegas replaces Manhattan, such an important a part of Hammer's world, and Pat and Velda make only cameo appearances.

MAC: *The first time I visited Mickey was at his invitation after we'd met at Bouchercon in Milwaukee. The second came when Jim Traylor and I interviewed him for* One Lonely Knight: Mickey Spillane's Mike Hammer *(1984).*

Jim and I quickly learned we couldn't keep up with Mickey. We were in our early thirties and he was almost twice our age, but he ran us ragged. His vitality and energy were staggering. We settled on a strategy—Jim would handle the morning interrogation and I would take over in the afternoon. Evenings, we just struggled to keep pace with him.

One night Mickey handed us two incomplete manuscripts—one for The Big Bang, *the other for* Complex 90—*as "bedtime reading." We read into the night, trading off manuscripts. Jim took some notes. There hadn't been a Hammer novel since 1970 and this was 1983!*

On my next trip—on the advice of a phone call from Dave Gerrity—my goal was to get Mickey to write the blurb he'd offered for my novel, True Detective *(1983). Mickey picked me up at the Myrtle Beach airport. Over the next several days, we talked as we rode around the area. On a back road, a long, deadly looking snake slithered across the blacktop and Mickey slammed on the "Carolina Cadillac" brakes so as not to run over it.*

He turned the squinting hazel eyes on me and said, "I wouldn't kill a snake. . . . But some people?" He shrugged and the snake made it to safety and we rode on.

One morning, going to pick up biscuits at Hardee's, he paused in the parking lot to set loose that gaze on me again. "What's this about you wanting to be your generation's Mickey Spillane? I'm your generation's Mickey Spillane."

Dave Gerrity was a frequent, friendly presence. He lived in nearby Pirate Cove trailer park in a mobile home Spillane owned.

When it was time for Mickey to drive me back to the airport, I still hadn't found the nerve to ask for that blurb. Gerrity said, "Mickey! For Pete's sake, write Max that blurb you promised."

"Oh yeah!" Mickey said, as if remembering something on the stove was burning. He ran into his office and I could hear him, batting out the blurb. He jogged out and handed it to me. "Hope this'll do."

"One of the best books I ever read," it said. "Mickey Spillane."

"That'll do just fine," I said.

Years passed before I asked Jane why Mickey put up with me. I was a liberal (which of course Spillane defined as a "radical"). I never served in the military. I lived on the Mississippi River but avoided boats. I couldn't pitch a tent much less build a house.

"Mickey has lots of friends," Jane said. "From all walks of life. But since Dave died, you're the only one he can talk writing with."

Gerrity had passed away in 1984 at fifty-nine, after suffering badly with cancer. In his writer pal's last days, Mickey convinced Dave to convert to the Witnesses.

Late at night, my host would lead me to his third-floor office. He would tell me about stories he had in mind. He would share the surprise endings of Mike Hammers he intended to write—me on a little couch watching like a kid in school, him on his feet, gesturing and acting it out, like he was telling ghost stories around a campfire on the beach back at Breezy Point. He would hand me a brittle old manuscript and sit in a chair and smile as I read it, enrapt. And we would talk about the craft of writing. The man who pretended not to care about writing cared more than anyone else that I ever met in this game.

◆

The non-Keach but Bernstein-produced *Come Die With Me: A Mickey Spillane's Mike Hammer Mystery* aired December 6, 1994, a backdoor pilot with an unlikely Hammer in Rob Estes (*Silk Stalkings*) and a platinum blonde Velda in Pamela Anderson (*Baywatch*). With San Diego posing as Miami Beach (in for Manhattan) and big-band music giving way to a Latin salsa score, *Come Die With Me* is a wretched attempt to reboot Hammer for a new, younger audience.

Bernstein provides another chorus line of Hammerettes, buxom babes who find Estes irresistible—one with a stalled car wants a "jump," another goes door-to-door collecting for "the milk fund," ad infinitum. These sexist embarrassments defeat any notion of a hip young Hammer, who brags that "sleaze is his meat," divorce cases his specialty.

A grim death-by-airbag ending does represent a contribution from Spillane. The writer gave it to Bernstein, who used it as a shocking finish to an otherwise forgettable travesty.

In 1997, Jay Bernstein enlisted Keach to return as Hammer in a more modestly budgeted series, *Mickey Spillane's Mike Hammer, Private Eye*. Twenty-six episodes were shot for syndication.

Velda is portrayed by blonde Shannon Whirry, a veteran of R-rated erotic features. The younger Whirry necessitates a surrogate father-and-daughter relationship for Hammer and Velda. This Velda is briefly entangled romantically with Hammer's young associate, Nick Farrell, played by Shane Conrad. Pat Chambers is not on board; actor Peter Jason plays Captain Skip Gleason. Neither Nick nor Skip are characters from any Hammer novel.

The revival lacks the production values of the previous Keach offerings, with its underdressed sets, negligible guest stars, and routine, often downbeat plots. As with the original films noir, chiaroscuro cinematography lends an appropriate ambience that disguises budgetary limitations. The saving grace is once again a self-assured Keach, carrying the series off with humor and style.

It was good to see him back in the trench coat one last time.

In 1998, producer Jay Bernstein and star Stacy Keach join Mickey at his 80th birthday party.

Mickey (as attorney Neil Ekhardt) with Patty McCormack in *Mommy's Day*, 1997.

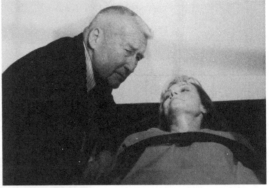

Mickey and MAC visit the Tower of London while attending a Spillane film retrospective at the National Film Theatre in London in 1999.

Mickey's Grand Master Edgar.

CHAPTER TWENTY-TWO

GRAND MASTER

Mickey Spillane seemed, if anything, prouder of his success as a beer salesman than as a bestselling author—that is, writer.

"I've done more [Lite Beer] commercials than anybody," Spillane told *Coast* magazine in 1985. The other pitchmen were mostly well-known athletes. "The All-Stars are great even though they're amateurs," he said. "The commercials are fun to do . . . and [the proceeds] are fun to spend, too."

Mickey made over $100,000 a year doing the one-minute spots and the personal appearances they generated.

Eddie Gossage of Miller Brewing Company said at the time, "[Spillane] leans to a masculine audience. He's a real presence. He transcends time."

The writer had done commercials before—Lifebuoy soap, Braniff Airways, even Piels, a regional beer. In *Lite Reading*, Frank Deford writes, "Mickey came off as a definite character in his [first] commercial. . . . It took another year and a half before the agency began to understand this sufficiently—to present athletes as themselves. . . . Only when the Spillane influence began to spread did the campaign become a true critical phenomenon."

In airports, people would shout at Mickey, "Where's the Doll?" And actress Lee Meredith would similarly be asked constantly where Mickey was. The unlikely duo were in big demand for in-person events.

Meredith recalled in 1998, "On the road there were many, many women that would go up to him and say, oh Mickey I've read all your books and absolutely love them."

When Mickey and the Doll were given red branded manager jackets, he asked her on the phone if she'd worn hers out in public yet. She had, and wondered why everybody was talking to her and being so nice.

"Now . . . picture this big beautiful blonde walkin' down Hollywood Boulevard," Spillane said, "in a bright red jacket with the Miller logo on the back that said, 'Tastes Great.' I said, don't ever wear that out like that, geez!"

Meredith, recalling those days warmly, said, "It went on for eighteen years, we did the commercials. Eighteen years of friendship and traveling. It was really great."

"That's the best gal I ever worked with," Spillane said of his co-star. "She was giving—always on time and well-rehearsed."

The All-Star fame contributed to Spillane appearing as the guest murder victim on *Columbo* on January 18, 1974. The producers wanted a real, recognizable author for "Publish or Perish."

"I always wanted to play a corpse," Mickey said. "The only scene I had with Peter Falk I was dead as a doornail." Told he'd be wearing his own things, he was annoyed when "some idiots took me down to Rodeo Drive and bought a thousand dollars' worth of nondescript clothes!"

The Lite Beer campaign lasted until 1991, over eighty commercials filmed, with the elaborate 1986 "Case of the Missing Case" showcasing Mickey with the Doll on his arm as they searched for a missing case of Lite Beer. In the twist ending, the culprit proves to be Rodney Dangerfield wearing a Mickey Spillane mask. But the beautiful woman with Rodney is wearing a mask too—Mickey Spillane in drag; in other words: *The Doll was a man!*

That Spillane's creativity, and his bank account, were satisfied by the Lite Beer gig—with writing all but sidelined—may come as a surprise to some; but not to those who knew him well. He insisted he got his inspiration from "the urgent need for money." Further, he saw himself as an entertainer and was drawn to performing at least as much as writing. The assumption that his religious faith kept him from producing fiction seems misjudged.

Nonetheless, in 1988—with the Lite Beer campaign winding down and television drawing new attention to Mike Hammer—Mickey Spillane sat down to write a novel instead of a TV-movie treatment he'd been considering for Bernstein, for a possible Keach TV movie.

The Killing Man (1989) holds its own with the best of the mid-period Hammer novels; its texture and mood as important as the story being told, and presenting a character study of an older, more world-weary Hammer, still up to the game. A bizarrely mutilated corpse in his office, and a badly beaten Velda, wake the beast in Mike Hammer; a taunting note from the killer pinned to the dead man's head says: "YOU DIE FOR KILLING ME. *Penta.*" Once again, Mike is immersed in high-level corruption and murder, but for the first time he's dealing with a new breed of assassin: a serial killer who has been in the government's employ. Mike is compelled once again to kill, this time to defend himself and his beloved Velda.

Spillane's ability to paint word pictures remains as vivid as ever:

> *Some days hang over Manhattan like a huge pair of unseen pinchers, slowly squeezing the city until you can hardly breathe. A low growl of thunder echoed up the cavern of Fifth Avenue and I looked up to where the sky started at the seventy-first floor of the Empire State Building. I could smell the rain. It was the kind that hung above the orderly piles of concrete until it was soaked with dust and debris and when it came down it wasn't rain at all, but the sweat of the city.*

With the exception of the two "kids' books," Spillane had not published a novel in sixteen years. Yet *The Killing Man* is a masterful exercise in first-person private-eye prose. The novel's relentless pace and occasional explosions of violence—sex and violence still the exclamation points of his writing—are only slightly marred by the retread of a *One Lonely Night* plot device and Hammer solving the case at the last minute by sheer accident.

For *The Killing Man*, he received from NAL a record $500,000 advance. And whether prescience or simply kismet, Spillane was about to feel the urgent need for money.

While he and Jane were in California helping daughter Britt move in for her first year at Stanford in 1989, Hurricane Hugo was making landfall. Friends who'd been left to watch the house—with the storm sitting off the Atlantic Coast—did not take the precautions the Spillanes had requested. The windows had not been boarded up and the cats, and even Jane's car, had gone unattended.

Hugo cut a deadly path across the Southeast: twenty-six South Carolina residents would die (eighty-two Caribbeans preceding them) and countless others were left homeless, with ten billion dollars of havoc wreaked. The Spillanes—unable to fly into South Carolina with airports shut down or runways clogged as people fled—took a rental car through leveled forests to the inlet where the house that had stood for thirty-five years had been gutted. Only Spillane's small office on stilts remained, a precarious, stubborn survivor.

In *Life with Mickey*, Jane Spillane wrote: "Through a labyrinth of fallen trees, cracked limbs, and washed-up miscellany, we saw a torn up and broken-down home with shattered windows, warped staircases, and ceiling bowing under the weight of pressure of water-logged floors."

A boat was waiting for them in the living room on a dirty puddle of sewage-fouled water, as if parked there.

"The boat had gone right through the living room wall," Jane wrote, "leaving a gaping hole in the house and allowing whatever elements and animals to get in. . . ."

A pelican was sitting on the front porch looking like he belonged there more than the homeowners. Rather than chase the bird off, Mickey fed it bread. Later—as he once had with a spider—he got indignantly disgusted with the bird for paying him back by bothering Jane.

The damage was unbelievable—the second-floor stairs warped into wooden waves, the first floor one gigantic puddle, trees down in the yard, a rowboat sitting on the outdoor bar, doors, tables, cabinets flung around the yard as if in preparation for an *Alice in Wonderland* tea party. Gone, likely looted, was the original painting for *One Lonely Night* and a portrait of Spillane by his old comic-strip artist, Ed Robbins.

This was a house with thirty-five years of memories, in an area Mickey had loved since that flyover during the war.

"Ya make Mother Nature mad and this is what you get," Spillane said philosophically.

Okay, then—he would put up a bigger and better house. Rebuilding it would be fun, a new experience he was looking forward to. He'd lost his old junk—he shrugged—so he'd get new junk.

"With characteristic grit," Jack Bettridge wrote in *Mine*, "he started over, building a heavy-duty dream house, everything over code, twelve electrical outlets to a room, four wet bars."

He employed a crew of the best craftsmen in the area and moved among them, like a film director, or perhaps just someone who had experience building houses. When the insurance adjustor suggested just repairing the original structure, Spillane just shooed him off the property.

"If you're going to do it from scratch," he said, "do it right."

The result was a humble three-story mansion built on the memory of its predecessor, a knotty-pine sanctuary within, Jane's touches apparent ("[F]loral fabrics, and lots of Americana bric-a-brac," *Vanity Fair* said). Rockers on the porch, expansive kitchen and living room, chamber-like bookshelf-lined office, another cozier office on the third floor, which—with that survivor on stilts—made three.

He would soon have books going on the manual typewriters in each.

MAC: *In the little office on stilts, or the big one on the main floor of the rebuilt house, he would hand me partial manuscripts and send them home with me—the two Jim Traylor and I had read among*

*them, which otherwise would have been lost to Hugo. He sent all
kinds of things home with me.*

"If I need it," he said, "I'll know where to find it."

Sometimes, as with The Consummata *or the unproduced
screenplays for* The Saga of Cali York, The Green Woman,
and The Menace, *he'd say, "Maybe someday we'll do something
with these."*

Our first project was gathering previous uncollected novellas into
Tomorrow I Die *(1984) for Mysterious Press, whose publisher Otto
Penzler also valued Spillane. Two more such collections followed.
Together, Mickey and I co-edited four NAL non-Spillane anthologies,
including* A Century of Noir. *But the project that excited Mickey
most was a return to comic books.*

*In 1994 Martin Greenberg approached me at a Bouchercon about
a new company, Big Entertainment, who were starting a line called
Tekno Comics. Marty specialized in anthologies from science-fiction
and mystery writers, and had published stories by both my wife Barbara
and myself. As creative director of Big Entertainment, he wondered if
I might approach Mickey about a Mike Hammer comic book.*

*Tekno Comics sought famous names to attach to comic
books—for example, Leonard Nimoy created* The Primortals *and
Gene Roddenberry's estate licensed an unrealized non–Star* Trek
project.

*I approached Mickey, who was against licensing Hammer—it
might step on Jay Bernstein's toes. I suggested a science-fiction
variant, and Mickey was immediately on board.* Mickey Spillane's
Mike Danger *took Hammer's precursor, cryogenically froze him
in the 1950s and thawed him out in a darkly comic politically
correct future.*

*Laurie Silvers and Mitchell Rubenstein, who had created the
Sci-Fi Channel, launched Tekno at Disneyworld, where Mickey
and I joined fellow stablemates Nimoy and Neil Gaiman for*

promotional events. My most vivid memory is walking with Barb along the beach, while ahead of us two kids—Mickey Spillane, 77, and his godson, Nathan Collins, 11—were laughing and teasing each other, Mickey bumping into him, Nate bumping back, the bigger kid telling the littler one how to eat worms.

Mickey and I did several other Tekno events, including one at Griffith Observatory and a signing at Mall of America, and the comics line got off to a great start. I did the writing but Mickey stayed current on the script, getting a big kick being in comics again. On Late Night with Conan O'Brien, *Mickey carried the ball and I got an up-close look at his mastery of handling promotion. We agreed to do a signing at San Diego Comic-Con.*

Meanwhile, I was prepping my first independent film, Mommy. *Mickey had agreed to play the attorney for Patty McCormack, doing a grown-up variation of her famous* The Bad Seed *(1956) role. He'd be "shot out" in a day, doing me this favor knowing I'd raised the money in my own little town, and his name would help on the video box. We would meet in San Diego and do the* Mike Danger *signing, then fly back together to Iowa where shooting began on Monday.*

But when I arrived at the hotel in San Diego, I learned Mickey had been rushed to the ER the night before. He was very ill—a scratch on one of his legs had become infected. I told the Tekno Comics team, and the con, to cancel the signing—we needed to get him back to South Carolina as soon as the doctors allowed.

Mickey was having none of it. He pulled himself up and appeared at the Tekno Comics booth to sign autographs and chat with fans. Behind his back, I arranged for the three-hour session to be cut to one. I told Mickey I could fly him in at the end of the Mommy *shoot and do his scenes then. He refused, saying he knew how much that would screw up production. Then I got word to Jay Bernstein to come down and talk Mickey into going home.*

Jay came quickly down from LA and I stood outside Mickey's hotel room for fifteen minutes while they talked within; it almost sounded like an argument. I had never met Jay before and feared he might think I was taking advantage of Mickey, trying to pressure him into doing the shoot.

But Jay stepped out, shut the door behind him, and quietly said, "You have to let him do this for you. He wants to do this for you."

So Mickey flew back to Iowa with me. When we changed planes at Chicago, he refused a wheelchair and I helped him along, my mind racing. I did not want to be the man who killed Mickey Spillane. But he insisted on being there for the first day of my shoot.

When we arrived at the Moline Airport, my wife had a look at Mickey's swollen, reddened leg and said, "We'll be going to the ER now."

We did. He was given treatment and medication. The next day he performed beautifully. He had a little trouble with his lines, but was otherwise fine. He was great. He was Mickey Spillane. My writer friend Matthew Clemens accompanied Mickey on the plane back to South Carolina.

Two years later we did a sequel called Mommy's Day *and Mickey came back for it. Because he'd had trouble with his lines before, I had cue cards ready for him. He frowned.*

"What are those for?" he said, as close to angry as I ever saw him. "Get those out of here."

He knew his lines, all right. And everybody else's.

The Mike Danger *comic book generated a movie option. We met in New York at Miramax in Tribeca and sat at a big confer-ence table with Mitch Rubenstein of Tekno, Marty Greenberg, various Miramax staffers, and Harvey Weinstein, who told Mickey he was a big fan, raving about reading* I, the Jury *as a kid. Unfortunately, we weren't there to discuss* I, the Jury, *which Weinstein seemed to want Mickey to replicate.*

The film czar suggested Mickey write a Mike Danger novel; they had a publishing arm, after all. When Mickey pointed out that he and I were partners, Weinstein said, "He can write the screenplay."

Mickey agreed to write a Mike Danger novel. My heart sank, knowing how little writing he'd done in recent years. But he surprised me—within a month came a draft of a Mike Danger time-travel novel, and it was terrific. But it wasn't anything like what Weinstein wanted.

They never published the book and the option lapsed. Still, Mike Danger *had a respectable two-year run as a comic book—the longest of any Tekno Comics title.*

Whenever I told Mickey I wanted to write his biography, he insisted he'd one day do it himself. But he cooperated when I proposed a documentary about his life and work. In 1998 I brought a camera crew from Des Moines to Murrells Inlet. On the first morning at Mickey and Jane's home, I heard the young crew members talking about all the fun they intended to have in Myrtle Beach that night.

I said, "See that little old man over there? He's going to run your asses off today, and tomorrow, and the next day. You will be spending your evenings recuperating in your hotel rooms." Which is exactly what happened.

Mike Hammer's Mickey Spillane *(1998) debuted at the noir film festival in Courmayeur, Italy; I was a guest and Mickey was interviewed by satellite on a big screen. Mickey and I were invited to show the film at the National Film Theater in London as part of a Spillane retrospective that included* Kiss Me Deadly *and* The Girl Hunters. *Mickey and I were interviewed on stage before a packed house. I stayed uncharacteristically mum—these people weren't here to see me—but interviewer Adrian Wootton knew me well and tossed me a hot-potato question.*

"I understand there's one thing you and Mickey don't agree on—Kiss Me Deadly."

And I said, "Yes. Mickey hates it. But it's a great film and a huge part of his legacy. For a mystery writer to endure, there has to be at least one great film made from his work. Would Hammett be Hammett without Bogart and John Huston? Chandler without Bogart and Hawks? Look at Agatha Christie, everything from Witness for the Prosecution *to* Murder on the Orient Express. *Mickey will live forever in part because of* Kiss Me Deadly *and Robert Aldrich."*

Throughout this little speech, Mickey gave me a very strange, distant look, the payoff of which came in one of his last interviews. Asked which big screen Mike Hammer he liked best—next to himself—Mickey said, "Ralph Meeker."

On April 27, 1995, at the Sheraton New York Hotel, Mickey Spillane was named a Grand Master by the Mystery Writers of America at their fiftieth annual awards dinner. The Private Eye Writers of America had beaten them to the punch, recognizing Spillane's importance by giving him their life achievement award, the Eye, in 1983.

In *Mystery Scene* magazine, Lawrence Block—also an MWA Grand Master—revealed that, behind the scenes, resentment and condescension toward Spillane still existed.

"[T]he pro-Spillane contingent argued that Mickey was enormously influential," Block wrote, "that he had not only brought a whole generation of new readers to crime fiction, but that in so doing he had spawned the whole world of hardboiled paperback original fiction . . . [which] owed their very existence to the new market Mickey and Mike Hammer had called into existence."

But Block also noted that "[T]he anti-Spillane crowd pointed out that, influential though they might well be, Mickey's books were essentially crap. The plots were dumb, the characters lacked any semblance of depth, the underlying philosophy was brutish, and the writing itself was heavy-handed and crude." It was not the place of the MWA, these naysayers said, to reward popularity.

The six hundred in attendance at the awards ceremony—at which Quentin Tarantino won an Edgar for *Pulp Fiction*, a film overtly referencing *Kiss Me Deadly*—appeared to be anything but an anti-Spillane group. Charmed by his amusing acceptance speech, taken by his gracious demeanor, everyone seemed eager to at least catch a glimpse at the Lite Beer All-Star, this living legend of mystery fiction. Many stopped to shake his hand and/or get an autograph, Lawrence Block among them.

Donald E. Westlake—who as Richard Stark wrote *The Hunter*, basis of the influential neo-noir *Point Blank* (1967)—witnessed "firsthand the arc of Spillane's redemption with the Mystery Writers of America, from being a pariah for years to receiving the organization's Edgar Award." An MWA Grand Master himself, Westlake—talking to *Vanity Fair*'s Cliff Rothman—credited Spillane with "breathing life into one-dimensional detective heroes." Considering the writer's work dated but important, Westlake was among those who fought behind the scenes for Spillane's recognition.

Jealousy among authors is nothing new, nor is hypocrisy, but Mickey Spillane nonetheless accepted the tribute gratefully and carried the Edgar Award home to go on an honored shelf in his main-floor office. He displayed the PWA Eye there, as well, recovered from the detritus of Hugo and as battered as the private eyes it was named for.

This overdue and by any yardstick great honor may have led to what followed—Mickey Spillane began what would be the final Mike Hammer novel published during his lifetime.

In *Black Alley* (1996), an older, world-weary Hammer and an ever-loyal, patient Velda postpone their long overdue marriage to search for a missing fortune—$89 billion—the location of which a crime family is convinced (quite correctly) that Mike knows.

Various unfinished Hammer novels in Spillane's files often explore the theme of a weakened Hammer, returning to New York City after a recuperative period in hiding following a near fatal fire fight (see the posthumous *Kiss Her Goodbye*, 2011, completed by MAC). In *Black Alley* and the unpublished Mike Danger novel, the detective's absence from Manhattan (by any name) appears to spring metaphorically from the infected-leg health crisis of 1995.

"Writing is a fantasy situation," Spillane told Hank Nuwer with Orbit in October 1983. ". . . There's a lot of scenes, a lot of situations that are real, that really happened to me. Those are things that you take and you elaborate on and build up. . . ."

Also, Hammer's return as a damaged warrior is Spillane's way of depicting his return to writing—it had been seven years since *The Killing Man*—and to present Mike Hammer aging to an extent that Mickey felt he could not directly acknowledge. For years he had kept Hammer his own age, but now he froze the character in his midforties.

"I got older, but he didn't," Spillane said of Hammer to *Los Angeles Times* writer Beverly Beyette in 1989.

Also, in *Black Alley*, Mickey was playing it cagey with his readers. He was back in the Jehovah's Witnesses, where he'd taken criticism over *The Killing Man*. The words "shit" and "fuck" had turned up in the text from this writer who in real life used "golly" and "gee." And the older Spillane was a more mellow, socially conservative person. By making Mike Hammer a shadow of his former physical self, playing down the usual violence would go unquestioned; and of course Mike's doctor tells him that sex is out till he's fully recovered.

The latter relates to Mickey's revisionism where Velda and Mike are concerned. They seem never to have consummated their long love when earlier novels make it clear they'd been sexually active for years, starting on that hillside in *The Snake*. Write it off as coy, senior-citizen sex play.

Black Alley is clearly a rumination on old age. Hammer's mellow masculinity is greatly appealing, and his warm relationship with Velda is believable and very much an equal partnership. For writer and character, both often dismissed as misogynist, the love and respect between Mike and Velda should put such nonsense to rest.

As early as 1955, Spillane spoke of writing one last Hammer novel, though of course he went on to write *The Girl Hunters*, *The Snake*, *The Body Lovers*, and *Survival . . . Zero!* Then in the 1970s, he began threatening a much longer book of a length similar to *The Erection Set*.

Black Alley seems to be that book, having evolved into a projected two-book set—the second, *King of the Weeds*, intended as a direct sequel. He was particularly taken with the concept of $89 billion dollars in cash, squirreled away somewhere by the mob. Central to *Black Alley*, this plotline does not play out until the posthumous *King of the Weeds* (2014).

Mike Hammer's Mickey Spillane.

CHAPTER TWENTY-THREE

WHERE'S MY TRENCH COAT?

Journalists visiting the Spillane casa in Myrtle Beach expecting a trench coat and pork-pie hat, or maybe a Lucky dangling from tough-guy lips, were instead greeted (as was Art Harris of the *Herald Tribune*) by "a stocky fireplug of a man with a menacing gray crewcut and a bullneck" wearing khaki shorts, a black T-shirt, and sneakers, an intimidating effect mitigated by "mirth lines etched about pale blue eyes." Peter Lennon of the Manchester, England, *Guardian* described the Spillane face as "a boulder trying to express something but not trying too hard." Beverly Beyette of the *LA Times* encountered a self-identified "beach bum" wearing "a black sweatshirt, white deck pants and Topsiders on sockless feet."

Spillane discussed his wardrobe with *Esquire* magazine in December of 1972. "I own two suits and a sports jacket," he explained. "Clothes mean little to me." Wide ties were "like a throw rug around the neck." But he owned "the best diving gear, the best flying gear in the world." Clothes, he said, were "just something you wear in the city."

But in the city, those two suits of his were custom-made by Richard Bennett, the distinctive hats made especially for him by Dobbs. Haircuts, however, he either handled himself or at barbershops outside Air Force bases.

Of his beach life, Spillane said to *Writer's Digest*, "There's always fish to catch or something to do or a book to read. If there's no books to read, I'll write one."

In the last decade of his life, Mickey Spillane published little but seemed to be writing constantly. While he published only two novels in that period, he was always working on more than one in each of his three home offices. Despite his laid-back manner, he clearly heard the ticking clock of a man in his eighties.

"Time becomes very important to you as you get older," he told *Coast* magazine. "Money is good to have but time is important. I don't have to write a book, but I want to."

The second part of the saga begun by *Black Alley* and its $89 million mob stash would, he insisted, be the final Mike Hammer novel. He was fascinated by the notion of so much cash hidden away in a mountain cave, like something out of the swashbuckling novels and adventure pulps he gulped down in his youth. He had also been working intermittently on *Something's Down There*, an outright adventure novel that would draw on his nautical interests, somewhat in the Peter Benchley fashion. When Benchley published a novel called *The Deep* (1976), Spillane sent the author a telegram saying, "Mine sold four million. Hope yours does as well."

He liked the idea of a retirement community for cops and that became *Dead Street* (2007). Several false starts grew into a manuscript nearly completed before his passing.

Something's Down There and *Dead Street* were third-floor office projects. *The Last Stand* (completed but published posthumously in 2018) apparently began in the big office downstairs. The ancient office on stilts, never remodeled and a time machine into the 1950s, was Mike Hammer's domain.

Many of Mickey's close friends were dying: Ray Wilson and Roscoe Fawcett in 1980, Dave Gerrity in 1984, Hy Gardner in 1989. He began naming characters in the new books after his surviving buddies—Jack Stang was the Hammer-ish lead of *Dead Street*, Don Watts a sea captain in *Something's Down There*, Joe Gill is the pilot hero of *The Last Stand*.

Several Hammers in progress indicated new ideas kept elbowing their way to the front of the line. The most dramatic of those came in the wake of the terrorist attacks of September 11, 2001, after which *King of the Weeds* (2014) was set aside and *The Goliath Bone* (2008) took over.

You stand at the heart of New York City and look east to where the twin monuments once stood, gargantuan edifices that reached into the sky, proclaiming wealth and power and hopefully indicating peace. There's an oddball silence there now, not the absence of noise, but the stillness of sounds that people make, like laughter and satisfaction. As they go by that once-busy avenue that houses the magnificent businesses of the world, they avert their eyes, their voices become subdued but, if you listen real close, you can hear someone swear at the bastards who tried to murder a city. It's an empty space now, but someday the snakes who live for destruction across the ocean in their own empty spaces of sand and caves would meet the snapping teeth of the avengers.

Two things were clear: Mike Hammer had a worthy foe again, and Mickey Spillane didn't really hate New York at all.

He had so many manuscripts going, in his unspoken race against the clock, that when he mislaid the first third of so of *The Goliath Bone*, he just shrugged and started over. That was nothing unusual for this writer. When his car was stolen with *The Body Lovers* manuscript under the seat, he said he just hated losing that car, but could always write the book again in a couple of weeks. (Both were recovered.)

During his final decade, Spillane pursued numerous interests in addition to writing, none more dear to him than conservation. Once again, commercial development had encroached upon his quiet lifestyle in its natural setting—workers installing water and sewer lines, yet another dirt lane giving way to pavement, the stretch of condos and beach houses of Garden City across the sound—getting from Spillane his idea of profanity: "Progress!"

Pointing across the backwater inlet past his yard, Spillane told journalist Cindi Clemmer, "This creek used to be full of crabs, clams and fish. Not anymore."

Mickey struck up a friendship with the much younger Paul Vernon, a sculptor and orthodontic technician, who shared the mystery writer's love of sport fishing.

On their first meeting, Vernon said, "He asked me questions that only a person who had been around the water enough would know—about the ecosystem, and what was being caught . . . [he had] a knowledge of anything to do with the ocean. After all, he'd been a diver."

When he became aware of Vernon's conservation work, Spillane said, "Well, you know, there's a lot of ways to raise money. We have plenty of golf tournaments around here, but a fishing tournament would be great."

Vernon began asking around at the area marinas and got an overwhelmingly favorable response. He and Spillane organized a Mickey Spillane Celebrity Fishing Tournament. The heavy lifting went to Vernon, while Mickey concentrated on getting backing from Miller Lite, and rounding up some fellow All-Stars as well as a few NASCAR drivers and an actor named Stacy Keach.

The event ran three years, was backed by Polaroid, Johnson Outboards, and Hummingbird Electronics, the proceeds going to marine conservation. Vernon and Spillane, from the latter's "Mudboat Marina," went on to co-host the *Carolina Billfish* series seen on Turner's SportSouth Network.

By the midnineties, however, Spillane was spending a few months in the fall with old friend George Wilson near Granville, New York. In a letter to MAC, he wrote of "not [being] the sand and surf nut I once was. After forty-two years I want the mountains back with snow and ice and strange wind noises."

In 1995, he reported, "This new place is great. I changed my approach to it—instead of building the new wing first, we're redecorating and refurbishing the house part so Jane can come into something beautifully livable, an old *real* carriage house with touches like a Swiss chalet."

Later Mickey wrote, "My ski bum's home is ready and waiting, wood cut and seasoned for the fire, groceries on the shelves and all I have to do is clean out some dead flies from the summer, take the cover off the typewriter and go to work."

In September 1998, in Murrells Inlet, he reported, "Finally, it's quiet on the roadways with the tourists gone, the creek has some boats with locals fishing and a sense of coolness has replaced the usual heat." Still, he had already bought an October 8th ticket ("Frequent Fliers upgrade to First Class!") to Granville.

But by the turn of the twenty-first century, the north country was losing its charm, and so was old age. He would frequently say, "I'm not an old man, I'm a young man something bad happened to."

"This eighty-two years old bit is a pain," he wrote. "I got nobody to play with. George doesn't ski." Another old friend older than Mick was "stooped and thin, mentally and spiritually fit, but aging fast." Even in letters, though, Mickey loved to shock: "I'm embarrassed to tell anybody that I had another wet dream that nearly knocked me out of bed. Wow!"

In Murrells Inlet, Mickey and Jane lived a quiet life. When Jane's daughters were with them, he cooked breakfast every morning, taking them to school if they missed the bus. As he had for years, he collected Blue Willow dishware (covered dishes were his Holy Grail). He and Jane would sit on the veranda, gazing out across the sandbars and chatting, chimes making music in the breeze, the occasional speedboat growling by. At the airport he might send a reporter off with a gift bag of Dunkin' Donuts, but only after making a quiet pitch for the Witnesses. "There's good news," he'd say. "Do you want to live forever?"

At Christmas, Jane would decorate the interior of the new house with a vengeance worthy of Mike Hammer, erecting a Manhattan-size city of Christmas villages. Mickey, who as a Witness claimed not to celebrate Christmas, secretly arranged and prepaid for fifty Christmas villages to be sent to her after his death, little ongoing presents from a loving husband.

In 1999, Jane, outraged over what she and Mickey considered a miscarriage of justice in a murder case, ran for district attorney on an anti-corruption ticket. "It's only an administrative job," she told Peter Lennon of the *Guardian*. "But three days before voting they passed a law saying you can't be a district attorney without a legal background. So I have a law called after me—the Jane Spillane Bill."

Vanity Fair's Cliff Rothman noticed that Spillane would inject outrageously sexist comments into the conversation to try to get a rise out of the politically opinionated Mrs. Spillane, as when he said to the reporter in front of her, "You remember when they'd send to Europe for a wife?"

Jane said someone in Beverly Hills walked up to her and asked, "How does it feel to be married to that male-chauvinist pig?" Her reply: "I love every minute of it."

He had mellowed politically—the man who walked a Communism-spouting partygoer through closed French doors in the 1950s, who had flirted in several senses of the word with Ayn Rand in the 1960s, who had branded anyone left of center as radical in the 1970s, now told journalists, "I am not a liberal or a conservative." To which Jane said, "Yeah, right. He's as conservative as they come."

When health issues began to crop up, Spillane took them in stride.

In 1991, "Mickey woke up and saw two of me," Jane said. He was rushed to the hospital and diagnosed with a mild stroke. "He begged the doctor to fix it," she said, "saying one of me was enough."

He recovered in two days and went on a blood thinner, which would figure in a much worse scare years later.

When in 2002 Spillane submitted *Something's Down There* to NAL, the editorial response was unenthusiastic and reminiscent of the long-ago rejection of *For Whom the Gods Would Destroy*. The latest regime might be willing to publish the seagoing adventure if Mickey rewrote it as a Mike Hammer—after all, his new hero's name, Mako Hooker, was already similar. Mickey declined. The publishing house Spillane had helped build turned his new novel down.

Approached with a Spillane manuscript, David Rosenberg at Simon & Schuster thought it might be a prank—he didn't know Mickey was still alive! The publisher told *Vanity Fair* that he had "swooned at the possibility" of publishing a new Spillane novel, which he described as "both a whodunit and a what-done-it."

Something's Down There (2003)—an adventure yarn with touches of Peter Benchley and Clive Cussler—has a scope and word count well beyond typical Spillane, though its subject matter and tone are consistent with his books for young readers, told in the same, rare-for-Spillane third person.

The reader is teased with the possibility of a sea monster destroying ships in the Caribbean, and Mako Hooker is a "retired" spook intrigued by this local mystery. Soon a movie production company, a branch of the CIA, and various nefarious characters share Mako's interest.

Something's Down There reflects not only the mature Spillane's love for the sea but for telling stories, and even a love for people that is quite at odds with Mike Hammer's defiant misanthropy. Hooker is at once evocative of Spillane himself and a nod to Ernest Hemingway and his valedictory *The Old Man and the Sea* (1952).

But while old fisherman Santiago loses his marlin to the deadly shark, Mako Hooker is not deterred in his quest as a mako shark trails his boat throughout the novel. Hooker conquers both the mako and the mythic "eater" mechanism that has plagued the islanders. Mako Hooker is at peace with the world; so is Spillane.

No rage storms through the final Spillane novel published during his lifetime. Unlike Hemingway, Spillane is not dreaming of recapturing youth—he has accepted the natural world, found peace, and walked away with the love of his life. The journey is over. The mythic quest complete.

"There are surely enough of Spillane's original fans left," *Publisher's Weekly* predicted, "to rack up respectable numbers for this enjoyable flashback to an earlier age." But that did not prove to be the case. And other reviewers were less kind.

Spillane's final completed novel, *The Last Stand*—published posthumously and paired with a previously unpublished (but more typical) 1950s novella, "A Bullet for Satisfaction"—indicates further the writer's move away from mystery and into adventure. In it, pilot Joe Gillian makes an emergency landing on an Indian reservation and stumbles into a search for rare minerals led by the federal government. Along the way he meets a true love, Running Fox, and Big Arms, a tribesman at first an adversary but ultimately a trusted friend.

In 2005, Jane, visiting her daughter Britt in Virginia, had difficulty reaching her husband. She sent a friend to check on Mickey and a scene out of a literal bloody murder mystery awaited. Blood spattered the long flight of exterior steps and the stairs inside to the second floor. The friend found Mickey, seemingly unconscious or worse, in scarlet-streaked sheets.

The mystery writer was just asleep, however, and easily roused. He had tripped over one of their cats and tumbled down the sixteen exterior steps. He crawled back up the stairs and into the house, leaving a gruesome trail thanks to his blood thinner, and on up to the bedroom, where he got under the covers and went to sleep. Cranky over the unnecessary fuss, Mickey allowed himself to be taken by ambulance to the hospital, where he stayed for two days. He'd broken no bones and a raft of tests turned up nothing.

> MAC: *When I first met Mickey, and kidded him about having written him a hundred letters in return for one, he must have set about to even up the score. Over the next twenty-five years, he sent me forty-some letters and many packages of "goodies," like the printing plate of an ad in the* New York Times *for* I, the Jury, *a color photostat of the 1940s proposed* Mike Danger *comic book cover by Harry Sahle, and the original dedication page to me for* Black Alley.
>
> *We spoke frequently on the phone and often he called me, after which I would look at Barb, shake my head, and say, "Mickey Spillane just called me." I never took for granted our relationship, both personal and business, but could never quite believe this man was in my life. Whether he wrote or called, he always inquired after his godson Nathan, now over six feet tall, who he referred to variously as "the Giant," "el giantico," or "the trumpeter"—Mickey had his own trumpet refurbished (once played by Harry James) and sent to Nate. Mickey always remembered Barb, who was "my lovely wife" and "the blonde."*
>
> *In July 1992 I traveled to Murrells Inlet to testify in court as to the value of the (likely stolen)* One Lonely Night *painting lost in Hugo. He and I talked the evening before in his tiki bar in his backyard. He spoke of his anger with the looters who ravaged his home in the storm's aftermath. In his eyes was a Mickey Spillane I'd never seen*

before, a Mike Hammer burning with rage; he put his hands out in front of him and squeezed them into fists, and told me vividly what he would like to do the thieves. Then his body relaxed and fists were fingers again, and he said, "But I'm not like that anymore. I don't do that now."

In 1999, my documentary Mike Hammer's Mickey Spillane *made its American premiere at the University of Iowa Library in Iowa City. Sweet revenge—I had been something of a black sheep at the U of I for writing hard-boiled fiction and various papers on Spillane at the Writers Workshop, including an essay comparing the novel and film of* Kiss Me Deadly *when its importance was just a twinkle in the eyes of French film critics and Paul Schrader.*

Mickey and Jane attended the premiere and stayed at the Hotel Muscatine where, four years before, he had billeted after arriving with a dangerously swollen, infected leg, insisting the show—my show—must go on. In our house for the one and only time, he sat at our dining room table and patiently signed all my Spillane first editions.

A letter from him—always single-spaced and on his distinctive "Mickey Spillane Productions" letterhead—was always a thrill. In one of the first missives (undated) he wrote, "I always enjoyed the [comics] business. The only hard part was describing the sound a guy made on the way down from a thirty-story building. There was EEEEEEeeeeee, YYYiiiiii OGHrrrrrrrr, then splat."

In a late letter, he wrote, "Today it's warm again. I like it either too hot or too cold, but the intermediate weather is not my cup of tea. One day I'll find my little niche and build my log cabin there. Cut logs stacked in the back yard, chickens in the coop, a good cook in the kitchen, a few Smith-Coronas with a bushel of ribbons and a BT-13 on a nearby airstrip. Great, huh?"

In March 2000—the day after his birthday—he wrote, "Maybe I won't quit doing the Mike Hammer books after all. Though I'd hate to die halfway through one."

In June 2006 he called me, sounding chipper. But his news was grim: he'd been diagnosed with pancreatic cancer. My wife's father received that same diagnosis and, like so many, had gone quickly. Mickey was upbeat about treatment possibilities. Perhaps a week later he told me he'd completed The Last Stand *and wanted me to have a look at it. He sent it, I read it, and called to tell him how much fun it was. He was pleased with the book—to have finished it, under the circumstances, and with the way it came out. In the meantime, he was getting back to the final Hammer novel-in-progress,* The Goliath Bone, *looking forward to finally getting Velda and Mike hitched.*

His next call betrayed a hint of tiredness—just a hint—as he said, "I'm doing well with Goliath Bone, *but if I can't finish it, would you?"*

I said, "Yes, of course, but I hope the need won't arise." I told him it was the greatest honor I could ever be paid.

And then I heard myself say, "I love you, Mickey."

"I love you, buddy," I heard him say.

Italics and all.

On July 17, 2006—six weeks to the day of that deadly diagnosis—Mickey Spillane passed away in the Tidelands Hospice in Georgetown, South Carolina. A memorial service was held July 29, 2006, at the Jehovah's Witness Kingdom Hall. On August 26, 2006, his family and friends celebrated his life on the lawn of his Murrells Inlet home. Among those sharing warm memories and anecdotes were Jane Spillane, Jane's daughter Britt Ellinger, Mickey's daughter Caroline Hill, Max Allan Collins, Don Watts, and Paul Vernon.

Media coverage on his passing was extensive. The *New York Times* called Spillane the "Critic-Proof Writer of Pulpy Mike Hammer Novels." The AP, in a widely circulated story, said, "Mickey Spillane, the macho mystery writer who wowed millions of readers with the shoot-'em-up sex and violence of gumshoe Mike Hammer, died Monday. He was 88."

On July 14, 2011, Business 17 was renamed Mickey Spillane Waterfront 17 Highway. Spillane was inducted into the South Carolina Academy of Authors in 2012.

Jane Spillane actively sought to preserve and promote her husband's memory and accomplishments. In 2012 and 2013, she taught a class for Coastal Carolina University called "My Life With Mickey" and in 2014 her book of that name was published. She appeared on local TV and spoke at luncheons, civic clubs, museums, the University of South Carolina, and book clubs all around the state. She was also a guest lecturer at Coastal Carolina University in their literature classes.

Posthumous honors and accolades are all well and good, but memories keep a dead man living—memories and books, in this man's case. Jane Spillane sits on the deck where she and her husband would watch the sun's rays and the water's shimmer conspire to create colors and patterns, broken suddenly by a mullet's silvery sideways leap, then splash. Black legs nimbly motivate the white bodies of egrets patrolling the shoreline. Looking across the sandbars at dusk, Jane notes the twinkling lights of Garden City, but only a speedboat or two bring close the species Mike Hammer so distrusted.

Yet Mike Hammer and his papa only pretended not to care about people. Fans were his customers. His neighbors were his friends. Sometimes the line nicely blurred.

One night Mickey left for Bible study at the Kingdom Hall, then rushed back minutes later. Her husband didn't take Bible study lightly; now here he was home again.

"Jane, where's my .45? Where's my holster? Where's my hat? Where's my trench coat?"

She asked this man in a perfect black suit, Bible in hand, what was wrong. Why was he trying to grab a gun and suit up like some private eye?

"Because," he said, deadly serious, "they're staking out the gas station around the corner and they're getting ready to rob this woman and the attendants aren't allowed to have guns behind the counter to defend themselves."

Jane thought, *Oh my God, he is going to get himself killed!*

Somehow Mickey was already in his hat with his shoulder holster on, .45 snugged in place, climbing into his trench coat. He had become Mike Hammer. An eighty-year-old Mike Hammer.

As he went out the front door, he told her to call the sheriff's office—as if Hammer were ordering Velda to get Pat Chambers. She did as she was told: "Mickey's on the way to the gas station right now to break up a robbery." The deputies rushed out, but the gas station was just around the corner from the Spillane house, less than a quarter of a mile—Mickey had the jump on them.

The rest Jane learned from witnesses and the deputies.

Night—about nine P.M. Spillane in his new white Ford pickup pulled into the gas station parking lot. The female attendant at the register was a neighbor and Mickey was not about to let anything happen to her. The car he'd seen parked, waiting for the right moment, was still there. Two menacing-looking men got out on either side. They approached the gas station's glass-and-steel door.

The white pickup's rider side door opened and out into a light ground fog climbed a broad-shouldered figure in pork-pie hat, suit, and unbuttoned trench coat. Hat brim turned down, hiding his eyes, the man moved toward the two "customers," trench-coat tail trailing.

Mickey Spillane cut across their paths, lifted his eyes as he drew back the trench coat with his left hand, filled his barrel chest with air, and let them see the holstered .45 under his arm. They scrambled back into their car and squealed off. Mickey went inside to check on the woman behind the counter.

Later the Spillanes learned there had been a string of robberies of all-night gas stations in the area by a pair answering the description of the suspects, who were picked up that night carrying illegal, unregistered weapons.

Mike Hammer was not seen in the Inlet again.

Margaret Kirk of the *Philadelphia Inquirer* asked the writer about the final Hammer novel he had been promising for years, the one he always said he was "about three weeks shy" of completing. He said he wanted it to be a farewell. In it, he wanted to say something to all the readers over the years who ignored the critics.

"Thank you people," Mickey Spillane said. "I appreciate you reading my books."

THE SPILLANE FILES

TIMELINE

1918

- March 9: born in Brooklyn, New York
- Baptized Frank Michael in father's Catholic Church
- Baptized Frank Morrison in mother's Protestant Church
- John Joseph Spillane calls his son Mickey; Anne Catherine Spillane calls her son Babe

1919

- Spillane family moves to Elizabeth, New Jersey

1924

- "Morrison" Spillane in Public School 88, Queens
- Honor Roll, class 1AB

1926

- June: enrolls in Theodore Roosevelt Junior High School (Elizabeth, New Jersey)

1927

- Enrolls in St. James Episcopal Methodist Sunday School

1929

- June 14: performs as "King of the Weeds" in operetta *The Stolen Flower Queen*
- Reads Alexander Dumas and Herman Melville

1932

- Writes book report on *The Age of Fable* by Thomas Bulfinch
- June: graduates from Theodore Roosevelt Junior High School

1935

- September: enters as a senior at Erasmus Hall High School, 911 Flat-bush Avenue, Brooklyn, New York
- Writes stories and articles for *Elizabeth* (New Jersey) *Daily Journal* (at least one about bootleggers)

1936

- Erasmus Hall Yearbook, *The Academy*: "By the palette and the brush/ Here's one who could amount to much"
- Home address: 1211 Church Avenue, Brooklyn

About 1933–38

- Sells fiction to slick magazines and pulps

1938/1939/1940

- Works as a lifeguard at Point Breeze, Long Island (Breezy Point)
- Meets Wilma Sterling from Rockaway Point

1939

- Attends Kansas State Teachers College (Kansas State College), Man-hattan, Kansas—"The Little Apple"
- Member of Phi Delta Chi fraternity
- On football team (varsity) and swim team (intramural)
- Sells stories to New York markets, turning in carbon copies to his English classes
- Army records state he was an English major

1940

- Pictures of Spillane and Ray Wilson appear in *The Reveille*, yearbook of Kansas State College
- Back in New York by fall, working in Gimbel's department store base-ment ("selling robes," according to *Vanity Fair*)

1940–42

- Writes comic stories and two-page short "fillers" for Funnies, Inc. (49 W. 45th Street, New York City)
- Works as associate editor for Louis Jacquet
- Joe Gill introduces him to brother Ray, writer at Funnies, Inc.
- Works with comics legends Stan Lee, Carl Burgos (Human Torch), Bill Everett (Sub-Mariner), and Jack Kirby and Joe Simon (Captain America)
- Creates "Mike Danger" comics character, drawn by artist Harry Sahle
- "Mike Lancer" story sold to *Green Hornet* (in 1942)

- December 8, 1941: volunteers for United States Army
- December 1941–September 1942: editor at Funnies, Inc.
- October 19, 1942: enters active service

1943

- July 28: Air Corps commission becomes official
- Aviation Cadet, class 43-G AAF Advanced Flying School, Mariana, Florida
- Commissioned Second Lieutenant: Instructor of Cadets in Basic Training at the Greenwood Basic Flying School (Greenwood, Mississippi)
- Meets Mary Ann Pearce, secretary at army base

1945

- March 19: marries Mary Ann
- Receives training and combat fighter assignment in P-51s, but does not see combat
- January 4–February 4: at Napier Field, Dothan, Alabama
- October 14: separation date from active army
- Military occupation listed as "Fighter Pilot"
- October 8: promoted to First Lieutenant, enlists in Air Corps Reserve for five years: Officers Reserve Corps
- "Mustering out" paperwork addressed to 808 Beverly Road, Brooklyn, New York (Kings County)

1946

- Writes freelance comics and fillers
- With Joe and Ray Gill, starts Spillane/Gill Studios, 2212 Vanderveer Place, Brooklyn, New York
- Makes sales to Timely Comics
- Converts Mike Danger comic book into Mike Hammer mystery novel
- Claims to write *I, the Jury* in nine days
- Velda Sterling named for Spillane's girlfriend from Breezy Point: Wilma Sterling (Velda's last name not revealed until *The Goliath Bone*, 2008)
- Ray Gill contacts John F. "Jack" McKenna, who has connections at Dutton
- McKenna passes *I, the Jury* to Roscoe Fawcett, who will distribute if Dutton/Signet publishes it
- June 10: signs contract with agent McKenna
- Builds house with help of friends George Wilson and Ray Gill at Newburgh, New York, property. During construction lives in army surplus tents
- December: receives $1,000 advance for *I, the Jury* and uses money to complete cement-block house on Rock Cut Road, Newburgh, New York

1947

- *I, the Jury* published by E. P. Dutton
- Five thousand copies printed

1948

- April 30: receives VA real estate loan for $1,750; VA eligibility card issued
- December: *I, the Jury* paperback published (Signet #699)
- Dutton shelves second Mike Hammer (*For Whom the Gods Would Destroy*), fearing it would hurt Spillane's sales. Manuscript is passed back and forth from Spillane to editors for many years; not published until 1996 as *The Twisted Thing*

1949

- May 10: Spillane's AF unit at Stewart Field, Newburgh, New York, deactivated
- July 2: daughter Kathy Spillane born

1950

- September 25: son Ward Joseph Spillane born
- *My Gun Is Quick* published by Dutton
- *Vengeance Is Mine!* published by Dutton

1951

- *One Lonely Night* published by Dutton
- November 17: joins Jehovah's Witnesses
- *The Big Kill* published by Dutton
- *The Long Wait* published by Dutton (first non-Hammer novel)
- December 3: review ("A Slaughter for a Quarter") in *Time*
- Races hot rods in Newburgh, New York

1952

- *Kiss Me, Deadly* published by Dutton (last book of Spillane's contract with Dutton). *New York Times* and *New York Herald Tribune* bestseller. 75,000-plus copies sold (big numbers for a hardback of that era)
- Paperback of *I, the Jury* has its 21st printing (11 million copies of his five paperbacks sold)
- Biographical article appears in *Life*
- May: articles in *Saturday Review* ("Decline and Fall of the Whodunit") and *Harper's* ("Dames and Death")

- Signs movie deal with Victor Saville for $210,000 (announced in *Variety*, Christmas Eve)
- First postwar visit to Myrtle Beach, South Carolina

1953

- Paperback of *I, the Jury* has its 29th printing (1.6 million copies sold)
- *Kiss Me, Deadly* appears in paperback (Signet #1000)
- Spillane short novel "Everybody's Watching Me" serialized in first four issues of *Manhunt*
- Start of eight-year novel hiatus
- Spoofed in two films: Fritz Lang's *The Blue Gardenia* and Vincente Minnelli's *The Band Wagon*
- November 6: savaged in *Saturday Review* ("Mickey Spillane and his Bloody Hammer")

1954

- Stars in John Wayne–produced circus film, *Ring of Fear*
- First *Mike Hammer* TV pilot (with Brian Keith)
- TV: *Person to Person* (series 1, episode 25) with Edward R. Murrow, CBS-TV on March 19, live from Newburgh
- TV: *The Texaco Star Theater* (series 6, episode 11), reciting "The Night Before Christmas"

1955

- Rumored undercover work for FBI into narcotics ring
- Reviews/articles in *Good Housekeeping*, *Look*, *National Parent Teacher*, and *New Statesman*
- Referenced in Academy Award–winning film *Marty*
- June 7: son Michael Spillane born
- TV pilot for *Mickey Spillane Presents* announced but perhaps not produced; not picked up by a network

1956

- TV: *Tennessee Ernie Ford Show* (series 1, episode 4)
- Works with Robert Fellows on various scripts for movies and proposed TV series
- Begins work on the lost *One Lonely Night* script
- January 1–June: "Mickey Spillane Writes" column for *Greensboro* (North Carolina) *Daily News*

1957

- Works with Robert Fellows and Gene Roddenberry on proposed TV show, *Murder by Spillane*
- May 18: daughter Caroline Spillane born

1958

- January 15: purchases Murrells Inlet home
- Referenced in movie *Separate Tables* (Burt Lancaster wrote Spillane asking permission)
- *Mickey Spillane's Mike Hammer* TV series (with Darren McGavin); it will run until 1960

1959

- Uncredited appearance on "Sea Hunt" (with Lloyd Bridges) as a scuba diver

1960

- Proposed Mike Hammer Broadway musical ("Oh Mike!")

1961

- September 8: *Life* profile, "Soft Side of a Hard Egg"

1962

- TV: *The Tonight Show Starring Johnny Carson* (series 1, episode 56) on April 1
- June 19: Gay Talese interview in *New York Times*
- Announces "a serious war novel," the apparently unwritten *The Stragglers,* about an Air Force B-17 crew
- Divorced from Mary Ann Pearce
- Shoots feature film *The Girl Hunters* in Manhattan and the UK, playing Mike Hammer; co-stars Shirley Eaton, "golden girl" in the James Bond movie *Goldfinger*
- TV: *The Tonight Show Starring Johnny Carson* (series 2, episode 76)
- TV: *Hy Gardner Show* (show #352) on January 6
- Medically qualified, United States Air Force
- May 2: now a colonel, part of the 354th Tactical Fighter Wing, Myrtle Beach Air Force Base
- June 7: favorable review in *Time* ("I, the Actor") of Spillane's role in *The Girl Hunters*
- July: tongue-in-cheek but not negative Terry Southern article in *Esquire* on Spillane writer/actor

1964

- November 6: in Malibu, California, marries Selma (Sherri) Malinou of Providence, Rhode Island

1965

- First of academic articles: Frederick Duke, "*I, the Jury*: Allegory of McCarthyism," *Hexagon*, 1, no. 4, pp. 43–59
- Erle Stanley Gardner discusses Spillane and Carroll John Daly in "Getting Away with Murder," June *Atlantic*

1966

- TV: *Today Show* on February 9
- May 28: in Los Angeles, California, signs contract for musical "Mike" with Robert Fellows, Charles Tannen, and Tay Garnett (The Mike Company)
- Kingsley Amis includes Mike Hammer in "My Favorite Sleuths" in December *Playboy*

1967

- Has 7 of the top 10 in Alice P. Hackett's *80 Years of Bestsellers*
- Johnny Mercer writes songs for "Oh, Mike!" Broadway show; they resurface in *The Complete Lyrics of Johnny Mercer* (2009)
- Discussion and correspondence with Roy Rowland and Robert Fellows regarding possible Tiger Mann movies
- TV: *The Joey Bishop Show* (season 1, episode 27)

1969

- Takes over as producer after Robert Fellows dies during preproduction of *Delta Factor* film. Shoots in Nashville and Puerto Rico; Sherri has a supporting role
- John Cawelti discusses "The Spillane Phenomenon" in the *Journal of Popular Culture* and the *University of Chicago Magazine*

1970

- TV: *The Mike Douglas Show* (series 10, episode 5)
- TV: *The David Frost Show* (series 2, episode 208) on June 17 and (series 2, episode 232) on July 24

1971

- Works with Hollywood PI Fred Otash on Los Angeles background for novels

1972

- Publicity articles about *The Erection Set* in *Penthouse*, *Gallery*, and *Esquire*
- January: in Chicago for wife Sherri's nightclub act at Mister Kelly's
- July: *Delta Factor* PR tour
- TV: NBC *First Tuesday* (similar to *60 Minutes*) program about Communism on December 5
- TV: mystery guest on *What's My Line?* in December

1973

- January: Sherri in *Oklahoma!* at Union Plaza Hotel, Las Vegas
- Spillane returns to Murrells Inlet
- TV: appears on *Parkinson* (series 2, episode 35) in the UK on March 3
- May 8: with Sherri in Chicago at Mister Kelly's
- July: shoots first Miller Lite Beer commercial with Lee Meredith; begins an 18-year run

1974

- TV: *Columbo*, "Publish or Perish" (series 3, episode 5, as writer Alan Mallory) on January 18

1975

- TV: *Dinah!* on June 13 (with Dinah Shore)

1976

- September: article and cover photo in *Writer's Digest*

1979

- Middle-grade book *The Day the Sea Rolled Back* wins Junior Literary Guild Award
- Spillane issue of *The Armchair Detective*, Fall

1981

- Special guest at Bouchercon in Milwaukee
- *People* magazine paints positive picture of Spillane as children's writer

1982

- Middle-grade book *The Ship That Never Was* published
- TV: *Late Night with David Letterman* on May 6

1983

- April 7: divorce from Sherri finalized

- October 30: marries Jane Rogers Johnson
- Receives the Eye, Lifetime Achievement Award from Private Eye Writers of America

1984

- *Mickey Spillane's Mike Hammer* TV series with Stacy Keach premieres in January on CBS-TV
- Presents award for Outstanding Drama Series at the 36th Primetime Emmy Awards

1987

- TV: *The Dick Cavett Show* with Robert B. Parker, Evan Hunter, and Dilys Wynn
- September 3–5: hosts Sea Scouts Fishing Festival, Murrells Inlet, South Carolina

1988

- March 4: Mickey and Lee Meredith travel to Atlanta for fundraiser to combat child abuse

1989

- Death of longtime friend Hy Gardner (1908–89)
- September: Hurricane Hugo destroys most of the Spillanes' home in Murrells Inlet. Looters take rare items, including *One Lonely Night* paperback-cover painting
- Receives $500,000 advance for *The Killing Man*, first Mike Hammer novel since 1970

1990

- Receives Private Eye Writers of America best short-story award for *Playboy* abridgement of *The Killing Man*

1991

- Distinguished Service Award from Fort Hays State University (Kansas)

1993

- Suffers a stroke

1995

- Tekno Comics begins publishing *Mickey Spillane's Mike Danger*
- Spillane appears in Max Allan Collins movie (*Mommy*)

- Named Grand Master by Mystery Writers of America (MWA)
- August 15: appears on *Late Night with Conan O'Brien* promoting *Mike Danger* comic book

1996

- *Black Alley* published; receives $1.5 million advance
- Spillane plays role in *Mommy's Day* (released 1997)

1997

- *Mike Danger* comic book ends two-year run

1998

- March 9: 80th birthday celebration at Oliver's Lodge in Murrells Inlet. Bernstein, Keach, and Collins attend

1999

- July: National Film Theatre in London, screenings of *I, the Jury* in 3D, *Kiss Me Deadly*, Blake Edwards's *Mike Hammer* pilot, documentary *Mike Hammer's Mickey Spillane*. Interviewed on stage alongside MAC by Adrian Wootton

2002

- Special guest at Palm Springs Film Noir Festival

2003

- Simon & Schuster publishes *Something's Down There*, Mako Hooker filling in for Mike Hammer. It is dedicated to his daughter Caroline, "a real product of the beach"

2004

- June 3: Mary Ann [Spillane] Taylor (née Pearce) dies

2005

- Receives honorary Doctor of Humane Letters from Coastal Carolina University, Conway, South Carolina

2006

- July 17: Spillane dies in Murrells Inlet. He had been at Tidelands Hospice
- Funeral at Kingdom Hall of the Jehovah's Witnesses

- Celebration of Spillane's life held outside his Murrells Inlet home
- October 26: son Michael dies

2012

- "Spillane Sunday" at Coastal Carolina University
- April 14: Mickey Spillane Tribute at the Strand Cinema in Georgetown, South Carolina; Jane Spillane introduces *Kiss Me Deadly* and *The Girl Hunters*

2013

- August 10: son Ward dies

MICKEY SPILLANE'S
AUTOBIOGRAPHY

[Mickey often said that he was going to write his own autobiography. The following fragment is the only part of that document found in his papers. It does, however, answer several questions about his youth, including his love for flying airplanes. Minor corrections have been made.]

Life is never lived at the beginning. Life, it seems, is lived only in retrospect, from a vantage point of age that is capable of reflection without the disadvantage of disillusionment with still a hope of future years ahead.

Life is fun.

Life is silly.

Life can only be enjoyed by the young and you never have to be young to get young. As long as you can enjoy life, you *are* young.

Looking back is no disaster. It's a cram course for the future and as long as there's life, there's a future, from the single moment to countless years.

So buckos, here's my past, a prediction of the future, and nothing of the present because that is always with us from each microsecond to each microsecond. The big *now* is so minuscule that we can only see on either side of us and NOW becomes the experience of yesterday and the hope of tomorrow. NOW to me is writing this to see if I really did enjoy the big past and will profit from it by a better future that gives life more meaning and greater fulfillment as we learn how to spend it.

◆

I was born in Brooklyn, New York, March 8th or 9th, 1918, nine months and several days after the marriage of my parents. It seems that they wed during the time of my mother's monthly cycle (poor Dad)(he really must have loved her) and the first cracker out the box must have begat me. These were the days before The Pill and should upset the Catholic Church's teachings on rhythm control of birth.

Or possibly, it was a pox because Ma was Protestant and Dad an Irish Catholic and neither converted, choosing instead to be married plan and simple by an old-fashioned minister who couldn't care less for the mix-up.

However, Dad got back at ritualistic churchiness. With Ma nine months down the road he caught pneumonia, was dying when the priest came in to give him the last rites of the church, and when my mother wasn't invited in for the so-called absolution, my old man threw the cleric out with my mother's approval and got so damn made he wouldn't die and that was the end of Romanism in our house.

They never knew when I was born. A few minutes after I was delivered cold turkey fashion in a cold water flat the time was a few minutes after twelve midnight, so the arbitrary time became March 9th and I'm just as glad there's some doubt about it because at my age now I have a reason for not bothering to remember birthdays. They're only numbers anyway, kids.

And that takes care of the first year. We moved to Elizabeth, New Jersey, when I was about eighteen months and my most memorable experience was, first . . . getting off the tittie. Being old fashioned, Ma kept me breast-bound for two years, not that I'm complaining. Today I'm a leg man first, a tit man second, possibly the gimmick Ma used to kick me out of the nest.

Apparently some of the more "progressive" neighbors reached old Ma and talked her out of depriving her kid of his security, so she reached for the burnt cork, painted her nipple black and when I was about to take hold of the swamp rabbit with gusto, she grimaced, gasper that the "the boogie" (as we fondly called it in those days) was sick . . . I almost upchucked, but that was the end of that. For quite a while I didn't even want a surreptitious peek at the thing.

End of second year.

At three I showed everybody how brave I was.

Until then I had never been further away from home than three houses down the block. My foot had never been in the gutter without ma's hand around mine. Oh . . . one exception. Once I was allowed to run down the street to meet Dad as he came home from work and I felt like Captain Cook, world traveller.

Then the iceman came around. Now *there* was an experience. The old, plodding horse that knew every stop, the cold, beautiful smell of wet wood and fresh chopped ice, the rickety wagon with the little step on the back, the spare tongs, apron and pick hanging on the hooks, and all glorious little chunks on the floor any kid could pick up and suck on if he could reach that far.

But I was brave. Man, was I brave. I didn't reach. I got on the step, and with everybody watching climbed into the wagon and was busy scooping up the pieces to hand out like popsicles when the wagon started to move.

Move? No, that's wrong. It took off down the street at a formidable rate, the familiar little universe of mine still visible from the confines of the wagon disappearing into nothingness like a train going down the track at one step a second from old Dobbin who was simply making his rounds.

But have you ever been *seven* houses from home when you were three? My screams were neighborhood-wide and I was promptly rescued by an amused iceman who had the decency not to embarrass me in front of my friends, asked me what kind of ice I wanted, deciphered a tearful "big-little" piece to mean medium, gave me some extras to restore face with the gang, then put me back on my sidewalk and pointed in the direction of my house. After a few different lies I was a momentary hero.

I never climbed back into an ice wagon again.

Then I was four.

I made believe I was going to school by walking as far as the corner with kids really going to school, ran back to the house and started over again. It got tiresome after a while so I took up reading. The longest word in the world at that time was CHESTNUT. Then ELEPHANT. They both have the same number of letters, but elephant sounded longer. What the hell was a chestnut, anyhow? Later it was CONSTANTINOPLE, and still later PROANTITRANSUBSTANTIATIONISM, which I finally translated, but that was much later.

That same year a tough girl socked me on the head with a stocking that had a potato in it on Halloween and when my mother wiped my tears and repaired my witch's costume, I went out and knocked her off the porch with a banana stalk and broke her arm. Nobody ever knew who did it to her, but she shouldn't have been sitting on the railing anyway with eight feet of space under her.

I felt a lot better than I did when I got out of the ice wagon.

When I was five I could read and write.

When I was six I could read and write better. I was vaccinated.

When I was seven I went to school and had nothing to do because I could already read and write.

When I was eight they skipped me because they thought I was a genius and put me in a class with a lot of Polacks who knocked the crap out of me.

When I was nine I beat up my first Polack and I felt good again.

It was a long time before I beat up another Polack. They kept growing bigger than me.

◆

Depression time. Haircuts were thirty-five cents on my corner, but ten blocks away you get them for thirty cents and that was a big saving. The only trouble was, I still wore short pants when everybody else had long ones, having even outgrown knickers. And the barbershop was in Polack Town where I was fair game. Every other Saturday Operation Terror-Stricken went into operation.

It was their backyard and I couldn't get away. I could get in, but just try to get out. This generation with their silly long hair never knew what it was like to get flatted out on the sidewalk while everybody gave you "the barber's itch" on the back of the head with warty knuckles. You got up bawling with frustration, got a few more belts in the mouth for good luck, had our shirttails ripped off, your fly opened with a backhanded "home run," and if you were lucky you got away without catching a rock in your back.

I caught hell at home for "playing" too much, but if I could have earned a nickle in those days it would have been spent at Tony Cushion's barbershop on the corner.

However, too much gets to be enough after a while. Next to the hated barbershop was a grocery store and sooner or later the wheel has to turn. It always does. Just wait long enough and it'll go around.

Black Saturday for the Polacks came the day they delivered the bananas. Ah, my old friend, the stalks. What a magnificent weapon. It should be used in combat. Delicately poised with the thin end in your hand, the heavy end ready to come around, the body of it so freshly firm that it can knock a man kicking, yet so pneumatic will never leave a mark on an unconscious form, it is the most formidable of handy, cheap, and devastating clubs ever devised by nature.

Being a devious little slob, I watched them gather on the corner knowing they had an hour of anticipation before I came out with a fresh haircut ready for by bimonthly beating. But I was looking past them at the pile of debris the grocer was throwing out, that lovely, warm feeling of knowing the garbage man didn't come around until the next day. I even had my stalk picked out as I skirted past the enemy, grinning a little fatuously like maybe if I was nice they wouldn't hurt me too much.

Damn, if they only knew how long that haircut took. Twice I saw kids go by, kick some of the stalks around, pick up one and discard it in the gutter.

But they never touched my stalk.

I didn't wait for the Wild Tiger lotion that day.

Always before I let the barber douse me and rub me so I would be safe that much longer. Not this time. I paid him the thirty cents and went next door. I remember I was almost laughing.

They didn't realize the immensity of the weapon. Maybe they didn't consider it a weapon at all. I really don't think they did. They had brainwashed themselves into complacency like we did with the Japs before Pearl Harbor and let me walk up, my stalk dragging behind me disconsolately, my face a feigned mask of gulping indifference.

Retreat was cut off. Advance was halted. Every avenue of escape was bottled up.

But there's always got to be one. The Leader. The Führer. Big teeth, nasty grin, tough guy attitude with the gang at his back while he took the first swipe and generously handed you over to the mob. And that was Iggy.

So as he went into his act where his utter ferociousness was to make me break and run into their arms, I stepped into him with one beautiful, calculated swing of the banana stalk, caught him square in the mouth, and had the extreme pleasure of watching blood squirt all over his shirt before his head hit the sidewalk and put him out like a light. The sound of his skull popping the concrete was the grandest music I heard before I whipped the stalk around again and saw with amazement another two tangle into one bunch of arms and legs piled against the Bond Bread box and knock over the milk bottles.

That did it. It was Polack day for me then. I nailed three more before they all finally escaped.

I talked my mother into letting me get another haircut the following Saturday. I didn't need it, but I said I was doing a play on Monday. I picked out a new banana stalk from the National Grocery Store ahead of time. The other one had gotten soggy from practice on fenceposts.

Saturday came and nobody was there. I was very disappointed.

Monday came and I made friends with Iggy. We stayed friends until he was killed in the war.

Then I was ten.

Nothing much happened in those days. They were making way for the new highway and moving houses on eight-by-eight timbers pulled by teams of horses and one of the watchmen gave me a pailful of manure to bring home for my mother's flowers. I walked it back two miles balancing it on the seat of my bike and just before I reached the house I spilled it. I smelled terrible and caught hell.

That was the year I peed in my father's shoes. Not deliberately, in case some psychologist is reading. I loved my mother and father. Peeing in the old man's shoes was an accident.

We lived in an unheated house on Bayway with the toilet off the kitchen. I got up to pee in a semi state of consciousness and somehow got disoriented. Dad had left his shoes under a kitchen chair and when I reached the spot, thought it was the bowl, tipped the chair back, figuring it was the seat, and peed. It left Dad's shoes flooded. So when Dad went to put on his brogans, you can imagine what happened. Shoes were made pretty watertight in those days. He wanted to wham me, but Ma stepped in and managed to make a case for me that it was better than wetting the bed. At least I tried. Now I think it would have been better if I had wet the bed. Dad only had one pair of shoes.

(One unmentioned biographical point just recalled: At age six we moved from Bayway to Brooklyn, New York, where I started school, lasted a few months before the call of the wild overcame the folks and we moved right back into the same house on Bayway in a Simmons Mattress Company truck supplied by the landlord and for a little kid it was a happy homecoming.)

In those days Elizabeth was still largely unpaved and lit with gas lamps. Progress was just around the corner to spoil the pleasure of undoing the lamplighter's work (or helping him at it), and ruin the lovely network of channels made by Model Ts, early Buicks, and Durants that flowed so swiftly after a rainstorm you could hardly run as fast as a shingle heading downhill.

Now Ma had graduated from the sixth grade while Dad managed his dropout program to culminate at the fourth. Higher education came only to the special ones then and neither of my folks came under that category. But opportunity is there for anybody.

Ma was known as Petition Annie.

In a neighborhood of even more unschooled people, having a fine mind, an even temperament, a gentle nature, but determined attitude . . . and not being burdened by a large family, me being the only begat, Ma took it upon herself to improve the lot of Bayway.

Much to the consternation of politicians, to whom only the downtown area of Elizabeth had any importance, Ma got up petitions. Ah, what petitions. Hell, she led the original freedom marches. Pleasures were simple then, and a double file of women six blocks long carrying hampers of lunch, a campout on the steps of the board of education brought happiness to the neighborhood and an immediate reaction from city hall. The new school was upped hurriedly while the politicos were still wiping the sweat off their faces, but before their hankies were dry a new petition was under way.

In two fell swoops Bayway was paved and electricity was installed in place of the gas lamps. I often wondered what happened to the lamplighter. It was technology that replaced him, but he sure must have hated Petition Annie.

In the meantime, dear old dad was unwittingly about to become Mayor of Elizabeth.

Dad was gregarious. He could always "mortify" Ma at any party when he had a couple of belts of homemade booze, but he sure didn't lack for invitations. He wasn't too big, but he was strong as a bull and acrobatic as hell. His act that was my favorite was a backflip when he was showing off to the kids that was always highlighted by a magnificent fart when he tucked and that brought the house down and mortified Ma again. In all the times I tried it I could never manage a fart like he could and he wasn't even trying.

Somehow he got to know all the politicians and Polacks at the same time and became the gentle mediator. Whenever a Polack wound up in jail it was "Yonnie" the family called upon to bust the offender out. Many a time I remember squads of them standing in the parlor, that inner sanctum open only on special occasions, listening to the tearful pleas, watching the hat wringing and then telling them not to worry.

I was too young to know how he did it, but he did. The next day the jail doors opened and someone was home with his family.

In those days, Elizabeth, like Gaul, was divided into three parts. North Elizabeth, Elizabeth, and South Elizabeth. In those days Polacks had cousins. Man, did they have cousins! Nobody ever had cousins like the Polacks. He was the near undoing of the local political machine. Those nuts didn't know about Polacks having cousins and the special kind of grapevine they brought over from Poland that could, if patented, put A. T. and T. right out of business.

Somehow Dad's benevolence got around. "Yonnie" was the special friend of the underprivileged and could get things done. Maybe not much really, but when you're in the can, getting out is *plenty*. He could un-confiscate still, get cut rate prices for kegs of beer for Polack picnics, work a little deal at Ellis Island to get another cousin into the states and placed at Standard Oil or Simmons Mattress Company.

By the time for the new mayor to be elected came along, cousin told cousin and the word was out. Everybody wanted "Yonnie." North Elizabeth and South Elizabeth ganged up on middle Elizabeth and whether they liked it or not, Yonnie was going to be mayor.

Dear old Dad didn't necessarily relish the thought of being mayor. Neither did the politicians. Elizabeth was a swing city and there were Polacks all over the state and Dad stood a damn good chance of being Governor of New Jersey the next time out once the grapevine really went into operation.

So once again the parlor was opened. This time it wasn't the Polacks asking for favors. It was pasty faced men from uptown and one guy straight out of Trenton and *they* were wringing their hats trying to talk Dad into forgetting the whole thing.

I used to think Dad made a mistake in going along with them, but now I know better. He cancelled the deal out, went around making speeches about how, if they wanted him, they should really vote for the incumbent, and they did just as he asked them to. After that, Dad could call his own shots whenever he felt like it. He never made governor, but he was just as big.

He still farted when he did backflips.

There are eras in a person's life that begin in memorable fashion and become more memorable as time goes on. Memorable, however, subject to change. At first it's exciting, shattering, spectacular, then becomes a little unbelievable, dissolves into a time-you-can't-speak-about-because-nobody-would-believe-you-anyway, becomes a little shamefaced memory, then years later erupts into a crazy comedy because there wasn't much you could have done about it anyhow and wouldn't have wanted to if you could have.

Titled, *The Day of the Rape*. Not somebody else's . . . *mine*. And not really to be semantically technical. No maidenhead was struck a blow, no full genital encompassment occurred. Hell, the particular of the event I recall the most vividly was having a mouth so dry I couldn't swallow for lack of spit or squeeze a squeak out of the pipes. And that propellor. That damn prop.

Her name was Grace somebody, she was in her late twenties, a bleached blonde and built with more curves than the Indianapolis Speedway. Her boyfriend was a hood who got knocked off a year later in a hijacking incident and back in the early thirties she wore bikinis before they were invented or maybe it was just her underwear. I remember they were silk, you could see through them when they were wet and mostly she'd climb into a pair of linen boy's shorts and a halter affair when she dressed up. Twice she was arrested for indecent exposure . . . and remember, this was when the *men* had to wear tops on their bathing suits.

Sandbar McDougal had run his cruiser up on another shell bank and bent his prop. There was too much party going on at his place for him to bother about so he had Lennie and me go down at low tide, wrench the bronze screw off, and since he had already sent his car off for another case of booze, he asked Feeney Swithers (who liked to be called Spud) for the use of his bullet-proof Lincoln. Feeney was crocked out and couldn't care less, so to get rid of Penny Pordolo, who wouldn't give him any when he was drunk, and have time to make out with her sister Annie, he told her to drive me to Atlantic Beach where the machine shop was.

Lennie decided to go along for the ride and hopped in the front with her. I was alone in the back seat with the prop.

Until Grace Somebody decided to go too and she slid in next to me with the wet soaking through the pink things into the white linen shorts.

I was fourteen.

The prop was too heavy to hold in my lap so I put it on the floor. That was my mistake. Mistake?

So Grace made me slide over and put her head in my lap. And stuck her feet on the windowsill.

I could barely see the top of Lennie's head over the front seat but I could hear him giggling at whatever Penny was saying. Actually, I wasn't listening because of what Grace Somebody was doing. Innocently, I supposed the constant turning of her head was because she was watching the top of the telephone poles go by through the windows, and innocently I supposed the way she held my trembling hands on her chest was because actually there was no other place to put them, and innocently I supposed the physical condition that was happening to me was because I was a dirty young man who shouldn't have peaked at that book they were all laughing about on the dock.

Then Grace Somebody looked at me and smiled, "My, don't you get excited quickly?"

Speak I couldn't. Swallowing was impossible. My lips were parched, my tongue was a dry rasp, my throat was a desert, so I grinned weakly and wondered what she meant by excited. There was none of the thrill of diving from a low bridge into shallow water, none of the anticipation of a hard tackle into a ball carrier, no chilling experience seeing the world upside down from an open cockpit biplane.

There was just the horror of knowing a mature woman had her head in my lap and could tell that I was in a state of erectile shock. Up to now spin-the-bottle had been a big sex adventure. I never knew when she let my hands go. Her fingers were button-deft and home-runned me with absolute dexterity and before I could recover enough to even try for a protesting squirm or sound—it was over and done with and all she did was turn her head up to me with a strange smile and say, "My goodness!"

I could still see the top of Lennie's head. He was giggling again, talking about going clamming. Talking about playing baseball. Hell, I wanted to tell him, yell at him what it was to be a man and I couldn't even get a squeak out.

Grace Somebody was still smiling and there was a funny expression in her eyes. Her ministration had been eminently professional and exquisitely wonderful, but at the perverse age of fourteen, nature was unable to control or reduce the structure of her product through a single physical release no matter how capably applied, and there I was, still in that state of dynamic tension and with the machine shop only a few blocks away, I was about to be embarrassingly disclosed as a

[The manuscript ends abruptly at this point.]

MICKEY SPILLANE ON WRITING

"Sex and violence are punctuation marks in a story."

"Critics don't decide anything. Publishers don't decide. The public is the one who decides everything."

"Writers don't have talent. Writers have mechanical aptitude."

"Nobody reads a book to get to the middle."

"If you're a singer you lose your voice. A baseball player loses his arm. A writer gets more knowledge, and if he's good, the older he gets, the better he writes."

"The first page sells this book. The last page sells your next book."

"All you need is a typewriter, $3 worth of paper and a mailbox and you're in business."

"Authors want their names down in history; I want to keep the smoke coming out the chimney."

AYN RAND AND
MICKEY SPILLANE

In a 1964 *Playboy* interview, Alvin Toffler asked Ayn Rand about modern American novelists.

"My favorite is Mickey Spillane," Rand told Toffler.

"Why do you like him?"

"Because he is primarily a moralist. In a primitive form, the form of a detective novel, he presents the conflict of good and evil, in terms of black and white. He does not present a nasty gray mixture of indistinguishable scoundrels on both sides. He presents an uncompromising conflict. As a writer, he is brilliantly expert at the aspect of literature which I consider most important: plot structure."

Rand—author of the hugely popular novels *The Fountainhead* (1943) and *Atlas Shrugged* (1957) and creator of the Objectivist philosophy—was an unlikely Mike Hammer fan. ("Spillane gives me the feeling of hearing a military band in a public park.")

In *The Romantic Manifesto* (1969), Rand uses excerpts from Spillane's *One Lonely Night* and Thomas Wolfe's *The Web and the Rock* to demonstrate the superiority of the former and the deficiencies of the latter. Rand writes:

> *Let us compare the literary style of two excerpts from two different novels reproduced below. Both are descriptions of the same subject: New York City at night. Observe which one of them re-creates the visual reality of a specific scene, and which one deals with vague, emotional assertions and floating abstractions.*

First excerpt:

Nobody ever walked across the bridge, not on a night like this. The rain was misty enough to be almost fog-like, a cold gray curtain that separated me from the pale ovals of white that were faces locked behind the steamed-up windows of the cars that hissed by. Even the brilliance that was Manhattan by night was reduced to a few sleepy, yellow lights off in the distance.

Some place over there I had left my car and started walking, burying my head in the collar of my raincoat, with the night pulled in around me like a blanket. I walked and I smoked and I flipped the spent butts ahead of me and watched them arch to the pavement and fizzle out with one last wink.

Second excerpt:

That hour, that moment, and that place struck with a peerless co-incision upon the very heart of his own youth, the crest and zenith of his own desire. The city had never seemed as beautiful as it looked that night. For the first time he saw that New York was supremely, among the cities of the world, the city of the night. There had been achieved here a loveliness that was astounding and incomparable, a kind of modern beauty, inherent to its place and time, that no other place nor time could match. He realized suddenly that the beauty of other cities of the night—of Paris spread below one from the butte of Sacre-Coeur, in its vast, mysterious blossoms of nocturnal radiance; of London with its smoky nimbus of fogged light, which was so peculiarly thrilling because it was so vast, so lost in the illimitable—had each its special quality, so lovely and mysterious, but had yet produced no beauty that could equal this.

. . . Observe the difference in their methods. There is not a single emotional word or adjective in Spillane's description; he presents nothing save visual facts; but he selects only those facts, only those

eloquent details, which convey the visual reality of the scene and create a mood of desolate loneliness. Wolfe does not describe the city; he does not give us a single characteristic visual detail. He asserts that the city is "beautiful," but does not tell us what makes it beautiful. Such words as "beautiful," "astounding," "incomparable," "thrilling," "lovely" are estimates; in the absence of any indication of what aroused these estimates, they are arbitrary assertions and meaningless generalities.

Brought together by their mutual editor/publisher Victor Weybright, Spillane and Rand had drinks and dined, exchanged occasional warm letters, and in 1959 appeared on the Mike Wallace interview program together.

In Scott McConnell's *100 Voices: An Oral History of Ayn Rand* (2010), Wallace recalled: "Mickey Spillane came to an Objectivist party with, as I recall, an alarmingly ancient ex-burlesque queen; it was either Sally Rand or Georgia Southern. Ayn greatly admired Spillane's novels in those days, thought he wrote in essentials and dealt with characters clearly representing good and evil. That night, Mickey did something I never saw any male do with Ayn Rand. Right in front of everybody, in an innocent, breezy way he flirted with her, and I think she got a big kick out of it."

In *100 Voices*, Spillane spoke of their friendship:

> *[We had lunch] in a very fancy Belgian restaurant in New York City in September 1961. It was so hoity-toity that they only stayed open for a couple of hours a day, and they had a very high-class group of waiters—very intellectual. Lunch started at eleven, and we met then, and before we got finished, that place was jammed with reporters and people. We didn't leave there until about seven at night. By that time, all the waiters and whatnot in that restaurant had got into a circle around where we were yakking away, and they were just sitting there listening.*

> *It wasn't the case that we were professional friends. We were friend*
> *friends. There was a lot of laughing together and we had a good time*
> *talking about things. There was nothing really deeply serious about*
> *our conversations. We weren't discussing world problems. . . . It's just*
> *that we enjoyed each other's company.*

Spillane often said he admired both *The Fountainhead* and especially *Atlas Shrugged*, but if pressed would admit he'd never made it through John Galt's thirty-three-thousand-word speech.

JIM TRAYLOR MEETS
MICKEY SPILLANE

ummer, 1972, two of my fellow English graduate students at Georgia State University (GSU) in Atlanta and I (Jim Traylor) are on the way to see Mickey Spillane. They're along for the lark; I'm going to see the man who has written some of my favorite mystery novels.

I became a Spillane fan after reading the twenty-five-cent copy of *The Big Kill* in 1959 (at the age of thirteen)—the one that had the small rectangular picture of tough-looking Spillane on the back cover and the words "A Mike Hammer Thriller" in bold letters on the front.

I never anticipated meeting Spillane. In fact, true to his belief of appearing only where "the people" buy books—supermarkets, Kmarts, PXs, and the like—Spillane was scheduled to appear at the GEX (Government Employees Exchange) in Chamblee, Georgia. Gloria Henderson, one of my friends and fellow graduate student at GSU, remembered that I loved Spillane's books. She told me about his visit and jokingly suggested we go to meet Spillane and get an autographed book. I agreed and another friend/fellow graduate student, Finn Bille, came along to take pictures.

It was a low-key affair. Spillane was promoting his latest book, *The Erection Set*, which featured a nearly nude picture of his then-wife, Sherri, on the cover. Spillane commented later that on the paperback edition the publishers had put a strip across Sherri's breasts that did not appear on hardcover dustjacket. He was amused that "high-priced customers" got that extra attraction for their money.

We weren't sure what to expect. At that time I didn't know many of the Spillane anecdotes that have now become a part of my consciousness. We arrived quite early to await his entrance. We stood around a display rack featuring the two different editions of *The Erection Set*—one with the nearly nude Sherri and the other with an extremely sedate orange cover—and a large poster blow-up of the nude cover.

Shortly thereafter Spillane and a friend ambled in as if they were going out for a beer. The friend was Sid Graedon from Signet books who organized the promotional tour. Spillane was dressed in slacks and a pullover T-shirt, looking very fit and macho with this *big smile* on his face. The smile never left.

He answered all my questions. God only knows what they were. Spillane, as anyone who ever met him knows, was a gracious man who had considerable patience. Although I'm sure he must have answered these same questions hundreds of times, he answered them once again for me. He kept talking almost as if he were an actor on stage. I paid him the homage due to the bestselling mystery writer come to visit his people and then stepped out of line to let the other fans who had come for their chance to meet the *man*.

Spillane paid special attention to Gloria, quite a striking blonde, making her feel at ease, telling her little stories, and putting his arm gently around her. Then just as quickly, her turn was over and Spillane was talking with another lady who had a young child. My photographer friend Finn was busily snapping pictures. He took some wonderful shots showing Spillane's true appreciation of people, especially his love for children.

We lingered until all the autograph seekers wandered away and Spillane and his pal were the only ones left. We went back over for another talk. Sherri was not with him even though on a local radio talk show that morning he had indicated she would be. I asked him about that. He said she was busy getting ready for another part of the promotional tour. The guy from Signet was getting all the material ready to move. It was obvious that the visit was over. I asked for the poster, and he was gracious enough to autograph it as well as the book: "Hi, Jim! As you can see Sherri is a hard girl to keep clothes on."

Even then there was a spark in the back of my mind. While Spillane was talking to his public, I asked Sid Graedon if I wrote a book on Spillane, did he think Signet would consider publishing it. He looked at me with amusement, said something like, "Sure. Send it to us," expecting no doubt never to hear from me again.

But the concept was there. I shared very little time with Spillane, but he gave me countless hours of entertainment with his heroes and tough guys. Perhaps the story could have ended there.

Yet the story continued. My friends encouraged me to write the book and quit just talking about it. One day in November 1980, while at GSU's library, I noticed a special Mickey Spillane issue of *The Armchair Detective*. One article was by a man I did not know until several years later, my co-writer Max Allan Collins. While working on my manuscript, I decided to try to contact the author of the article I'd liked best from *The Armchair Detective* special edition on Spillane—Max Collins, scripter for the *Dick Tracy* comic strip and also a mystery writer. I received in return a short note from Max on bold stationery with Nolan (his hard-boiled crook character) on one side and Dick Tracy on the other, asking just what was this Spillane project I was working on. He had just completed a ten-thousand-word article on "The Mick" for the mystery writer's volume of the *Dictionary of Literary Biography*. (I did not even know at the time that one of the *Dick Tracy* characters is actually named "Jim Trailer.")

The rest of this story is the history of this book: new friends, much time rereading books read previously just for joy, and the culmination—the publication of this volume.

WAS FRANK MORRISON
"FRANK MORRIS"?

Pulp historian Will Murray is among those who (like co-authors Collins and Traylor) suspect the Frank Morris–bylined pulp stories published in 1947–49 may be by Frank Morrison "Mickey" Spillane.

"There was also a Frank D. Morris contributing to *Collier's* at about that same time," Murray wrote MAC in 2010. "Most of his work has a military theme consistent with Spillane's military service at that time. . . . [T]he earliest Morris pulp story, a two-parter in *New Mystery Adventures*, was published in the same year that Spillane claimed to have broken into the pulps, 1936. This was at least good circumstantial evidence, as is the Frank Morris *Collier's* story that ran in '35. Spillane once said that he sold to the slicks first, then pulps, then comics. Everything fits."

Murray also points out that a Morris-bylined story in *The Shadow* in 1938 includes characters named Mike Hammer and Tiger Marsh.

Frank Morris–authored stories published in the window between *I, the Jury* and *My Gun Is Quick* include: "Easy Money," *Thrilling Detective*, August 1947; "Moider da Bum," *Best Detective*, December 1947; "Body in the Boat," *Private Detective*, May 1948; "Movieland Kill," *Hollywood Detective,* May 1948; "Location for Murder," *Hollywood Detective*, August 1948; "Don't Wake the Dead," *Thrilling Detective*, August 1948; "The Cold Hand of Murder," *Super-Detective*, June 1949; and "Picture Me Dead," *Hollywood Detective*, October 1949.

Spillane himself shrugged off his possible secret identity: "Aw, that's just some guy imitating me," when of course it was too early for any

Spillane imitators to have arisen. The timing of the publication, however, is indicative—it's a period during which Spillane needed money and was actively freelancing.

"Movieland Kill" is narrated by private eye Andrew Blane—red-headed, Irish, a Spanish speaker who says "Nuts" frequently. He packs a .38; his Captain of Homicide pal is Ed "Big Brain" Baughn. Imelia Suadino (a victim) gets a long descriptive paragraph about her good looks, and Sam Rhym (another victim) "was as dead as Moses."

"Location for Murder" is narrated by Joe Kane (a talent scout for a studio). Joan Merrick is a "small girl with nice legs and a nicer shape . . . standing there huddled against the doorway to keep from being drenched . . . clothes were plastered against her." Rain and pulchritude—Spillane hallmarks.

"Don't Wake the Dead" is in third person, starring Rick Luggan, private eye. Lovely Caral Teresi "pushed the door closed and followed Luggan into the room. Her wide hips swayed as she walked and her every movement was rhythm and grace." The war is referenced: "Dimly he heard feet pounding in the hall. Then, like that other time on Saipan, Luggan passed out. . . ."

"Picture Me Dead" is narrated by Pat Conley, a studio guard for Polychrome Films, 5'11", 185 pounds. Drives a Buick, says "Nuts" a lot. Sally McLain "stood there in front of me, and she was something to see. Skin a light pink, with a few scattered freckles on her dimpled cheeks. With my lips I could have touched the top of her head, she was so little. Nice brown hair, too, curling softly at the shoulders. . . . What I had against her was her legs. They were too skinny."

"I have four of the 'Frank Morris' stories," Spillane expert Stephen Mertz wrote to MAC in 2021, "and to my mind, given various elements in their writing, it would be more difficult to *disprove* the notion that these are Mickey's work. The story with the most well-defined Spillane motifs is 'Location for Murder.' . . . We get the first-person hardboiled narration, the narrator arriving from out of town looking for the killer of his pal, a blonde doll and, oh yes, the rain ('. . . it seemed like night, with the dark sky hovering over the city and the skies falling apart'). One more quote: 'My head felt hot and cold at the same time and the bells started ringing again. I was out on the ropes and didn't know it.' Sure sounds like Mickey to me."

All of this is, of course, circumstantial. But while Mickey exaggerated, he never outright lied, and his insistence on writing for the pulps—as had Hammett and Chandler, after all—may well mean that Frank Morrison Spillane was also Frank Morris.

THE OTHER
MICKEY SPILLANE

Hell's Kitchen crime boss Michael "Mickey" Spillane, known as the Last Gentleman Gangster and rival of the notorious Westies, flourished in the 1960s and '70s.

Paddy Whacked (2006), T. J. English's book on Irish-American gangsters, tells of mobster Spillane refusing to talk before a grand jury.

"Finally," writes English, "the exasperated assistant D.A. asked: 'Well, can you tell me this: Are you related to the other Mickey Spillane? The famous writer?'" This one question did get a response, as the Hell's Kitchen Spillane leaned into the microphone and said, 'No. But I'd be happy to change places with him at the moment.'"

The Murrells Inlet Spillane said in 1998, "Now this guy gets himself killed . . . the newspaper says, 'Mickey Spillane Killed In Gangland War.' And some idiot [reporter] decides that's me and makes a big column out of it. Now my daughter Caroline says, 'He's not dead, I just talked to him.'"

Michael J. Spillane, gangster, was killed outside his apartment in Queens on May 13, 1977.

MICKEY SPILLANE BOOKS
BY PUBLICATION DATE

1947	MH	*I, the Jury* [MH = Mike Hammer]
1950	MH	*My Gun Is Quick*
1950	MH	*Vengeance Is Mine!*
1951	MH	*One Lonely Night*
1951	MH	*The Big Kill*
1951		*The Long Wait*
1952	MH	*Kiss Me, Deadly*
1961		*The Deep*
1962	MH	*The Girl Hunters*
1963		*Me, Hood!* (UK)
1964	MH	*The Snake*
1964		*The Flier* (UK)
1964		*Return of the Hood* (UK)
1964	TM	*Day of the Guns* [TM = Tiger Mann]
1965	TM	*Bloody Sunrise*
1965	TM	*The Death Dealers*
1965		*Killer Mine* (UK)
1966	TM	*The By-Pass Control*
1966	MH	*The Twisted Thing*
		[written in 1949 as *For Whom the Gods Would Destroy*]
1967	MH	*The Body Lovers*
1967		*The Delta Factor* [Morgan the Raider]
1968		*Killer Mine* (USA)
1969		*Me, Hood!* (USA)
1969		*The Tough Guys* (USA)
1970	MH	*Survival . . . Zero!*
1972		*The Erection Set* [Dogeron Kelly]

1973		*The Last Cop Out* [Gillian Burke]
1979		*The Day the Sea Rolled Back* (middle-grade)
1982		*The Ship That Never Was* (middle-grade)
1984		*Tomorrow I Die* (short stories)
1989	MH	*The Killing Man*
1996	MH	*Black Alley*
2001		*Together We Kill* (short stories)
2003		*Something's Down There* [Mako Hooker]
2003		*Primal Spillane: Early Stories 1941–1942* [Revised and Expanded 2018 (comic-book "fillers")]
2004		*Byline: Mickey Spillane* (stories; nonfiction)
2007		*Dead Street* [with MAC] [Jack Stang]
2008	MH	*The Goliath Bone* [with MAC]
2010	MH	*The Big Bang* [with MAC]
2011	MH	*Kiss Her Goodbye* [with MAC]
2011		*The Consummata* [with MAC] [Morgan the Raider]
2012	MH	*Lady, Go Die!* [with MAC]
2013	MH	*Complex 90* [with MAC]
2014	MH	*King of the Weeds* [with MAC]
2015	CY	*The Legend of Caleb York* [CY = Caleb York] [MAC novelization of unproduced Spillane screenplay]
2015	MH	*Kill Me, Darling* [with MAC]
2016	MH	*Murder Never Knocks* [with MAC]
2016	MH	*A Long Time Dead: A Mike Hammer Casebook* (short stories) [with MAC]
2017	MH	*The Will to Kill* [with MAC]
2017	CY	*The Big Showdown* [MAC, with Spillane characters]
2018	CY	*The Bloody Spur* [MAC, with Spillane characters]
2018	MH	*Killing Town* [with MAC]
2018		*The Last Stand* (includes "A Bullet for Satisfaction," with MAC)
2018	MH	*Mickey Spillane's Mike Hammer: The Night I Died* (graphic novel) [with MAC]
2019	MH	*Murder, My Love* [with MAC]
2019	CY	*Last Stage to Hell Junction* [MAC with Spillane characters]
2020	MH	*Masquerade for Murder* [with MAC]
2020	CY	*Hot Lead, Cold Justice* [MAC, with Spillane characters]
2021	CY	*Shoot-Out at Sugar Creek* [MAC, with Spillane characters]
2022	MH	*Kill Me If You Can* [with MAC]
2022		*The Menace* [MAC novelization of unproduced Spillane screenplay]

MIKE HAMMER BOOKS IN
CHRONOLOGICAL ORDER OF NARRATIVE

* = with MAX ALLAN COLLINS

2018	*Killing Town (1st MH attempt, ca. 1945)
1947	I, the Jury
2012	*Lady, Go Die! (I, the Jury sequel attempt, ca. 1945)
1950	My Gun Is Quick
1950	Vengeance Is Mine!
1951	One Lonely Night
1951	The Big Kill
1952	Kiss Me, Deadly
2015	*Kill Me, Darling
2022	*Kill Me If You Can
1962	The Girl Hunters
1964	The Snake
2017	*The Will to Kill
2010	*The Big Bang
1966	The Twisted Thing (2nd completed MH)
	[written in 1949 as For Whom the Gods Would Destroy]
2013	*Complex 90 [sequel to The Girl Hunters]
2016	*Murder Never Knocks
2016	*A Long Time Dead: A Mike Hammer Casebook
1967	The Body Lovers
1970	Survival . . . Zero!
2011	*Kiss Her Goodbye
1989	The Killing Man
2020	*Masquerade for Murder
2019	*Murder, My Love
1996	Black Alley
2014	*King of the Weeds [sequel to Black Alley]
2008	*The Goliath Bone

MICKEY SPILLANE
SHORT FICTION AND ARTICLES

"Together We Kill" (January 1953, *Cavalier*)

"Everybody's Watching Me" (January–April 1953, *Manhunt*; serialized in four issues)

"The Girl Behind the Hedge" (October 1953, *Manhunt*; aka "The Lady Says Die!")

"The Night I Died" (1953; Mike Hammer)—unproduced radio play, converted by MAC in *Private Eyes* (1998)

"The Pickpocket" (December 1954, *Manhunt*)

"Tonight My Love" (1954, released as 33⅓ and 45 rpm records *Mickey Spillane's Mike Hammer Story*)

"The Screen Test of Mike Hammer" (July 1955, *Male*)

"Tomorrow I Die" (February 1956, *Cavalier*)

"Sex Is My Vengeance" (October 1956, *Cavalier*)

"Stand Up and Die!" (June 1958, *Cavalier*)

"Me, Hood!" (July 1959, *Cavalier*)

"I'll Die Tomorrow" (March 1960, *Cavalier*)

"The Seven Year Kill" (July 1960, *Cavalier*)

"Kick It or Kill" (July 1961, *Cavalier*)

"The Affair with the Dragon Lady" (March 1962, *Cavalier*)

"Hot Cat" (April 1964, *Saga*)

"The Bastard Bannerman" (June 1964, *Saga*)

"The Big Bang" (January 1965, *Saga*; aka "Return of the Hood")

"Death of the Too-Cute Prostitute" (October 1965, *Man's Magazine*; aka "Man Alone")

"The Gold Fever Tapes" (1973, *Stag Annual* #15)

"The Dread Chinatown Man" (August 1975, *True*)

"Toys for the Man-Child" (August 1975, *True*)

"The Killing Man" (December 1989, *Playboy*; Mike Hammer)*

"Black Alley" (December 1996, *Playboy*; Mike Hammer)*

* abridged editorially at *Playboy*

MICKEY SPILLANE
COLLECTIONS (CONTENTS)

"Sex Is My Vengeance"

"Trouble . . . Come and Get It!"

"The Gold Fever Tapes"

"Everybody's Watching Me"

2001   *Together We Kill*

"Together We Kill"

"The Night I Died" *

"I'll Die Tomorrow"

"The Veiled Woman" **

"The Affair with the Dragon Lady"

"The Dread Chinatown Man"

"Toys for the Man-Child"

"Hot Cat" (aka "The Flier")

* radio play converted to prose by MAC for Spillane

** ghosted by Howard Browne for *Fantastic*, Nov/Dec 1952

2004   *Byline: Mickey Spillane*

"The Killing Man"

"Black Alley"

"Tonight, My Love"

"The Duke Alexander"

"Down, Down for Gold"

"I Rode with the Hot Rod Moonshiners"

"Sawdust in My Shoes"

"You Can't Rock a Stock 'Jock'"

"Speaking of Speed"

"Sports Car Fiesta"

"Tough, Fast and Beautiful"

"I, the Driver"

"The Enjoyment of Women"

"The Trouble with Violence on TV"

"Secrets of a Private Eye"

"Blondes are a state of mind" (poem)

"Tangled up in Blue"

"Mickey's Myrtle Beach Memories"

Green Hornet #10: Mike Lancer: "The Syndicate of Death"

Crime Detector #3: "Meet Mike Danger, Private Eye"

Crime Detector #4: "Mike Danger, Private Eye—Murder at the
    Burlesque"

Fan Letter to Carroll John Daly (ca. 1953)

2016   *A Long Time Dead: A Mike Hammer Casebook**
         "The Big Switch"
         "Fallout"
         "A Long Time Dead"
         "Grave Matter"
         "So Long, Chief"
         "A Dangerous Cat"
         "It's in the Book"
         "Skin"

                                    * stories begun by Spillane and completed by MAC

2022   *Kill Me If You Can*
         75th anniversary Hammer novel includes five bonus uncollected Spillane/
             Collins stories:
         "There's a Killer Loose!" (August 2008, *Ellery Queen Mystery Magazine*)
             [from unproduced Spillane radio script]
         "The Big Run" (October 2018, *Ellery Queen Mystery Magazine*)
             [from unproduced Spillane TV script]
         "The Punk" (Spring 2018, *Mystery Tribune*)
             [from unproduced Spillane TV script]
         "Tonight, My Love" (October 2018, *The Strand*)
             [expanded from *Mickey Spillane's Mike Hammer Story* LP script]
         "Killer's Alley" (March 2021, *Ellery Queen Mystery Magazine*)
             [expanded from 1953 screen-test script]

MICKEY SPILLANE'S
MIKE DANGER

(with MAC)

Tekno Comics/BIG Entertainment, Inc. (1995–97)
    [Each issue contains 24 story pages.]
Volume 1, #1 (September 1995): "Danger Ahead"
Volume 1, #2 (October 1995): "Danger in the Future"
Volume 1, #3 (November 1995): "I, the Jury"
Volume 1, #4 (early December 1995): "Old New York"
    [Cover states "Soon to be a MIRAMAX MOTION PICTURE"]
Volume 1, #5 (late December 1995): "Sin Syndicate"
    [Inside cover: "Mickey Stays up Late": appearance on NBC's *Late Night with
        Conan O'Brien*]
Volume 1, #6 (early January 1996): "Man Out of Time"
Volume 1, #7 (late January 1996): "Death in Duplicate, Chapter 1: A Dangerous Past"
Volume 1, #8 (February 1996): "Death in Duplicate, Chapter 2: A Perfect Wife"
Volume 1, #9 (March 1996): "Death in Duplicate, Chapter 3: The Head Man"
Volume 1, #10 (April 1996): "A Child in the Future, Part 1: Sunday in the Park"
Volume 1, #11 (May 1996): "A Child in the Future, Part 2: Escape from New York"
Volume 2, #1 (June 1996): "Virtual Man"
Volume 2, #2 (July 1996): "Bring Me the Head of Michael Danger"
Volume 2, #3 (August 1996): "A Brand New Me"
Volume 2, #4 (September 1996): "A Woman Called Mann"
Volume 2, #5 (October 1996): "Time Heels"
Volume 2, #6 (November 1996): "The Paradox Rule"
Volume 2, #7 (December 1996): "The Red Menace, Part 1: Abduction"
Volume 2, #8 (January 1997): "The Red Menace, Part 2: Look to the Skies"
Volume 2, #9 (February 1997): "The Red Menace, Part 3: Better Dead"
Volume 2, #10 (April 1997): "The Red Menace, Part 4: Close Encounter of the Worst
    Kind"

SELECTED TELEVISION, MOVIES, AND AUDIO

More extensive information is available in Collins and Traylor's *Mickey Spillane on Screen* (2012).

Television:

Mickey Spillane's Mike Hammer (1958–59)
Syndicated TV series airing 1958-1960, produced by Revue Productions in Hollywood, California; MCA-TV exclusive distributor. The series was in production for two seasons of 39 episodes each. Darren McGavin as Mike Hammer and Bart Burns as Captain Pat Chambers (latter not in every episode). Preceded by 1954 pilot produced by Richard Lewis, written/directed by Blake Edwards, starring Brian Keith as Mike Hammer; despite initial acceptance, rejected by CBS-TV president William Paley.

Mickey Spillane's Mike Hammer in "Margin for Murder"
TV-movie ("backdoor" pilot) airing October 15, 1981, on CBS-TV. Kevin Dobson as Mike Hammer. First Jay Bernstein *Mike Hammer* production.

Mickey Spillane's Mike Hammer: "Murder Me, Murder You"
TV-movie ("backdoor" pilot) airing April 9, 1983, on CBS-TV. Stacy Keach as Mike Hammer. Tanya Roberts as Velda does not appear in ensuing series. Don Stroud as Captain Pat Chambers.

Mickey Spillane's Mike Hammer: "More Than Murder"
Two-part episode of the series presented as a TV-movie airing January 26, 1984, preceding series official premiere on January 28. Stacy Keach as Mike Hammer; Lindsay Bloom as Velda; Don Stroud as Chambers.

Mickey Spillane's Mike Hammer (1984–85)
CBS-TV series produced by Jay Bernstein Productions and filmed at The Burbank Studios in Burbank, California, for Columbia Pictures Television.

Ten episodes broadcast from January through April 1984 for season one. Fourteen episodes broadcast from September 1984 through January 1985 for season two.

Stacy Keach as Mike Hammer; Lindsay Bloom as Velda; Don Stroud as Captain Pat Chambers; and Kent Williams as Assistant DA Lawrence D. Barrington. Danny Goldman as Ozzie the Answer; Eddie Egan as Hennessey; Eddie Barth as Ritchie; Lee Benton as Jenny; Ben Powers as Moochie.

The Return of Mickey Spillane's Mike Hammer
TV-movie first airing April 18, 1986. A second "backdoor" pilot.

Stacy Keach as Mike Hammer; Lindsay Bloom as Velda; Don Stroud as Captain Pat Chambers; Kent Williams as DA Barrington; guest star: Lauren Hutton.

The New Mike Hammer (1986–87)
Essentially a continuation of the previous series, again produced by Jay Bernstein Productions in Los Angeles. Mickey Spillane's name is not used in the title for this iteration, his credit appearing just before the screenwriters in each of the 22 episodes from September 1986 to May 1987.

Stacy Keach as Mike Hammer; Lindsay Bloom as Velda; Don Stroud as Captain Pat Chambers.

Mickey Spillane's Mike Hammer: Murder Takes All
TV-movie first airing May 21, 1989.

Stacy Keach as Mike Hammer; Lindsay Bloom as Velda; Don Stroud as Captain Pat Chambers; guest star: Lynda Carter.

Come Die With Me
TV-movie first airing December 6, 1994 (unsuccessful "backdoor" pilot). Generally considered the worst Hammer film.

Rob Estes as Mike Hammer; Pamela Anderson as Velda; Darlanne Fluegel as Captain Pat Chambers; Kent Williams as Jugs.

Fallen Angels: "Tomorrow I Die"
Aired November 5, 1995, on Showtime. Adapts the novella of the same name, faithful but for a darker ending, the only aspect of the production Spillane disliked.

Bill Pullman as Rich Thurber; Dan Hedaya as Auger; Heather Graham as Carol Whalen.

Mickey Spillane's Mike Hammer, Private Eye (1997–98)
One syndicated season of 26 episodes. Jay Bernstein brought back Stacy Keach after the failure of the Rob Estes pilot.

Stacy Keach as Mike Hammer; Shane Conrad as Nick Farrell; Shannon Whirry as Velda; Peter Jason as Captain Skip Gleason; Kent Williams as Deputy Mayor Barry Lawrence; Malgosia Tomassi (wife of Stacy Keach) as Maya Ricci.

Film:
I, the Jury (1953)
  Blu-ray, ClassicFlix: 2022
The Band Wagon (1953)
  DVD: Warner Brothers
The Long Wait (1954)
  Not commercially available
Ring of Fear (1954)
  DVD: Paramount 2005

Kiss Me Deadly (1955)

    Blu-ray/DVD: Criterion 2011

My Gun Is Quick (1957)

    DVD: MGM 2011

Blu-ray: Kino 2020

The Girl Hunters (1963)

    DVD: Image 1999

    Blu-ray/DVD: Scorpion Releasing 2014

The Delta Factor (1970)

    Not commercially available

I, the Jury (1982)

    Blu-ray: Kino 2016

    DVD: Twentieth Century Fox Cinema Archives 2015

Murder Me, Murder You/More Than Murder (1983/1984)

    DVD: Sony Pictures Home Entertainment

Mickey Spillane's Mike Hammer (TV pilot 1954)

    [On *Black Box* DVD compilation; see below]

Mickey Spillane's Mike Hammer (1958–59)

    DVD: NBC Universal 2011

Columbo (season 3), "Publish or Perish" (January 18, 1974)

    DVD: Universal 2013

Mickey Spillane's Mike Hammer Private Eye (1997–98)

    "Song Bird" DVD: Gator Home Entertainment 2002

    DVD: Tango Video 2005

    "A New Leaf" DVD: Hollywood Entertainment 2006

The Black Box: Shades of Noir (2006)

    DVD: Neo-Noir/Troma (2005)

Includes feature films *Mommy* and *Mommy's Day* with Spillane; Blake
    Edwards/Brian Keith 1954 *Mike Hammer* TV pilot; documentary
    Mike Hammer's Mickey Spillane (1999); with shorts "Eliot Ness: An
    Untouchable Life" and "A Matter of Principal," and non-Spillane-
    related *Real Time: Siege at Lucas Street Market* (2001).

Mommy/Mommy's Day (1995/1997)
>   Blu-ray (double-feature): VCI Home Video 2020

Audio

Numerous abridged and unabridged audios of Spillane (and Spillane/Collins) novels issued by various publishers, often read by Stacy Keach.

>   Selected original works:

New Adventures of Mickey Spillane's Mike Hammer

"The Little Death" (script by Spillane/MAC), 2009

>   Blackstone audio, full cast with Keach as Hammer

New Adventures of Mickey Spillane's Mike Hammer

"Encore for Murder"* (script by Spillane/MAC), 2011

>   Blackstone audio, full cast with Keach as Hammer
>
>   *play version with Gary Sandy as Mike Hammer performed at the International Mystery Writers Festival, Owensboro, Kentucky, in 2012; Ruth Eckerd Hall's Murray Theatre, Clearwater, Florida, January 2018; and Muscatine Art Center Benefit, Muscatine, Iowa, September 2022.

COMPLETING MICKEY SPILLANE

Max Allan Collins

A week or so before his death, Mickey Spillane told his wife, Jane, "Take everything you find around here and give it to Max—he'll know what to do." In doing so, he paid me the greatest honor I could ever imagine.

A short while later, Jane said to him, "Mickey, you know Max isn't a Jehovah's Witness—he's not going to censor the sex and violence." And Mickey said, "I'm fine with that."

With my wife Barb—who writes the *Antiques* humorous cozy mystery series with me—I went down to Mickey's home near Myrtle Beach, South Carolina, for a memorial tribute. We stayed with Jane and went through Mickey's three offices, in what Mickey said would be a "treasure hunt." We sat around the big dining-room table going through stacks of manuscripts. Now and then one of us would say, "I have a Hammer!"

Mickey had amassed a staggering number of unfinished works, many featuring Mike Hammer. Imagine going through Agatha Christie's papers and finding a dozen unfinished Poirot and/or Marple novels. Or a dozen unfinished Nero Wolfe's in Rex Stout's files, or James Bond chapters in Ian Fleming's desk, or . . . name your favorite deceased mystery author and just dream.

Some of the unfinished novels we found had been announced decades before. As a teenager I read in the *New York Times* "upcoming books" column of such forthcoming titles as *The Consummata* and *Complex 90*, never imagining they would not be on my shelf until I one day finished writing them. I recall Mickey telling me how pleased he was with the title of the new Mike Hammer he was working on, *King of the Weeds*—and, again, it's now on my shelf as a book co-written with him.

The manuscripts and associated materials were in various kinds of shape and included all sorts of things. I have been asked many times what the process is in completing these books. The one common factor in my approach is not to view this material—which Mickey, after all, set aside in most cases—as Holy Script. I have revised, expanded, and rewritten so that one hundred pages have become three hundred pages. If Mickey wrote around a scene, I provided it. If something seemed weak, I strengthened it. Some purists might scream at this. But I will say what makes me proudest is when a reviewer quotes two lines from a novel as prime Spillane examples, and one of them is Mickey's and the other is mine. Even better is when it's a sentence written by both of us.

Very briefly I will describe the process on each of the novels (thus far). As I set about the task, I chose not to assemble the unfinished novels in chronological order, but rather to work first with the longest manuscripts. These were usually about one hundred double-spaced pages.

The Goliath Bone (2008). Conceived by Mickey as the last Mike Hammer. He very nearly finished a draft—I had all but the last couple chapters. But he was racing against the clock, due to his failing health, and his manuscript was much shorter than usual, though it covered the span of the narrative, even jumping to the ending. He had provided only two action scenes—one at the start, another at the conclusion—and no murder-mystery element. I provided the latter and several more action scenes, and some general expansion. His final chapter became the basis of the second-to-last chapter, the murder-mystery requiring a new final one.

Mickey had misplaced the manuscript at one point, and—so typically of him—just started over. I found the missing draft and combined elements of the double chapters. I also found several takes on the opening, and combined perhaps four of those into what is now the first chapter. He had struggled with whether to start with a noirish mood piece or directly with action—I chose the former, because it was so beautifully written.

The Big Bang (2010). Mickey had completed a polished opening of one hundred pages. After a strong scene that is almost entirely his comes one written by me, a confrontation with a DA that Mickey had referenced but omitted. In this fashion, I expanded the one hundred pages into two hundred, with character and plot notes to guide me, with the last one-hundred-page section my work alone . . . though the shocking ending, one that Mickey said was his favorite, he'd shared with me verbally.

Kiss Her Goodbye (2011). Again, Mickey had written several opening chapters and these I combined. This was something of a disco-era comeback novel for Hammer, who had again (as in *The Girl Hunters*) been out of commission for a long spell. An alternate version of the first third presented an entirely different plot. I combined both plots into one, so I could use all the Spillane material. Mickey's character and plot notes were ample here.

Lady, Go Die! (2012). Among the most significant finds of all the manuscripts: a first attempt at a Mike Hammer novel after the acceptance of *I, the Jury*, which it refers to as Hammer's previous case. Elements here, including the setting and a corrupt small-town cop, indicate a first attempt at *The Twisted Thing*, but the plot is wholly different. I did not attempt this until I had several posthumous collaborations under my belt, because the first chapter was missing. I had to build some confidence before I could write a Mike Hammer first chapter with no Mickey to guide me.

I also wove in what would have been the first chapter of a different Hammer novel at about the midway point, because its serial-killer theme was similar. No notes on characterization or plot, but I knew at once where Mickey was going.

Complex 90 (2013). Mickey had one hundred pages of this *Girl Hunters* sequel. In his first chapter, Hammer is questioned by government agents about some wild adventures he's recently had behind the Iron Curtain. I used that as the outline of a flashback where we go to Russia with Hammer and experience everything firsthand. So for once a bunch of the front end of the book is mostly by me, and then I pick back up with Spillane material when the flashback is over. The novel was a chance to shore up some continuity issues caused by Velda's own Russian disappearance back in *The Girl Hunters*, and to settle up with one of the most memorable villains in the canon.

King of the Weeds (2014). One hundred pages of Spillane text included two plotlines and various reorderings of material and alternate chapters. Frankly, it was a mess, but a wonderful mess, especially the Moriarty-level villain, a serial killer targeting only police. Complicating matters: this was conceived by Mickey as a sequel to the then out-of-print *Black Alley* (1989), in which a cave filled with mob billions was central.

I wrestled with writing out the "billions" aspect, but knew Mickey had been fascinated by the notion of so much paper money in one place, so I gritted my teeth and left it in, really working to smooth things out and summarize *Black Alley* enough to ground new readers. The ending, another of Mickey's favorites, he'd shared with me several times. The one book I had been dreading to deal with turned out to be perhaps the most rewarding.

At this point, I had completed the six substantial Mike Hammer manuscripts—as well as the non-Hammer *Dead Street* and *The Consummata*—which had been my minimal goal. Now I set out to develop his shorter Hammer novel fragments, ranging from twenty-some to around forty pages, sometimes with notes, sometimes not.

Kill Me, Darling (2015). One of the best and trickiest fragments, this was a false start on *The Girl Hunters*, with the espionage plot that removed Velda from Hammer's life replaced by her going to Miami Beach and inexplicably becoming involved with a powerful gangster there. But the opening was word-for-word the same as *The Girl Hunters*. So I used another unpublished first chapter from the files, with Hammer similarly drunk and in a foul mood, and used plot material there to tie in with Velda going MIA. Then I picked up where the manuscript and *The Girl Hunters* took different routes. Mickey designed the book as the follow-up to *Kiss Me,*

Deadly, and finds Hammer in an alcoholic hole out of which he must climb to find, and rescue, Velda.

Murder Never Knocks (2016). I had only a twenty-six-page opening this time, but also plot notes and the ending, rare proof of Mickey's claim that he wrote endings first. With the opening and the closing (both powerful), and a strong premise, my collaborator left me in fine shape.

A Long Time Dead (2016). This collection of Mike Hammer short stories gathers eight tales, published in *The Strand* and elsewhere, developed from shorter Spillane fragments. I'm pleased to say these stories garnered numerous PWA Shamus nominations, including a win for "So Long, Chief" (also an Edgar nominee).

The Will to Kill (2017). The shortest of the significant fragments at twenty-two pages, this one nonetheless found Mickey giving me everything I needed. A haunting noirish opening is followed by a scene with Mike's pal, Homicide Captain Pat Chambers, setting up an Agatha Christie–type mystery of grown spoiled rich kids hovering over their dead daddy's fortune. After a trip with Chambers to the upstate mansion, Hammer and I are on our own; but Mickey had once again shown us the way.

Killing Town (2018). This is the Spillane centenary Mike Hammer novel, fleshed out from a sixty-page fragment that was Mickey's first crack at a Hammer novel, probably in 1945. I had set this one aside, along with *The Last Stand*, so that the centenary could be celebrated via the publication of the first Hammer and the last completed Spillane novel.

The Hammer was tricky because Mike is a newly minted PI here, undercover and out of Manhattan, with neither Velda nor Pat Chambers on hand. The material was very pulp tough, as hard-hitting and violent as any of the first six Mike Hammer novels. But the vengeance aspect is mostly not present, although Mike's loyalty to the guys he served with in the Pacific comes to the fore.

Murder, My Love (2019) and *Masquerade for Murder* (2020) were the first time I had little or no Spillane prose to incorporate. They have been developed from one-page, single-spaced synopses that Mickey appears to have written with Keach TV movies in mind. I worked in a few fragments from Mickey's files—for example, the opening Manhattan description of *Masquerade for Murder* is his; so is the exchange between Pat and Mike about a vintage .45 versus modern weaponry.

Kill Me If You Can (2022), the seventy-fifth anniversary Hammer novel, has an interesting history. Following the enormously successful *Kiss Me, Deadly*, Dutton and Signet announced the new Hammer novel—*Tonight I Die*. Other than a mock-up glimpsed in the film *Ring of Fear*, however, it never emerged. In Mickey's files was an unproduced half-hour radio play of that name using Hammer—also scripts for the same story in both half-hour and hour TV formats with leads now called "the Mick" and "Miler" respectively (the Hammer named tied up by producer Victor Saville). I employed this vintage material to explore how Hammer reacted to Velda's apparent death on his way to the gutter—a bridge between *Kiss Me, Deadly* and *The Girl Hunters*.

My philosophy throughout has never been to "continue" the Mike Hammer series. I have no intention or desire to do original Hammer novels. The idea is not to continue, but to complete. To make sure that there is genuine Spillane content and contribution to each of these books.

BIBLIOGRAPHY

Adams, Henry. "The Amazing Success of Mickey Spillane." *Climax*, May 1959, pp. 17–21ff.

Appelbaum, Yoni. "Publishers Gave Away 122,951,031 Books During World War II." *The Atlantic*, September 10, 2014.

Arnold, Edward T., ed. *Conversations with Erskine Caldwell*. Jackson and London: University Press of Mississippi, 1988.

"At Home with Mickey Spillane." *New York Sunday News*, September 29, 1968, p. 11.

Auerbach, Erich. *Mimesis: The Representation of Reality in Western Literature*. Translated by Willard R. Trask. Princeton: Princeton University Press, 1953.

Avery, Kevin. *It's All One Case: The Illustrated Ross Macdonald Archives*. Seattle: Fantagraphics, 2016.

Bailey, Beth, and David Farber. *The Fifties Chronicle*. Lincolnwood, IL: Legacy, 2006.

Banks, R. Jeff. "Spillane's Anti-Establishmentarian Heroes." In *Dimensions of Detective Fiction*, edited by Larry Landrum, Pat Browne, and Ray B. Browne, pp. 124–39. Bowling Green, OH: Bowling Green State University, 1976.

———. "Spillane and the Critics." *The Armchair Detective*, Fall 1979, pp. 300–7.

Barbier, Larry, photographer. "Mickey Spillane's Dames." *Cavalier*, July 1955, pp. 15–19.

Barnfield, Graham. "Mickey Spillane at 81." *Guardian* interview at the National Film Institute, London, July 29, 1999.

Barson, Michael. "Just a Writer Working for a Buck." *The Armchair Detective*, Fall 1979, pp. 292–99.

Base, Ron. "Hey, boys and girls, Uncle Mickey's at the bar, and he has something just for you," *Chicago Tribune Magazine*, August 16, 1981, pp. 28–31.

Benton, Mike. *The Illustrated History of Crime Comics*. Dallas, TX: Taylor Publishing Company, 1993.

Berliner, Michael S., ed. *Letters of Ayn Rand*. Introduction by Leonard Peikoff. New York: Dutton, 1995.

Bettridge, Jack. "How Hard-Boiled is Spillane?" *Mine*, October 1990, pp. 47–48ff.

Beyette, Beverly. "Toughing It With Mickey Spillane." *Los Angeles Times*, March 26, 1989, *View* section, pp. 1ff.

Biederman, Patricia Ward. "Macho Man." *Atlanta Weekly,* December 11, 1983, pp. 8–10, 21.

_____."Softie." *Chicago Tribune Magazine*, April 8, 1984, pp. 30–34ff.

"Big Ugly Shamus." *Time*, December 3, 1951, p. 110.

Black, Catherine Perkins. "Mickey Spillane." *Coast*, September 29, 1985, pp. 16–17ff.

Blackford, Frank. "Spillane, with 10 million copies in print, has busy time autographing copies." *Norfolk-Virginian Pilot*, November 30, 1951.

Boucher, Anthony. *New York Times Book Review*: February 12, 1950, p. 14 [*My Gun Is Quick*]; August 5, 1951 [*The Big Kill*]; [*The Long Wait*]; and October 26, 1953, p. 33 [*Kiss Me, Deadly*].

Boyer, Ruth. Interview by JLT, 2007.

Brooks, Tim, and Earle Marsh. *The Complete Directory to Prime Time Network and Cable TV Shows, 1946–Present.* New York: Ballantine, 1979.

Bruccoli, Matthew J. *Ross Macdonald.* San Diego: Harcourt Brace Jovanovich, 1984.

Bullock, Elizabeth. "Gore and Gals." [Review of *Vengeance Is Mine!*] *New York Times Book Review*, November 5, 1950, p. 30.

Burke, Jackson. "Tough—and Two of a Kind." *Man's Conquest*, August 1955, pp. 18–19ff.

Burns, James MacGregor. *The Crosswinds of Freedom: From Roosevelt to Reagan—America in the last half century.* New York: Vintage Books, 1990.

Burrell, Maurice C., and J. Stafford Wright. *Today's Sects: Who They Are, What they believe, and how they differ from Key Christian Doctrines.* 2nd ed. Grand Rapids, MI: Baker House, 1983.

Butcher, Fanny. "I Write for Money." *Chicago Sunday Tribune Magazine*, July 18, 1953.

Cameron, Gail. "The Soft Side of a Hard Egg." *Life*, September 8, 1961, pp. 127ff.

Carlson, Peter. "Another in the Can." *People Weekly*, January 30, 1984, pp. 18–21.

Carter, Angela. "The *Men Only* Interview: Mickey Spillane." *Men Only*, June 1973, pp. 34–36ff.

Cassidy, J., ed. "It's Mickey Spillane, all right!" (interview). *Writer's Digest*, September 1976, pp. 18–20.

Cawelti, John G. "The Spillane Phenomenon." *Journal of Popular Culture*, 3 (Summer 1969): pp. 9–22. (Originally appeared in *University of Chicago Magazine*, 61, no. 5, March/April 1969.)

_____. *Adventure, Mystery, and Romance: Formula Stories as Art and Popular Culture.* Chicago: University of Chicago Press, 1976.

Chandler, Raymond. "The Simple Art of Murder." *Atlantic*, December 1944, pp. 53–59.

_____. *Raymond Chandler Speaking.* Edited by Dorothy Gardener and Katherine S. Walker. Boston: Houghton Mifflin, 1962, p. 233.

Christie, Paddy. "Lay off the broad, you guys, that's my wife." *Scottish Daily Express*, February 24, 1973, p. 7.

Clemens, Matthew V. "Mickey Spillane the Myth," "Mickey Spillane alias Mike Hammer," and "Mickey Spillane—The Dolls." *Femme Fatales*, December 1998, pp. 42–53, 60.

Clemmer, Cindi. "Murrells Inlet 'Tough Guy' Goes after the Bad Guys Again." *Myrtle Beach,* Summer 1986, pp. 42–46ff.

Collins, Max Allan, ed. *From the Files of . . . Mike Hammer: The Complete Dailies and Sundays by Mickey Spillane and Ed Robbins.* Neshannock, PA: Hermes Press, 2013.

Collins, Max Allan, director. *Mike Hammer's Mickey Spillane.* 1999 documentary included in the DVD set *The Black Box: Shades of Neo-Noir,* Neo-Noir/Troma, 2005.

Collins, Max Allan. "Mecca Spillane." *All About Beer,* April/May 1983, pp. 14–16ff.

_____. "Mickey Spillane." In *St. James Guide to Crime and Mystery Writers,* edited by Jay P. Pederson and Taryn Benbow-Pfalzgrat. Detroit: St. James Press, 1996. [Written in collaboration with James L. Traylor.]

_____. "Mickey Spillane in Hollywood." *Psychotronic Video* 28 (1998): pp. 34–42.

_____. "Mickey Spillane: Lord of the Ring." *Videoscope,* 60 (Fall 2006): p. 28.

_____. "Mickey Spillane's *Day of the Guns.*" In *1001 Midnights: The Aficionado's Guide to Mystery and Detective Fiction,* edited by Bill Pronzini and Marcia Muller. New York: Arbor House, 1986. [Written in collaboration with James L. Traylor.]

_____. "Mickey Spillane's Return to the Pulps." *The Thieftaker Journal Annual: Brass Knuckles and Back Alleys,* 2, no. 6 (1983): pp. 10–13. [Written in collaboration with James L. Traylor.]

_____. "Mickey Spillane's Tiger Mann." *The Armchair Detective,* 17, no. 1 (Winter 1984): pp. 74–79. [Written in collaboration with James L. Traylor.]

_____. "This is Mike Hammer." *Hardboiled* 2 (Fall 1985): pp. 11–14.

Collins, Max Allan, and George Hagenauer. *Men's Adventure Magazines in Postwar America.* The Rich Oberg Collection. Hong Kong: Taschen, 2008.

Collins, Max Allan, and James L. Traylor. *One Lonely Knight: Mickey Spillane's Mike Hammer.* Bowling Green, OH: Popular Press, 1984.

_____. *Mickey Spillane on Screen: A Complete Study of the Television and Film Adaptations.* Jefferson, NC, and London: McFarland & Company, 2012.

Cowley, Malcolm. "Sex Murder Incorporated." *New Republic,* January 11, 1952, "Books in Review" column, pp. 17–18.

Crawford, Herbert H. *Crawford's Encyclopedia of Comic Books.* Middle Village, NY: Jonathan David Publisher's [sic], Inc., 1978.

Curran, Bob. "Mickey Spillane: His Wildest Adventure as Mike Hammer." *Saga,* November 1963, pp. 21–23ff.

DeB., F. "Mike Hammer." *TV Guide,* March 29, 1958, p. 27.

Deford, Frank. *Lite Reading: The Lite Beer from Miller Commercial Scrapbook.* New York: Penguin, 1984.

DeFuccio, Jerry. "Nuggets: Missives from Mickey." *Alter Ego,* 3, no. 11, November 2001, pp. 42–43.

Doud, Earl. "Interview with Mickey Spillane: 'I Call Myself the Chewing Gum of American Literature.'" *Gallery,* March 1974, pp. 32–36.

Dugan, James. "Mickey's Giving Murder a Bad Name." *Macleans Magazine*, April 16, 1952, pp. 22–24ff.

Eaton, Shirley. *Golden Girl*. Foreword by Mickey Spillane. London: B. T. Batsford Ltd, 1999.

English, T. J. *Paddy Whacked: The Untold Story of the Irish American Gangster*. New York: HarperCollins Publishers, 2006.

Evans, M. Stanton. *Blacklisted by History: The Untold Story of Senator Joe McCarthy and his fight against America's Enemies*. New York: Crown Forum, 2007.

"An Ex-Wife's Suit Behind Him, Mickey Spillane Returns to the Easier World of Fiction." *People Weekly*, July 28, 1986, pp. 28-29.

Eyman, Scott. *John Wayne: The Life and Legend*. New York: Simon & Schuster, 2014.

Fetterly, Judith. "Beauty as the Beast: Fantasy and Fear in *I, the Jury*." *Journal of Popular Culture*, 8 (Spring 1975): pp. 775–82.

Fletcher, Connie. "Mickey Spillane." *St. Louis Post Dispatch*, March 16, 1984, J1ff.

Friedman, Mickey. "Vengeance Is His, Again." [Review of *The Killing Man*] *New York Times Book Review*, October 15, 1989, p. 43.

Gardner, Erle Stanley. "Getting Away with Murder." *Atlantic*, January 1965.

Garnett, Tay, with Fredda Dudley Balling. *Light Your Torches and Pull Up Your Tights*. New York: Arlington House, 1973.

Gaucher, Claire. "Meet Biff Elliot." *Motion Picture and Television Magazine*, October 1953, pp. 48–49ff.

Geherin, David. *The American Private Eye: The Image in Fiction*. New York: Frederick Ungar, 1985.

Gerrity, Dave. "The Soft Side of a Hard-boiled Mickey Spillane." *Family Weekly*, February 14, 1982, pp. 4–6.

Gerrity, Jon. Interview with JLT (2007).

Gill, Joe. "The Big Killing by Mickey Spillane." *Pathfinder*, March 5, 1952. [Cover: "A Bible studying author sells millions of books loaded with blood, violence and sex."]

The Girl Hunters (1963 film). Blu-ray with extra features including Collins commentary and interview footage of Spillane and Eaton. Scorpion Releasing, 2014.

Gorman, Ed, Lee Server, and Martin H. Greenberg, eds. *The Big Book of Noir*. New York: Carroll & Graf, 1998.

Gorman, Ed, and Martin H. Greenberg. *Pulp Masters*. New York: Carroll & Graf, 2001.

Hachett, Alice Payne. *80 Years of Best Sellers, 1895–1975*. New York: R. R. Bowker, 1977.

Halberstam, David. *The Fifties*. New York: Fawcett Columbine, 1993.

"Hammer in the Slammer." *TV Guide*, December 22, 1984, p. A-2.

Hargrove, Marion. "The Secret Life of Mickey Spillane." *Redbook*, June 1955, pp. 28–31ff.

Harper, Mr. "Dames and Death." *Harper's Magazine*, May 1952, pp. 99–101.

Harris, Art. "Mickey Spillane." *International Herald Tribune*, October 31, 1984.

Heller, Anne C. *Ayn Rand and the World She Made*. New York: Doubleday, 2009.

Hewitt, Tim. "Spillane: Toughest tough guy writes for children." *Sunrise* [Myrtle Beach, SC], December 16, 1979, pp. 8–9ff.

Hill, Caroline Spillane. Interviews with JLT (2006, 2007, 2021).

Hoberman, J. "The Thriller of Tomorrow." In booklet included in the package of the Criterion DVD/Blu-ray edition of *Kiss Me Deadly*, 2011.

Hopper, Hedda. "Film Actors Take Business Seriously Nowadays." *Los Angeles Times*, May 17.

Horberg, Bill. *"Her Hips Waved a Happy Hello."* Los Angeles: privately printed, limited edition of 500, 2002.

Hughes, Dorothy B. *Erle Stanley Gardner: The Case of the Real Perry Mason.* New York: William Morrow and Company, Inc., 1978.

Hunter, Evan. "Kiss Me, Dudley." In *The Comfortable Coffin*, edited by Richard S. Prather. Greenwich, CT: Gold Medal Books, no. K1297, n.d., pp. 162–68.

Hyams, Joe. "What Hollywood Thinks of Mickey Spillane." *Cue*, August 20–27, 1953, pp. 10–11ff.

"I, the Actor." *Time*, June 7, 1963, p. 51.

Johnston, Richard W. "Death's Fair-haired Boy: Sex and Fury sell 13 million gory books for Mickey Spillane." *Life*, June 23, 1952, pp. 79–80ff.

Jones, Robert F. "Mickey Spillane Chucks his Shamuses and Molls to write for a tougher audience: Kids." *People Weekly*, July 27, 1981, pp. 52–59.

Karas, Nick. "The Other Side of Spillane." *Argosy*, February 1974, pp. 58–62.

Kelly, Walt. *I Go Pogo*. New York: Simon & Schuster, 1952.

_____. *Uncle Pogo So-So Stories*. New York: Simon & Schuster, 1953. ["Muckey Spleen: the Bloody Drip," "Meat Hamburg Private Eye"]

_____. *The Pogo Peek-a-Book*. New York: Simon & Schuster, 1955. ["The Bloody Drip Writhes Again: from Gore Blimey"]

Keach, Stacy. *All in All: An Actor's Life on the Stage*. Lanham, MD: Rowman & Littlefield, 2013.

Kelley, David. "Mickey Spillane testifies at divorce suit trail." UPI Archives, July 9, 1986.

_____. "Spillane's ex-wife posed nude to promote books." UPI Archives, July 9, 1986.

Kimball, Robert, Barry Day, Miles Krueger, and Eric Davis, eds. *The Complete Lyrics of Johnny Mercer*. New York: Alfred A. Knopf, 2009.

Kirk, Margaret. "Mickey Spillane: The Tough Guy at 67." *The Philadelphia Inquirer Magazine*, April 6, 1986, pp. 34–38.

Kiss Me Deadly. Criterion Blu-ray/DVD, 2011. Includes condensed edit of documentary *Mike Hammer's Mickey Spillane*.

Koenig, David. *Shooting Columbo*. Aliso Viejo, CA: Bonaventure Press, 2021.

LaFarge, Christopher. "Mickey Spillane his Bloody Hammer." *Saturday Review*, November 6, 1954, pp. 11ff.

Lait, Jack, and Lee Mortimer. *Chicago Confidential*. New York: Dell, 1950.

_____. *New York: Confidential! The Lowdown on the Bright Life.* New York: Dell, 1948 [1951 edition].

_____. *USA Confidential.* New York: Crown, 1952.

_____. *Washington Confidential.* New York: Crown, 1951.

Lavine, Elliott, and Bob Stephens. "Dark Voyage: A Passage through 25 years of film noir." *The Perfect Vision*, 4, no. 15 (Fall 1992): pp. 120–32.

Lennon, Peter. "The hardest Jehovah's Witness in the world." *The Guardian* [US edition], Friday, July 23, 1999.

Lerner, Max. "Exponent of Sex and Sadism." *Town & Country*.

Lee, Stan. Typed letter signed to JLT, January 21, 1982.

The Long Haul of A. I. Bezzerides. [Documentary] Directed by Fay Efrosini Lellios, 21/31 Productions, 2007.

"*The Long Wait.*" *Chicago Daily News*, May 7, 1954, p. 20.

"*The Long Wait.*" Movie advertisement. *Chicago Daily News,* May 18, 1954, p. 20.

Lovisi, Gary, ed. *Paperback Parade: Mickey Spillane Special Issue!* August 1996, pp. 25–92.

Maltby, Richard. "'The problem of interpretation . . .': authorial and institutional intentions in and around *Kiss Me Deadly.*" *Screening the Past* 10, June 2000.

McConnell, Scott, ed. *100 Voices: An Oral History of Ayn Rand.* New York: New American Library, 2010.

McGavin, Darren. Interview [with Richard Valley]. *Scarlet Street,* Fall 1994.

McHugh, Bob. "A Serious Witness." AP news feature, Sunday, February 12, 1961.

MacShane, Frank. *The Life of Raymond Chandler.* New York: Penguin Books, 1976.

"Masters of Mystery." *Coronet*, February 1956, pp. 105-7.

Meredith, Lee. Interview with JLT (2008).

"Mickey ('Kiss Me Deadly') Spillane And His Wife, Sherri, End Their Unusual Stay-Apart Marriage." *People Weekly*, February 9, 1976, pp. 24-25.

"Mickey Spillane." *Current Biography*, September 1961, pp. 36-39.

"Mickey Spillane Puts the Finger on Mike Hammer." *Focus*, June 1953, pp. 16–17.

"Mickey Spillane's Ex-Wife Fails to Alter Nevada Divorce Ruling." AP: October 3, 1988.

"Mickey Spillane's 'I, the Jury.'" *Foto-rama*, October 1953, pp. 36–38.

Miller, Mary Carol, Donny Whiteheard, and Allan Hammons. *Greenwood: Mississippi Memories Volume II.* Greenwood, MS: West Washington Books, 2014.

Morris, Frank. "Location for Murder." *Hollywood Detective*, August 1948, pp. 60-73, 120.

_____. "Don't Wake the Dead." *Thrilling Detective,* August 1948, pp. 99-108.

Muller, Eddie. *Dark City: The Lost World of Film Noir*, revised and expanded ed. Philadelphia: Running Press, 2021.

Murphy, Mark. "Sex, Sadism and Scripture." *True*, July 1952, pp. 17-19ff.

New York Panorama: A Companion to the WPA Guide to New York City. New Introduction by Alfred Kazin. New York: Pantheon Books, 1984. [Original edition 1938].

Nolan, William F. "Carroll John Daly: the Forgotten Pioneer of the Private Eye." *The Armchair Detective*, October 1970, pp. 1-4.

_____. *Hammett: A Life at the Edge*. New York: Congdon & Weed, 1983.

Nuwer, Hank. "Mickey Spillane: Nailing Down the Man Behind the Hammer." *Satellite ORBIT*, October 1981, pp. 54ff.

Penzler, Otto, Chris Steinbrunner, and Marvin Lachman, eds. *Detectionary*. New York: Ballantine Books, 1971.

Peters, Fiona, and Rebecca Stewart. *Crime Uncovered*. Bristol, UK: Intellect Books, 2016. E-book.

Pomerantz, Gary. "Beach Bum." *Atlanta Journal-Constitution,* May 6, 1990, pp. M1, M4.

Powell, Gene. Interview with JLT (2007).

Powell, Rosemary Y. "Mary Ann Spillane Says: Keeping House is a Hard Job When Husband is Writing." *Charleston News and Courier,* February 28, 1961, p. 5A.

Pronzini, Bill. *Gun in Cheek: A Study of "Alternative" Crime Fiction*. New York: Coward, McCann & Geoghegan, 1982.

Pronzini, Bill, and Marcia Muller, eds. *1001 Midnights: The Aficionado's Guide to Mystery and Detective Fiction*. New York: Arbor House, 1986.

Propst, Andy. *You Fascinate Me So: The Life and Times of Cy Coleman*. Milwaukee, WI: Applause Theatre & Cinema Books, 1995.

Quigley, Carroll. *Tragedy and Hope: A History of the World in Our Time*. New York: The McMillan Company, 1966.

Rand, Ayn. *The Romantic Manifesto: A Philosophy of Literature*. New York: Signet, revised ed. 1975.

_____. Typed letter signed to Mickey Spillane, September 15, 1962.

"The Real Mickey Spillane." *Sir!,* September 1953, pp. 34–35ff.

Redman, Ben Ray. "Decline and Fall of the Whodunit." *Saturday Review*, May 31, 1952, pp. 8ff.

Robbins, Trina. *A Century of Women Cartoonists*. Princeton, WI: Kitchen Sink, 1993.

Rolo, Charles. "Simenon and Spillane: the Metaphysics for the Millions." *New World Writing No. 1,* 1952.

Rosenthal, Donna. "Mickey Spillane Secretly Wed to His Daughter's Childhood Pal." *National Enquirer* clipping, 1983.

Rothman, Cliff. "Mickey Spillane's Pulp Sensation." *Vanity Fair,* December 2003, pp. 336–39ff.

Roxon, Lillian. "That's No Naked Lady, that Mickey Spillane's Naked Wife." *Esquire,* August 1972, pp. 128ff.

Saville, Victor. *Evergreen: Victor Saville in His Own Words*. As told to Roy Moseley. Carbondale and Edwardsville: Southern Illinois University Press, 2000.

Shortell, Brad. "Mickey Spillane . . . most dangerous man in America?" *Confidential,* n.d., pp. 36ff.

Silet, Charles L. P. "Mickey Spillane: Interview." *Mystery Scene,* March/April 1996, pp. 32ff.

_____. "The First Angry White Male: Mickey Spillane's Mike Hammer." *The Armchair Detective*, Spring 1996, pp. 194–99.

Silver, Alain, and Elizabeth Ward. *Film Noir.* Woodstock, NY: Overlook Press, 1979.

"6 Spillane Yarns To Chill Film Fans." *New York Times*, December 20, 1952, p. 14.

"Slaughter For a Quarter." *Time,* December 3, 1951, p. 110.

Sloan, Doris. Typed memoir to JLT.

Smith, Bruce. "Mickey Spillane's Funeral." AP, July 18, 2006.

Somersett, Chris. "Hunt the Ripper." *Titbits*, June 3, 1967, pp. 20–21.

Southern, Terry. "Mickey Spillane as Mike Hammer [. . .]" *Esquire,* July 1963, p. 74. [Complete title is a paragraph long.]

Spillane, Jane. *My Life with Mickey.* As told to Andrew Lesh. Conway, SC: The Athenaeum Press at Coastal Carolina University, 2014.

Spillane, Mickey. "Blondes Are a State of Mind." *Men's Life,* October/November 1990, p. 107.

_____. "Choosing a Spillane Cover." *Penthouse*, 7, no. 1, 1972, pp. 56–57.

_____. "Comics Were Great—A Colorful Conversation with Mickey Spillane." Interview with Roy Thomas. *Alter Ego*, 3, no. 11, November 2001, pp. 33–41.

_____. "I, Mickey Spillane." Interview with Charles L. P. Silet. *The Armchair Detective*, Spring 1996, pp. 200–1.

_____. "Mickey Spillane: Interview." Interview with James L. Traylor. *Mystery Scene*, 23 (October/November 1989): pp. 15–16.

_____. "Mickey Spillane Writes." Various columns, *Greensboro Daily News*, January 1956 through May 20, 1956.

_____. "The Perfect Crime." *OMNI*, May 1987.

_____. "A Pulp Apprenticeship, Yes." *Report to Writers*, December 1951.

_____. "Sawdust in My Shoes." *Clyde Beatty Circus Official Program and Daily Magazine*, 1957, pp. 7ff.

_____. "Secrets of a Private Eye." *Quick*, September 29, 1952, pp. 55–57.

_____. "Speaking of Speed." *Motor Life*, August 1954, pp. 12–13, 40. [Cover: "Mickey Spillane Red Hot and Safe."]

_____. "The Trouble With Violence on TV." *TV Guide*, September 30, 1961, pp. 17–19.

_____. Typed letter signed to Ayn Rand, Friday, September 1961. [Rockcut Road, Newburgh, New York, letterhead, Spillane files]

_____. Typed letter signed to Ayn Rand. February 24, 1967. [Signed with full name—Mickey Spillane]

_____. "Writing Should Be Fun." *Memories,* April/May 1990.

"Spillane, Mickey." *Current Biography:* 42, 9 (September 1981): pp. 36–39.

"Spillane's Dames." *Dare*, June 1954, pp. 46–47.

Stanfield, Peter. *Maximum Movies Pulp Fictions: Film Culture and the Worlds of Samuel Fuller, Mickey Spillane, and Jim Thompson.* New Brunswick, NJ: Rutgers University Press, 2011.

Stang, Jack, Jr. *The Real Mike Hammer.* BookBaby 2012. E-book.

Steeger, Henry (Harry). Typed letter signed to JLT, August 20, 1987.

Steinbrunner, Chris, and Otto Penzler, eds. *Encyclopedia of Mystery and Detection*. New York: McGraw-Hill, 1976.

Stout, Rex. "An Interview with Rex Stout." *P.S. Magazine*, August 1966, pp. 20-24ff.

Talese, Gay. "It's a New Killer for Mike Hammer." *New York Times*, June 19, 1962, p. 29.

"Their Selves to Know." *Esquire*, December 1972, pp. 202–3.

"These Gunns for Hire." *Time*, October 26, 1959, pp. 48–50ff. [Cover: "The Corpse in the Living Room or the Private Life of the Private Eyes."]

Thomas, Dave. "The Case of the Blonde & the Mystery Writer's Mysterious Millions." *Star*, July 29, 1986, p. 5.

Tinkham, Charles B. "Anything by Spillane." *Book Week, Chicago Sun Times*, n.d., ca. 1969 or 1970, p. 4.

Tornabene, Lyn. "Lunch Date With Mickey Spillane." *Cosmopolitan*, 1963.

Traylor, James L. "Characternyms in Mickey Spillane's Mike Hammer." *The Armchair Detective*, 16, no. 3 (Summer 1983): pp. 293–95.

_____. *Dime Detective Companion*. Boston: Altus Press, 2011.

_____. "The Great Detectives: Mickey Spillane's Mike Hammer." *The Strand Magazine*, 26 (October 2008): pp. 65–66.

_____. "Mickey Spillane and Mike Hammer." *Clues*, 5, no. 2 (Fall/Winter 1984): pp. 9–19. [Written in collaboration with John A. Traylor, MD.]

_____. "The Violent World of Mike Hammer." *The Mystery FANcier*, 7, no. 6 (November/December 1983): pp. 13–20.

Valderrama, Carla. *This Was Hollywood*. Philadelphia: Running Press, 2020.

Van Biema, David, and Jack Kelley. "An Ex-wife's suit behind him, Mickey Spillane returns to the easier world of fiction." *People*, July 28, 1986, p. 28.

Van Buren, Raeburn. *Abbie an' Slats*. Syndicated Sunday comic strip, August 3 and 10, 1952. ["Mickey Spillgore"]

Vinciguera, Thomas. "Mickey Spillane's Works Keep Coming, 12 Years After His Death." *Wall Street Journal*, February 26, 2018.

Wakefield, Dan. *New York in the 50s*. Boston: Houghton Mifflin/Seymour Lawrence, 1992.

"Warden Adopts a Young Murderer." *Life*, April 12, 1948, pp. 55–56, 58.

Watts, Don. Interview with JLT (2008).

Weibel, Kay. "Mickey Spillane as a Fifties Phenomenon." In *Dimensions of Detective Fiction*, edited by Larry Landrum, Pat Browne, and Ray B. Browne. Bowling Green, OH: Bowling Green State University, 1976, pp. 114–23.

Weiler, A. H. "Mickey Spillane, Actor, On the Town." *New York Times*, November 18, 1962.

Wellek, Rene, and Austin Warren. *Theory of Literature*. 3rd edition. New York: Harcourt, Brace and World, 1956.

Weybright, Victor. *The Making of a Publisher: A Life in the 20th Century Book Revolution*. New York: Reynal & Company in association with William Morrow & Company, 1967.

"What's Mickey Spillane Up To Now?" *People Today*, April 18, 1956, pp. 18-21.

White, Theodore H. *America in Search of Itself: The Making of the President 1956–1980.* New York: Warner Books, 1982.

Whitehead, David. "The Hard-boiled Detective Novels of Mickey Spillane." *The Book & Magazine Collector*, November 1993, pp. 30–38.

Whiting, Frederick. "Bodies of Evidence: Post-war Detective Fiction and the Monstrous Origins of the Sexual Psychopath." *Yale Journal of Criticism*, Spring 2005, pp. 149ff. Accessed online via ProQuest.

Wilmot, Tony. "Take the Mickey with Mrs. Spillane." *Titbits*, April 12–18, 1973, pp. 18–19.

Wilson, George. Interview with JLT (2007).

Winn, Dilys, ed. *Murder Ink: The Mystery Reader's Companion.* New York: Workman Publishing, 1977.

WPA Guide to New York City: The Federal Writers Project Guide to 1930s New York. New York: Pantheon Books, 1982. [Originally published in 1939.]

Wylie, Philip. "The Crime of Mickey Spillane." *Good Housekeeping*, February 1955, pp. 54–55, 206–9.

Additional resources include:

Letters from Spillane to MAC, 1973–2003; letters from Ed Robbins to MAC, 1975; interviews with Jay Bernstein, Shirley Eaton, Stacy Keach, Jane Spillane, Mickey Spillane, and Paul Vernon by MAC for documentary, *Mike Hammer's Mickey Spillane* (1999), utilizing transcripts of interviews.

New American Library Archives, Fales Library, NYU Special Collections, New York University, Charlotte Priddle, Director.

Various Internet websites including (but not limited to) the International Movie Data Base Pro, Stacy Keach, Darren McGavin, William Horberg, Erasmus High School, Fort Hays State University, the Library of Congress, Comic Vine, Don Markstein's Toonopedia, Four-Color Shadows (Sergeant Spook), Digital Deli Too, Archive of American Television, Northjersey.com (Stan Purdy obit), Turner Classic Movies, and YouTube.

Mickey Spillane's personal script for *Ring of Fear.*

Hundreds of Spillane articles and photo spreads appeared over the years—particularly in the 1950s—and many of these have rated a glance but not a listing in this bibliography. Some, but not all, include such ephemera as *Bold*, *Dare*, *Focus*, *Foto-rama*, *Night and Day*, *Picture Digest*, *Picture Scope*, and *Quick*. A few, with specific articles, are included above.

ABOUT THE AUTHORS

MAX ALLAN COLLINS, a Mystery Writers of America Grand Master, won Private Eye Writers of America "Shamus" awards for his Nathan Heller novels, *True Detective* (1993) and *Stolen Away* (1993), and the PWA life achievement award, the Eye (2006). His graphic novel *Road to Perdition* (1998) became an Academy Award–winning film starring Tom Hanks, Paul Newman, and Daniel Craig. His produced screenplays include *Mommy* (1995) and *The Last Lullaby* (2008), based on his Quarry novels, also the basis of the Cinemax series *Quarry* (2016). In comics, he has scripted *Dick Tracy*, *Batman*, and co-created *Ms. Tree* and *Wild Dog*; his *New York Times* and *USA Today* bestsellers include *Saving Private Ryan* (1998) and *American Gangster* (2007). With his wife, Barb (as "Barbara Allan"), he co-authors the award-winning *Antiques* mysteries. He received an MFA from the University of Iowa Writers Workshop, where he wrote his first three published novels.

JAMES L. TRAYLOR was nominated for the Edgar Award by the Mystery Writers of America in 1985 for *One Lonely Knight: Mickey Spillane's Mike Hammer* (written with his frequent collaborator Collins). He is the author of *Hollywood Troubleshooter: W. T. Ballard's Bill Lennox Stories* (1985), *Dime Detective Index* (1986, revised and updated as *Dime Detective Companion*, 2011). With Collins, he co-authored *Mickey Spillane on Screen* (2012). His articles about noted pulp writers Carroll John Daly, W. T. (Todhunter) Ballard, Dwight Babcock, William R. Cox, and Mickey

Spillane have appeared in *The Armchair Detective*, *The Mystery FANcier*, *Clues*, *Hardboiled*, *The Strand*, and *The Oxford Companion to Crime and Mystery Writing* (1999). He received his doctorate in English Renaissance Prose and Poetry at Georgia State University, specializing in early realistic prose fiction. He writes short fiction about PI Bob Crawford.

INDEX